P9-AEX-745

SAGE Brief Guide to
MARKETING ETHICS

SAGE Brief Guide to
MARKETING ETHICS

Los Angeles | London | New Delhi
Singapore | Washington DC

Los Angeles | London | New Delhi
Singapore | Washington DC

FOR INFORMATION:

SAGE Publications, Inc.
2455 Teller Road
Thousand Oaks, California 91320
E-mail: order@sagepub.com

SAGE Publications Ltd.
1 Oliver's Yard
55 City Road
London EC1Y 1SP
United Kingdom

SAGE Publications India Pvt. Ltd.
B 1/I 1 Mohan Cooperative Industrial Area
Mathura Road, New Delhi 110 044
India

SAGE Publications Asia-Pacific Pte. Ltd.
33 Pekin Street #02-01
Far East Square
Singapore 048763

Printed in the United States of America

Library of Congress Cataloging-in-Publication Data

Sage brief guide to marketing ethics.

p. cm.
Includes bibliographical references.

ISBN 978-1-4129-9514-6 (pbk.)

1. Marketing—Moral and ethical aspects. 2. Business ethics.

HF5415.S228 2012 174′.4—dc22 2011006041

This book is printed on acid-free paper.

11 12 13 14 15 10 9 8 7 6 5 4 3 2 1

Executive Editor: Lisa Shaw

Acquisitions Editor: Deya Saoud Jacob

Editorial Assistant: Megan Krattli

Production Editor: Eric Garner

Typesetter: C&M Digitals (P) Ltd.

Proofreader: Carole Quandt

Cover Designer: Gail Buschman

Marketing Manager: Helen Salmon

Permissions Editor: Karen Ehrmann

TABLE OF CONTENTS

PREFACE

Commerce is by its very nature a normative enterprise. It is concerned with creating value for owners and other constituencies, ranging from the firm's immediate stakeholders, such as employees, customers, and suppliers, to the entire society within which the business operates. As a field of study, business ethics aims to specify the principles under which businesses must operate to behave ethically. Thus, business ethics focuses on issues such as those that have recently attracted so much public scrutiny: executive compensation, honesty in accounting, transparency, treatment of stakeholders, and respect for the environment. These are, in fact, perennial questions that accompany the long history of human economic activity and that will also be present through an indeterminate future.

Marketing ethics is the systematic study of how moral standards are applied to marketing decisions, behaviors, and institutions. Because marketing is a process inherent to most organizations, marketing ethics should be viewed as a subset of business ethics; thus, much of what is written about business ethics applies to marketing ethics as well. When the words "marketing ethics" appear in the general media or business press, the reports typically describe a marketing strategy, tactic, or policy that some constituency feels is "unfair" or "exploitive" or "deceptive." Often, the subsequent discussion turns to how marketing practices might become more consumer-friendly, socially compatible, or put in philosophical terms, how marketing might be normatively improved.

FORMAT

This guide to marketing ethics provides key terms and concepts related to marketing ethics in a short, easy-to-use format. It is intended to act as a companion for marketing courses or as a reference for students and practitioners who would like to learn more about the basics of ethical marketing.

The text is divided into five sections that contain important keywords that relate to those sections: *Business Ethics, Ethics and the Marketing Mix, Ethics and the Promotional Mix,* and *Special Topics in Marketing Ethics.* Each keyword entry is written by a scholar drawn from the fields of business and marketing ethics and is a comprehensive essay on such crucial topics as ethical issues in pricing, green marketing, and deceptive advertising. Each essay includes a list of references and suggested readings for each article so that readers can find more information on issues of particular interest to them. The AMA Code of Ethics is included in the Appendix of the book as a reference for current and future practitioners.

ACKNOWLEDGMENTS

We would like to acknowledge and thank Robert Kolb, editor of SAGE's award-winning *Encyclopedia of Business Ethics and Society,* whose contributions provided the foundation for this companion text.

We also wish to thank the reviewers, who assisted in finalizing the content for this text. They are:

Bruce A. Huhmann, New Mexico State University

Michael J. Messina, Gannon University

Herbert Sherman, Long Island University–Brooklyn Campus

Brent Smith, Saint Joseph's University

—The Editors of SAGE

PART I

Business Ethics

BUSINESS ETHICS

Although defining business ethics has been somewhat problematic, several definitions have been proposed. For example, Richard De George defines the field broadly as the interaction of ethics and business, and although its aim is theoretical, the product has practical application. Manuel Velasquez defines the business ethics field as a specialized study of moral right and wrong. Unfortunately, a great deal of confusion appears to remain within both the academic and the business communities, as other related business and society frameworks, such as corporate social responsibility, stakeholder management, sustainability, and corporate citizenship, are often used interchangeably with or attempt to incorporate business ethics. Relative to other business and society frameworks, however, business ethics appears to place the greatest emphasis on the ethical responsibilities of business and its individual agents, as opposed to other firm responsibilities (e.g., economic, legal, environmental, or philanthropic).

A BRIEF HISTORY OF BUSINESS ETHICS

The subject of business ethics has been around since the very first business transaction. For example, the Code of Hammurabi, created nearly 4,000 years ago, records that Mesopotamian rulers attempted to create honest prices. In the fourth century BCE, Aristotle discussed the vices and virtues of tradesmen and merchants. The Old Testament and the Jewish Talmud discuss the proper way to conduct business, including topics such as fraud, theft, proper weights and measures, competition and free entry, misleading advertising, just prices, and environmental issues. The New Testament and the Koran also discuss business ethics as it relates to poverty and wealth. Throughout the history of commerce, these codes have had an impact on business dealings. The U.K. South Sea Bubble of the early 1700s, labeled as the world's first great financial scandal, involved the collapse of the South Sea Company. During the 19th century, the creation of monopolies and the use of slavery were important business ethics issues, which continue to be debated until today.

In recent times, business ethics has moved through several stages of development. Prior to the 1960s, business was typically considered to be an amoral activity; concepts such as ethics and social responsibility were rarely explicitly mentioned. During the 1960s, a number of social issues in business began to emerge, including civil rights, the environment, safety in the workplace, and consumer issues. During the late 1970s, the field of business ethics began to take hold in academia, with several U.S. schools beginning to offer a course in business ethics by 1980. From 1980 to 1985, the business ethics field continued to consolidate, with the emergence of journals, textbooks, research centers, and conferences. From 1985 to 1995, business ethics became integrated into large corporations, with the development of corporate codes of ethics, ethics training, ethics hotlines, and ethics officers. From 1995 to 2000, issues related to international business activity came to the forefront, including issues of bribery and corruption of government officials, the use of child labor by overseas suppliers, and the question of whether to operate in countries where human rights violations were taking place. From approximately 2000 until today, business ethics discussion has mainly been focused on major corporate scandals such as Enron, WorldCom, and Tyco, leading to a new phase of government regulation (e.g., the Sarbanes-Oxley Act of 2002) and enforcement.

This current "scandal" phase of the business ethics field has tremendously enhanced its popular use. For example, a search in Google using the term *business ethics* (as of November 2005) generates over 88 million hits. Hollywood continues to portray important business ethics issues or dilemmas in movies such as *Wall Street, Quiz Show, Boiler Room, Erin Brockovich, The Insider*, and *Jerry Maguire* and even in children's films such as *Monsters, Inc.*

MORAL STANDARDS AND BUSINESS ETHICS

Although the field of business ethics covers a broad range of topics, the core of the field is based in moral philosophy and its use of moral standards (i.e., values, principles, and theories) to engage in ethical assessments of business activity. A literature review indicates that five moral standards have been applied in the field of business ethics to a greater extent and with greater consistency than others. Two moral theories are particularly dominant in the business ethics literature: utilitarianism and deontology. Utilitarianism, often expressed as a teleological or consequentialist framework, is primarily based on the writings of Jeremy Bentham and John Stuart Mill. Deontology (i.e., duty-based obligations)

3

is often expressed in terms of "Kantianism" (or more specifically as the principle of the categorical imperative), being primarily based on the writings of Immanuel Kant. In addition to utilitarianism and deontology, two other moral theories (typically considered deontological in nature) have been used extensively in the business ethics field: moral rights and justice (e.g., procedural and distributive). The fifth moral theory receiving attention appears to be moral virtue, being primarily based on the writings of Aristotle. The predominant use by business ethicists of these moral theories points toward their importance in the field. Other important moral standards that are also used (although to a somewhat lesser extent) in the field of business ethics include moral relativism, ethical egoism, and religious doctrine.

There have been several means by which moral standards have been applied in business ethics. Some of the more apparent ways are (1) individual ethical decision making; (2) organizational ethical decision making (e.g., policies and practices); (3) the moral evaluation of business systems (e.g., capitalism) and the marketplace (e.g., competition); (4) the relationship between business and society (e.g., corporate social responsibility); and (5) specific issues in business (e.g., affirmative action and discrimination, conflicts of interest, privacy, whistle-blowing, executive compensation, consumer protection or marketing, and international business). In conjunction with the above are the uses made of moral standards with respect to both teaching and research in business ethics.

BUSINESS ETHICS AS AN ACADEMIC FIELD

Richard De George might be considered the first to attempt to distinguish business ethics as a separate field of study. De George suggests that business ethics is a field to the extent that it deals with a set of interrelated questions to be untangled and addressed within an overarching framework. He argues that the framework is not supplied by any ethical theory (e.g., Kantian, utilitarian, or theological) but by the systematic interdependence of the questions, which can be approached from various philosophical, theological, or other points of view.

Despite business ethics being a relatively recent distinct field of study, several typologies have emerged. There appear to be five general approaches: (1) a normative and descriptive approach, (2) a functional approach, (3) an issues approach, (4) a stakeholder approach, and (5) a mixed approach. For example, in terms of the normative/descriptive approach, academic business ethics research is often divided into normative (i.e., prescriptive) and empirical (i.e., explanatory, descriptive, or predictive) methodologies. A functional approach attempts to divide the subject of business ethics into separate functional areas such as accounting, finance, marketing, or strategy. Others attempt to categorize business ethics by using an "issues" approach—in other words, by discussing issues such as the morality of corporations, employer-employee relationships, or other contemporary business issues. Another approach attempts to discuss the subject of business ethics from a stakeholder perspective (i.e., in relation to which stakeholder is most directly affected). For example, business ethics issues might be framed based on the following stakeholders: owners, employees, consumers, suppliers, competitors, the government, the natural environment, and the community. Finally, a mixed approach draws on aspects of several of the approaches (e.g., normative/descriptive, issues, and stakeholder) and appears to be the most popular approach used by business ethics academics. For example, quite often business ethics textbooks will commence with a normative discussion of moral theory and business systems. The discussion will then turn to a more mixed normative/descriptive discussion of the specific issues. In addition, many of the issues are tied to stakeholders, typically involving employees and customers.

In terms of business ethics research, in a review of the first 1,500 articles published in the *Journal of Business Ethics* from 1981 until 1999, Denis Collins found the presence of the following major business ethics research topics: (1) prevalence of ethical behavior, (2) ethical sensitivities, (3) ethics codes and programs, (4) corporate social performance and policies, (5) human resource practices and policies, and (6) professions—accounting, marketing/ sales, and finance/strategy.

MAJOR EARLY CONTRIBUTORS TO BUSINESS ETHICS

Several important early contributors to the field of business ethics, mainly through their initial textbook publications, include Norman Bowie, Richard De George, Manuel Velasquez, Thomas Donaldson, W. Michael Hoffman, Patricia Werhane, John Boatright, and many others too numerous to mention. John Fleming conducted a study in 1987 to determine among other things the most referenced authors, books, and articles in business ethics. The top five referenced authors were (1) Milton Friedman, (2) Christopher Stone, (3) Thomas Donaldson, (4) Peter French, and (5) Alasdair MacIntyre. The top three referenced books were (1) Christopher Stone, *Where the Law Ends*;

(2) Thomas Donaldson, *Corporations and Morality*; and (3) John Rawls, *A Theory of Justice*. The top three referenced articles were (1) Brenner and Molander, "Is the Ethics of Business Changing?"; (2) Peter French, "The Corporation as a Moral Person"; and (3) Milton Friedman, "The Social Responsibility of Business Is to Increase Its Profits."

BUSINESS ETHICS TODAY

Based on early efforts, the field of business ethics continues to flourish in both academia as well as the business community. For example, a search (as of November 2005) using the database ABI/Inform for the term *business ethics* found in scholarly journal articles generates over 11,000 hits. Several important academic journals now exist, including *Journal of Business Ethics, Business Ethics Quarterly, Business & Society, Business Ethics: A European Review,* and *Business & Professional Ethics Journal*, among others. Business ethics conferences are held annually, including those conducted by the Society for Business Ethics and the European Business Ethics Network. Every 4 years, the International Society of Business, Economics and Ethics organizes a World Congress on Business Ethics, often portrayed as the "Olympics of Business Ethics." Research centers such as Bentley College's Center for Business Ethics, Wharton's Zicklin Center for Business Ethics Research, or the Ethics Resource Center based in Washington, D.C., continue to support research efforts in the field of business ethics. Surveys suggest that approximately two thirds of the top U.S. business schools now teach business ethics as either a mandatory or an elective stand-alone course. In the corporate world, the growth of ethics officers as well as the Ethics & Compliance Officer Association, ethics programs (e.g., codes of ethics, ethics hotlines or helplines), ethics audits and reports, ethical investment, and even corporate business ethics awards highlight the growing practical importance of the field. Consulting efforts in the business ethics field appear to have grown significantly as well due to the various corporate scandals and the desire of firms to avoid them in the future.

Yet despite the growth of business ethics and the apparent acceptance of its importance among many, several issues are being debated. For example, can business ethics be taught? What factors actually influence ethical behavior? What should a firm's ethical obligations (i.e., beyond the law) consist of? Does ethical behavior actually improve the firm's financial performance? Is a firm capable of being held morally responsible, or only the firm's agents? How can business ethics best be integrated into a firm's corporate culture? These issues, as well as many others, remain to be examined and debated by those active in the business ethics field.

—Mark S. Schwartz

Further Readings

Beauchamp, T. L., & Bowie, N. E. (2004). *Ethical theory and business* (7th ed.). Upper Saddle River, NJ: Pearson.

Boatright, J. R. (2003). *Ethics and the conduct of business* (4th ed.). Upper Saddle River, NJ: Prentice Hall.

Collins, D. (2000). The quest to improve the human condition: The first 1,500 articles published in the *Journal of Business Ethics*. *Journal of Business Ethics, 26*(1), 1–73.

De George, R. T. (1987). The status of business ethics: Past and future. *Journal of Business Ethics, 6,* 201–211.

De George, R. T. (2006). *Business ethics* (6th ed.). Upper Saddle River, NJ: Pearson.

Donaldson, T., Werhane, P. H., & Cording, M. (2002). *Ethical issues in business: A philosophical approach* (7th ed.). Upper Saddle River, NJ: Pearson.

Fleming, J. E. (1987). Authorities in business ethics. *Journal of Business Ethics, 6*(3), 213–217.

Goodpaster, K. E. (1997). Business ethics. In P. H. Werhane & R. E. Freeman (Eds.), *Encyclopedic dictionary of business ethics* (pp. 51–57). Cambridge, MA: Blackwell.

Richardson, J. E. (2005). *Annual editions: Business ethics 05/06* (17th ed.). Guilford, CT: McGraw-Hill.

Velasquez, M. G. (2006). *Business ethics: Concepts and cases* (6th ed.). Upper Saddle River, NJ: Pearson.

THEORIES OF ETHICS

Ethics is the branch of philosophy that deals with morality. Ethicists are concerned with a wide range of topics, such as human nature; the meaning of life; the nature of value; how judgments are made; how judgments can be improved; how moral attitudes arise and change; and the workings of morally significant mental states such as love, hate, greed, envy, indifference, pity, desire, aversion, pleasure, and pain. Moral or ethical theories offer the means of understanding significant elements in these and other areas of inquiry.

Ethical theories tend either toward merely describing or toward both describing and judging. As a result, some moral theories seem to belong to anthropology, psychology, or sociology, while others look like instances of what ethics purports to study—that is, like moral doctrines or judgments. For this reason, a major distinction employed by moral theorists distinguishes descriptive from prescriptive, or normative, theories, or elements of theories.

Moral judgments tend to state that something is either good or bad or that something agrees or conflicts with our obligations. Consequently, a major division in moral theories is between theories of value (axiology) and theories of obligation (deontology). In each area, ethicists want to determine the meaning of moral judgments, their truth or falsity, their objectivity or subjectivity, how judgments are made, how they can be tested, how they can be justified, and the possibility of organizing judgments under first principles. A third major distinction places theories about the meaning of moral judgments in a category of their own called metaethics. Obviously, metaethical questions arise in all areas of ethics.

Prescriptive or normative moral thinking recommends at least one moral evaluation, or else it attempts the same for at least one moral obligation. Plato, Aristotle, the Stoics, the Epicureans, and the Cynics sought both to find the best kind of life and to strongly recommend the judgment that it was in fact the best. Others, such as Immanuel Kant, theorized about the nature of obligation and also provided grounds for justifying or recommending certain obligations. The theories of David Hume, Arthur Schopenhauer, Darwinism, and Logical Positivism exemplify the tendency to separate the task of description from that of prescription, or to eschew prescription altogether, in order to describe and organize moral judgments for the sake of understanding alone.

The unwavering pursuit of the metaethical question of the meaning of moral judgments brought many recent philosophers to the conclusion that moral judgments are not the sort of statements that can be true or false but instead express resolutions, preferences, feelings, demands, or other states of mind. Hume thought that they reported subjective feelings, so that a judgment such as "Insider trading is immoral" would not be understood as ascribing a predicate to insider trading but as saying something like "I disapprove of that act." A. J. Ayer, a Logical Positivist, believed that moral judgments did not report feelings but merely expressed them. For him, the statement "Insider trading is immoral" merely expresses a negative emotional reaction to stealing—along the lines of "Boo insider trading!" Such expressions are neither true nor false because they do not describe anything. Hume and Ayer represent the school known as Emotivism. A neighboring school, Prescriptivism, interprets "Insider trading is immoral" as an imperative, "Do not engage in insider trading," which is neither true nor false because it is a command rather than a description.

In value theory, the primary questions are first about the meaning of value terms, then about the status of value. With regard to meaning, the first question is whether value or goodness can be defined and, if so, how. For Plato and W. D. Ross, the good is indefinable, yet it names an intrinsic property of things, making it objective. For the Intuitionists, such as G. E. Moore, value is indefinable, objective, and absolute. Many ethicists believe that value can be defined so as to name something that is both objective and absolute, as did Aristotle, who defined the good as that at which all things aim. For others, the good has its seat in subjectivity and will be different for different persons or groups.

After the meaning and status of value, the chief concern in value theory has been the question of which things are of the highest value. The main answers have been a state of feeling, such as pleasure or satisfaction (Epicurus, Thomas Hobbes, John Stuart Mill); a state of the will, such as virtue (Epictetus) or power (Friedrich Nietzsche); or a state of the intellect, such as knowledge (Plato) or good intentions (Kant).

In the theory of obligation, similar questions have been posed. With regard to questions about the meaning and status of "right" and "wrong," Intuitionists hold that they name an indefinable, objective quality. Emotivists believe that right can have only an emotive, subjective meaning. Psychological and social thinkers typically hold that judgments of right and wrong indicate the attitudes of some person or group toward an act.

In response to the question of which things are right in the sense of their being morally obligatory, there are both teleological and nonteleological answers. For the teleologist, an act is right according to how much good it brings, or will probably bring, into the world. For the egoist, the amount of good brought to the agent is decisive (Epicurus, Hobbes), while for the universalist, it is the amount brought to the world as a whole (utilitarianism). Meanwhile, Thomas Aquinas and others have argued that an act is right according to its intent, so that an act with a comparatively better intent is a comparatively more righteous act. All these answers to the question of what is obligatory rely on a theory of value and, thus, make deontology dependent on axiology.

A fully deontological theory is supposed to hold that an act is obligatory regardless of its consequences for human happiness, ends, or other values. Deontologists, such as Kant, hold that right conduct can be determined by considering a priori principles, such as rights and laws. Kant's view was that objectively right conduct could arise from many sources, such as benevolence, prudence, or habit. However, the highest and the only morally significant motive for right action was respect for the moral law. If a course of action suggested by benevolence, pity, sentiment, or any other motive conflicted with the course indicated by moral law, respect for moral law ought to win out. The good will, the will truly searching for its duties so as to fulfill them, is supremely good for Kant, and the moral worth of an act is always guaranteed by the agent's intent to follow the moral law, regardless of any other motive or consequence.

Deontology is squarely opposed to teleological approaches to obligation because it holds that the end can never justify the means. Hence, violating another's rights cannot be justified by its serving a praiseworthy goal. Consequentialist theories, such as utilitarianism, hinge the goodness of conduct to its consequences and, hence, seem prepared to overlook a violation of rights as long as the consequences of the violation are highly valuable. In contrast, it has been said that the deontologist's motto appears to be "Let justice be done though the heavens fall." Kant argued that one must not lie even to save the life of an innocent man and that one must not commit suicide even when life has no further meaning or purpose. For Kant there can be no exceptions to moral laws because if they are to count as moral laws, they must at a minimum be universalizable. Hence, if suicide is immoral when life has purpose, it must also be immoral when it does not, and if lying to obtain a loan is immoral, lying must also be immoral in life-and-death situations.

Another version of deontology comes from theology, in which our moral duties are given by a deity. Divine command theories hold that regardless of any consequences for life or limb, we must do what the deity commands.

Virtue ethics is often described as an alternative to normative deontology because its normative elements concern the qualities of persons rather than the qualities of acts. Plato, Aristotle, and many Eastern systems of thought focus on what kind of person one ought to try to be rather than on which actions one ought to take or avoid. For Aristotle, who understood ethics as the branch of learning concerned with achieving the good life, the virtues are precisely those characteristics that make the character good and that lead to the good life. These include courage, prudence, wit, truthfulness, temperance, and justice, among others. Its detractors often say that virtue ethics is dependent on prescriptive moral judgments yet offers no insight into them.

Beyond theories of value and obligation, ethicists examine moral reasoning in their efforts to understand how our conduct is chosen and how moral judgments are or ought to be made. According to the Emotivists, a moral judgment comes about when one looks at an act or policy, consults one's sentiment, and pronounces morally about it. For teleologists, moral judgments are or ought to be made by considering the comparative amount of good or bad that an action can or does bring about. For Kantians, moral judgments ought to be made by considering the one obligation that determines all others—namely, to act so that you can at the same time honestly will that all others would act as you do. For divine command theorists, the will of the deity must be consulted in making accurate moral judgments.

One of the greatest challenges to all normative ethical theories lies in the problem of free will. We generally consider acts praiseworthy or blameworthy only if their agent could have acted otherwise. If we lack free will, we are apparently never able to do otherwise and, hence, our acts do not deserve either praise or blame. The school known as Compatibilism argues that belief in the moral status of human acts is compatible with an absence of free will. Incompatibilists, such as Nietzsche, argue that if we lack free will, statements about the moral status of human acts perpetuate a cruel myth.

A second, more contemporary challenge to normative ethics arises from the question of whether there are moral facts in the world and, if there are, whether moral judgments describe them. Moral realism answers that there are moral facts and that our judgments can describe them, and thus affirms at least three things: (1) that moral judgments are propositional, meaning that they can be either true or false because they attempt to describe features of the world; (2) that there are moral facts to be described; and (3) that moral facts are objectively present in the world, independent of our thoughts and feelings. Noncognitivism in ethics holds that moral judgments do not describe, and so are nonpropositional, and thus can be neither true nor false.

—Bryan Finken

Further Readings

Aristotle. (1984). *Nicomachean ethics* (*The Complete Works of Aristotle*, J. Barnes, Ed.). Princeton, NJ: Princeton University Press.

Ayer, A. J. (1952). *Language, truth and logic*. New York: Dover.

Hobbes, T. (1994). *Leviathan* (E. Curley, Ed.). Chicago: Hackett.

Hume, D. (2000). *A treatise of human nature* (D. F. Norton & M. J. Norton, Eds.). Oxford, UK: Oxford University Press.

Joyce, R. (2006). *The evolution of morality*. Cambridge: MIT Press.

Kant, Immanuel. (1985). *Grounding for the metaphysics of morals* (J. W. Ellington, Trans.). Indianapolis, IN: Hackett.

Mill, J. S. (1991). *Utilitarianism* (Collected Works of John Stuart Mill, J. M. Robson, Ed.). Toronto, Ontario, Canada: University of Toronto Press.

Moore, G. E. (1903). *Principia ethica*. Cambridge, UK: Cambridge University Press.

STAKEHOLDER THEORY

Every company exists in a network of relationships with social actors that affect and are affected by the company's efforts to achieve its objectives. Taken together, these actors are the company's *stakeholders*, implying that they hold a stake in its conduct. Typically, stakeholders of a for-profit company include its customers, employees, stockholders, suppliers, the local community, and many others groups.

Stakeholder theory is the term used to describe broadly the systematic study of these relationships, their origins, and their implications for how companies behave. As used in this context, the word *theory* raises serious problems. Social scientists who study stakeholder relations are interested in many empirical questions, such as why companies and stakeholders behave as they do and why companies succeed or fail. They use the word *theory* to refer to a specific set of cause-and-effect relationships used to answer such questions. The controversy (as explained below) is whether stakeholder theory, as a social science theory, points toward a unique set of causal statements about why organizations behave as they do that no other theory identifies. On the other hand, ethicists use the term *stakeholder theory* to describe a coherent and original answer to the central philosophical question in organizational ethics, How should organizations behave? There is less controversy about whether stakeholder theory is a form of ethical theory, though this does not mean that the theory's content is uncontroversial among ethicists. This entry discusses the development of stakeholder theory in both these contexts (social science and philosophy) and details its answers to both empirical and ethical questions.

HISTORICAL BACKGROUND

The term *stakeholder* is not a new one. It dates back at least as far as the early 18th century, where it sometimes appeared in British legal cases to describe a party holding a stake in a financial transaction. In the narrowest sense, a stakeholder was a neutral party to a transaction or wager who held the money in trust—literally holding the stakes. However, by the early 19th century—as detailed in the *Oxford English Dictionary*—the term had acquired a more expansive definition in two ways. First, its meaning expanded to include all parties to a financial interest, and second, it broadened to describe those parties holding an interest in the broader political system or commonwealth. In some sense, this more expansive use of the term would set the stage for its emergence as a term in the study of business and society.

While the term did not appear explicitly in writing about management for much of the 20th century, the notion that executives must pay attention to the demands of an organization's multiple constituencies has a long history in the early-20th-century precursors to the modern field of organization theory. Mary Parker Follett, an early American management thinker, portrayed the organization as nested in an environment of other actors, each mutually influencing and defining each other. To Follett, the manager's job was to integrate the conflicting interests held by these constituencies, and the success of the company depended, in no small part, on managers recognizing the need to (a) manage all relationships with as much attention as they traditionally paid to personal matters and (b) achieve some degree of creativity in how they dealt with conflicting demands.

Likewise, in his classic book *The Functions of the Executive*, Chester Barnard foreshadowed the eventual emergence of stakeholder thinking. For Barnard, an organization is a cooperative scheme, the result of a conscious effort by many people to work together. As such, an organization's survival depends on its relationship to its environment and its ability to satisfy those individuals interacting with it. The central role, in Barnard's thinking, of executive responsibility—the suppression of personal interest in service of the cooperative scheme—also heralds the eventual exploration of the moral side of stakeholder theory. Barnard introduces notions of balance and touches on questions of whether subordinates should be treated as having intrinsic value (valued for their own sake) or should be treated instrumentally (valued only for what they can do for the executive or the company). These are questions that, today, arise frequently in writing about companies and their stakeholders.

The early works of Follett and Barnard, though often neglected today, played some role in the emergence of the open systems view of organizations in postwar organization theory and, in turn, these authors laid much of the intellectual groundwork for theorizing about stakeholders. Efforts by Peter

Blau, W. Richard Scott, William R. Dill, and James Thompson all centered on the nature of the external environment in which organizations existed, paying particular attention to the nature of the *organization set*—the immediate relationships surrounding an organization. In the ensuing decades, the attention of most organization theorists would shift from the study of organization sets to organization fields, a higher level of analysis at which all organizations and their constituents interact to create institutional norms and rules. Yet the initial insight that a company plays multiple roles within a bounded set of actors would lay the groundwork for the advancement of stakeholder theory as a continuing effort to explore the nature of organization set interactions.

The term *stakeholder* emerged in the study of organizations and management in the early 1960s through the work of the Stanford Research Institute, in the work of Albert Humphreys and others. There, efforts to map program management processes and improve long-range planning techniques led to greater attention on the parties to a management process—that is, its stakeholders—and their role in determining the success of a change program. Both Kenneth Andrews and Igor Ansoff, early advocates of the study of corporate strategy, used the term explicitly and suggested that stakeholders might have something to do with the overall strategy formulation process in a company. However, the term did not attract much attention until the early 1980s with the publication of two books, Ian Mitroff's *Stakeholders of the Organizational Mind* of 1983 and R. Edward Freeman's *Strategic Management: A Stakeholder Approach* of 1984. Of the two, Freeman's has made the more lasting contribution to stakeholder theory.

FREEMAN'S SEMINAL CONTRIBUTION

R. Edward Freeman's book *Strategic Management: A Stakeholder Approach* (1984) is widely recognized as the first major work in stakeholder theory, though misunderstandings about its contents abound. It is, therefore, worth devoting some attention to the nature of Freeman's argument and its implications for the subsequent development of stakeholder theory.

The starting point for Freeman's book is to trace those previous schools of thought that lay a groundwork for thinking about a company's strategy in stakeholder terms. There are four primary schools—the corporate planning literature, open systems theory, the study of corporate social responsibility, and organization theory. For each, Freeman discusses the contributions made to the stakeholder concept. Chief among these contributors are the organization set theorists cited above, systems theorists such as Russell Ackoff, corporate strategists such as Ansoff, and business and society scholars such as Lee Preston and James Post. This section can, in some ways, be read both as a history of the stakeholder concept and as an intellectual genealogy indicative of the various circles in which Freeman was moving at the time that he was conceiving of and developing his approach to stakeholder management.

Freeman's definition of the term *stakeholder* remains the most commonly used (and is the basis for the definition provided above), despite frequent criticisms of its breadth. He writes, "A stakeholder in an organization is (by definition) any group or individual who can affect or is affected by the achievement of an organization's objectives" (p. 46). This definition also lays the groundwork for the visual figure, a hub-and-spoke diagram with the company at the center and stakeholders ranged around in a circle, most commonly associated with stakeholder thinking. Most subsequent writers, however, ignore Freeman's warning that if stakeholder thinking remains at such a generic level—ignoring the specific groups and complex interrelations that characterize actual company-stakeholder interactions—it would have little practical value.

The most obvious and lasting contribution of Freeman's book is the emergence of what has come, more recently, to be called instrumental stakeholder theory—the idea that companies that manage their stakeholder relationships effectively will survive longer and perform better than those companies that do not manage stakeholders well. (This entry will discuss more recent contributions to this stream of research.) In developing this argument, Freeman also offers what remains the most in-depth description of the actual practices and processes by which a company might be said to manage these relationships well. He suggests that stakeholder management "competence" includes a commitment to monitoring stakeholder interests, an ability to formulate strategies for dealing with stakeholders, sophistication in segmenting stakeholder needs, and the alignment of specific business functions (e.g., public affairs, marketing) to dealing with stakeholder needs. In essence, Freeman's book remains one of the most thorough "recipe books" for managers interested in stakeholder management, and far more than its contribution to theory, this remains its greatest strength.

As for Freeman's role in the emergence of an ethical literature on company-stakeholder relations, the genealogy is slightly more complicated. After all, Freeman's book contains little reference to the question of how companies should treat stakeholders, at least insofar as the question goes beyond merely prudential matters of survival or profit. The book contains only one passing reference to ethical and political theory (a stray citation of the writing of the philosopher John Rawls), and it would be a few years before Freeman would acknowledge that, only in later conversations, did he begin to explore seriously the question of stakeholders as moral agents. Yet Freeman's own training as a philosopher and his relationship to the burgeoning scholarly community of business ethicists probably created the conditions by which the 1984 book serves as a foundational work in ethics-based stakeholder theory, despite the fact that it contains little explicitly intended to kindle such discussion.

STAKEHOLDER THEORY IN ORGANIZATIONAL ETHICS

As stated above, stakeholder theory can be looked at as a marriage of two somewhat different theoretical enterprises—ethical and empirical. The first is the search for an ethics-based stakeholder theory. From its onset, in the early 1990s, this project started with several attempts by Freeman and other like-minded philosophers to formulate a so-called normative core from which to deduce the moral obligations of the company in dealing with its stakeholders. Many scholars thus sought to establish a clear philosophical foundation on which to ground statements about how companies *should* treat their stakeholders. Almost every major ethical theory—utilitarianism, property rights, feminist ethics, and Kantian deontology—offered some basis for relevant arguments.

At its heart, the quest for a normative core for stakeholder theory has clear roots in the more long-standing debate over the purpose of the corporation in a capitalist society. Ethicists tend to draw a sharp distinction between stockholder and stakeholder models of capitalism—the central question being "For whose benefit should the corporation be run?" The stockholder model, which received its most ardent defense from Nobel laureate Milton Friedman, holds that the corporation must strive to maximize returns for its shareholders. The property rights of its shareholders, the nature of fiduciary duties, the legal mandates surrounding corporate governance, and public policy considerations all offer some support for the stockholder model.

Set in opposition to this model, however, the stakeholder model holds that a corporation owes obligations to more than just the stockholders. For example, Thomas Donaldson and Lee Preston (in a widely cited article) argue that a more expansive notion of property rights allowed stakeholder groups to make legitimate claims on the value produced by the corporation. Each of the attempts to derive a normative core from some established school of ethical theory arrived at similar conclusions, though often from very different starting points. The object of the corporation, they argue, is to maximize stakeholder wealth—which includes but is not limited to stockholders.

With time, the pursuit of a normative, or ethics-based, stakeholder theory has gone beyond the simple pursuit of a normative core. Today, three major problems occupy ethicists interested in how companies should treat their stakeholders—identification, distribution, and procedure. Each has received attention in existing research but each demands further elaboration.

Identification

The problem of identification seems simple enough: Who should managers of a particular company identify as its stakeholders? Given the potentially vast number of actors claiming a stake in the company's operations, identification involves determining which actors truly have enough moral standing to be considered stakeholders. This is a moral problem rather than merely a question of description. A local business may well pay protection money to a local crime boss, and this person may affect and be affected by a company's actions. However, few ethicists would argue that crime bosses have moral standing vis-à-vis a company. Indeed, companies may well treat any number of social actors as salient (i.e., requiring attention) without considering them to have the moral standing afforded by ethics-based stakeholder theory.

From the earliest days of stakeholder theory, the identification problem has produced a great number of distinctions. Early stakeholder theorists spoke of stakeholders as either primary or secondary, indicating that some groups may have greater or lesser claims to stakeholder status. In a frequently cited article, Mitchell, Agle, and Wood suggest that the characteristics of power, legitimacy, and urgency not only determine who the company is likely to consider salient (an empirical question) but which groups merit this attention (a normative one).

It is, however, Robert Phillips's book *Stakeholder Theory and Organizational Ethics* that offers the most coherent and complete answer to the identification problem. Drawing on a principle of justice as fairness first articulated by John

Rawls, Phillips contends that a company should consider as stakeholders all those parties that participate in the cooperative scheme surrounding it. In other words, a company has an obligation to attend to the claims of parties insofar as it willingly receives benefits from them. Based on this notion of fairness, Phillips distinguishes between legitimate stakeholders (i.e., those that possess moral standing based on claims of fairness or reciprocity) and derivative stakeholders (i.e., those parties whose claims on a company are indirect, deriving from their relationship to a legitimate stakeholder). Thus, a company must recognize employees as a legitimate stakeholder because the company willingly accepts benefits from the employees' efforts; however, the company need not consider the labor union acting on behalf of employees a legitimate stakeholder, except insofar as their claims derive from their relationship to employees. In sum, Phillips grounds the debate over identification more firmly in the realm of ethical theory and offers one possible solution.

Distribution

The second and arguably greater ethical question in stakeholder theory is the problem of distribution, "How should a company distribute the value that it creates?" Of course, this is a highly simplified way to express the problem, as businesses tend to generate very different types of value (many of which are incommensurate with each other), operate over long time frames in which seeming trade-offs can worsen or resolve themselves, and generate enormous costs that may well be treated as morally different from the value the company creates. If a company damages the natural environment, for example, it deprives community members of certain intangible goods (peace of mind, quality of life) for which monetary value does not fully compensate. Many of the costs involved manifest over long periods of time, during which the immediate benefits to the company of polluting may place the company in better (or worse) position to remedy the environmental problems that arise. Finally, if the damage leads to deaths in the community, these costs are unlikely to fit naturally into a cost-benefit calculation along with returns to stockholders and employee salaries enjoyed by other stakeholders.

Despite the complexities, stakeholder theorists have continued to wrestle with the distribution problem. To a great degree, solutions to the distribution problem are set in contradistinction to the notion that companies (particularly corporations owned by stockholders) owe all their residual value to their owners. Alexei Marcoux, in an important article in the

Business Ethics Quarterly, mounts a vigorous defense of this principle. He contends that the notion that a company owes a fiduciary duty to shareholders—a duty to act first and foremost in the interests of shareholders—is the natural moral analog to other situations where fiduciary duties apply. Information asymmetries, the degree of possible harm, and the need for trust all create conditions where the company should acknowledge a fiduciary duty to it stockholders similar to that of doctor to patient or lawyer to client. Of course, this idea—equally present in Friedman's justification based on the property rights of owners—actually offers only an incomplete response to the distribution problem. After all, we may agree that shareholders, as owners of the company, deserve special consideration and still have few answers about the right way to distribute value and costs. Many of the decisions companies make and the trade-offs they address have only incidental impact on stockholder value.

In most such cases, the causal relationships are so tenuous as to make considerations of fiduciary duty and residual wealth not useful, if not altogether irrelevant, for solving the practical moral problems involved. Consider a simple example of an airline deciding how much airline baggage to allow on the airplane. Insofar as a company (rather than regulators) still gets to make this choice, managers must decide between passenger convenience and the well-being of employees—flight attendants are often injured trying to help passengers with oversized carry-on baggage. To say "the company should do whatever is best for the shareholder" is to say very little indeed. There is no evidence that baggage policies are a major determinant of customer preference and little more evidence that employee morale translates directly into financial returns in this industry. Indeed, fuel costs (a very important driver of profit in the industry) are not affected either way, as the baggage will end up somewhere on the airplane regardless of whether it is checked or carried aboard. The company is still left to decide how to distribute the good among two conflicting stakeholder claims. Though this is a trivial example, it may be more representative of the problems faced by management on a daily basis.

The general principle often attributed to stakeholder theory is that companies should distribute value broadly, that the company should be managed so as to create value for all its stakeholders. In specific terms, Phillips offers the clearest interpretation of this general principle. He argues that a company owes obligations proportional to the relative contribution that the stakeholder makes to the success of the cooperative scheme. Of course, by marking out such a specific position, Phillips exposes himself to critiques that the resulting allocations are still too narrow to be morally justifiable. After all, some groups (e.g., local communities) may offer few tangible benefits to a company, contributing little to the cooperative scheme, but still deserve some consideration if, for example, the company decides to erect a particularly ugly building that will destroy property values for miles around. Still, the distribution question awaits a more persuasive argument.

Procedure

The problem of procedure concerns the proper role of stakeholders in the formulation of strategies and policies that affect them: Does a company have an obligation to engage with stakeholders and invite their input into policy decisions? Regardless of the moral issues involved, many companies do offer ways for particular stakeholder groups to express their viewpoints. However, given that companies, especially very large corporations, can exercise a great deal of power (often on a par with governmental power) over customers, employees, and local communities, the question of whether managers owe an obligation to provide due process (e.g., via grievance processes, consultations, etc.) remains an important moral question.

Arguments in this vein tend to find their roots in one of two traditions. On the one hand, ethicists may choose to draw on the work of German philosopher Jürgen Habermas. Habermasian, or discourse, ethics hold that morally right decisions in a political context are only possible insofar as they are created through open public discussion and deliberation. The only way to honor man's nature as a reasoning being is to respect reason's role in the act of communication and deliberation. Applying this principle of communicative reason, Jeffrey Smith has argued that a company has an obligation to consult with its stakeholders so that the resulting decisions will not only be better but more ethically legitimate than those created in a vacuum.

A second perspective on the moral problem of procedure is the emerging discussion of multistakeholder dialogue. Though not necessarily rooted in any particular ethical theory, authors such as Jerry Calton and Stephen Payne, drawing on insights from William Isaacs and David Bohm, argue that dialogue is a natural and important facet of all human relationships and that suppressing dialogue in stakeholder relationships is both imprudent and unnatural. It is not clear, of course, what the extent of this dialogue must be—who should be involved, how long it should last—but Calton and Payne seem to suggest that these considerations should flow organically from the dialogue itself rather than according to any external constraints.

STAKEHOLDER THEORY AS SOCIAL SCIENCE

If stakeholder theory is (as suggested above) a marriage between two somewhat different theoretical enterprises—the ethical and social science traditions—the latter has been the more fickle partner. Many social scientists researching these interactions have done so while, more or less, accepting the notion that the normative project remains an essential part of stakeholder research. For these theorists, accepting that stakeholders have intrinsic value is a shared premise for stakeholder theorizing. In other words, the social scientist must accept a fundamental ethical principle and then embark on research that advances understanding either the empirical or the ethical implications of this premise. The ideal outcome, then, is some *convergent stakeholder theory*, a phrase coined by Thomas Jones and Andrew Wicks, in which both efforts combine in a hybrid that includes both a sophisticated morally grounded concept of how companies should treat stakeholders and an empirically robust causal chain linking such moral behavior to desirable outcomes.

A minority of social scientists doing research on stakeholders tend to reject this desire for convergence and see it as a threat to traditional assumptions about how to do proper social science. From this perspective, stakeholder research is merely one domain of scholarly activity that studies how companies and their stakeholders interact, and the relationship between the ethics- and social science–based traditions is, at best, at arm's length. There is, they might argue, no reason to privilege the ethics-based element of stakeholder research (as both ethicists and those seeking convergence have tended to do). Indeed, within this second camp, there is even considerable controversy as to whether there is such a thing as "stakeholder theory," if the term *theory* is interpreted solely in social scientific terms. They ask, Does stakeholder theory refer to some unique set of causal factors that theories of power, resource dependence, networks, and institutions do not encompass?

The interplay between these two camps serves as an intellectual backdrop against which good social scientific investigation of these interactions continues unabated. This section discusses the three main areas of investigation covered to date.

What Are the Effects of Stakeholder Management?

Building on the foundation laid by Freeman's (1984) book, one of the most popular subjects for study in the stakeholder research tradition has been the question of whether it matters (financially) how a company manages its stakeholder relationships. In other words, does stakeholder management actually correlate with widely valued outcomes such as profit or stock price?

In this realm, Jones's influential *Academy of Management Review* article from 1995 on instrumental stakeholder theory remains the central work. Jones argues there that the most important characteristic of a company's behavior toward its stakeholders is its moral quality, the presence or absence of dishonesty and/or opportunism. (It is worth noting, here, that this emphasis on morality as the distinguishing feature of good stakeholder management constitutes a departure from Freeman's original model of stakeholder management as largely concerning the procedures undertaken by the company.) Jones proceeds to argue that opportunism and dishonesty will tend to make stakeholders unhappy and lead to increased contracting costs, whereby stakeholders exact higher costs from the company up-front as a way of safeguarding against future opportunism. These costs translate into lower financial performance for the company. In contrast, companies that are honest and trustworthy in their dealings with stakeholders have more efficient contracting and achieve a competitive advantage. Jones then offers an extended list of specific practices (e.g., disproportionate executive compensation, poison pills, and greenmail) that qualify as opportunism and should, thus, correlate with lower financial performance.

A great deal of empirical research has been done to substantiate, either directly or indirectly, the claims of instrumental stakeholder theory. Much of this research has followed not from the theoretical claims of authors such as Freeman and Jones but from the corporate social responsibility literature that Freeman acknowledged as one of his intellectual antecedents.

Much research, of varying levels of scholarly rigor, has been conducted on the subject of the relationship between corporate social performance and financial performance. They address the rather simplistic question, Does "doing good" lead to "doing well"? Insofar as social responsibility can be taken as a rough proxy for stakeholder management, much research hints at the fact that stakeholder management can have some measurable effect on financial performance.

More persuasive, perhaps, is that genre of empirical research designed to test the specific theoretical propositions advanced by instrumental stakeholder theory. Berman's 1998 study of executive compensation, for example, suggests that companies with abnormally high levels of executive compensation do, indeed, underperform those that do not. Subsequent examinations of similar data also suggest that companies that attend to some important stakeholder issues (e.g., product safety and employee well-being) perform better than those that do not. But there is no evidence to suggest that this relationship occurs because the companies value stakeholders intrinsically; rather, it could occur because of the interaction between business strategy and the treatment of stakeholders.

Of course, it is worth noting that financial performance is not the only outcome variable of interest in stakeholder research. Broader questions of societal welfare may also arise from the ways that companies interact with their immediate stakeholders; however, these remain waters uncharted by stakeholder researchers.

What Are the Sources of Stakeholder Management?

A second interesting area for social science inquiry is the question of why companies adopt certain approaches to stakeholder management. Often branded "descriptive" stakeholder research, this research represents the least promising area of research for those interested in advancing convergent stakeholder theory and the most promising area for those seeking to study company-stakeholder interactions on their own terms. After all, to study how a company manages its stakeholders requires that theorists appeal not to "stakeholder theory" but to more established organization theories to account for a phenomenon (stakeholder management) that is interesting in its own right.

Two contributions to this genre stand out in particular; ironically, both were published in the same issue of the *Academy of Management Review* in 1997. Timothy Rowley's network theory–based account of stakeholder management posits that a company's approach to managing its stakeholders will depend, in no small part, on the company's structural position relative to its stakeholder set. Companies existing in dense networks of stakeholders or who are more central will behave different from those in less dense networks or who have less central positions. Rowley's efforts represent a groundbreaking attempt to conceive of the stakeholder set not as a traditional hub-and-spoke system evoked by simplistic readings of Freeman but rather as a web of interrelated groups tied both to the company and to each other. Yet, as network theoretical accounts of organizational phenomena grow more sophisticated, Rowley's effort seems only a simple first step in what must become a more elaborate model of company behavior.

Ronald Mitchell, Bradley Agle, and Donna Wood's article on stakeholder salience is the second important contribution to the descriptive genre. Mitchell, Agle, and Wood posit that stakeholders possess varying levels of three important characteristics—power, legitimacy, and urgency. Insofar as stakeholders possess more of each characteristic, they will be more salient in managers' thinking, receiving priority in decisions about how to allocate value. This model is a useful integration of important insights from various schools of organization theory (i.e., resource dependence, institutional theory, and social cognitive theories), and the ability to categorize stakeholders using these characteristics is a useful managerial heuristic. However, this account also raises stumbling blocks for those who would seek to build further stakeholder theory based on it. Subsequent researchers have (a) offered various interpretations (and misinterpretations) of the term urgency; (b) overlooked the article's emphasis on managerial perception (it is, after all, not how powerful and legitimate the stakeholder is but how powerful and legitimate managers perceive them to be that determines salience); and (c) ignored the extremely simplistic notion of salience, which serves as a vague proxy for the complexities inherent in classifying approaches to stakeholder management.

Indeed, these two contributions, though exemplary, offer two caveats to those who would understand why companies adopt certain approaches to stakeholder management. First, their appeal to existing schools of organization theory, though well-conceived, exposes the stakeholder research domain to the popular critique that stakeholder research has no theory of its own. Second, their emphasis on the causal factors involved (networks, stakeholder characteristics) rather than on the outcome (stakeholder management) does little to remedy the confusion (which must, by now, be apparent to the reader) surrounding how we conceive of stakeholder management. The practices cited by Freeman, the moral qualities of Jones, and the general orientations envisioned by Rowley, Mitchell, Agle, and Wood are all elements of a many-headed beast, and we have little reason to prefer one to the other, scattering the continued efforts of stakeholder researchers.

Why Do Stakeholder Groups Behave as They Do?

From a practical standpoint, a more interesting question for the manager is the issue of how to predict stakeholder behavior. This question forms the basis of the third and, at present, the most rapidly growing stream of stakeholder literature, asking "Why do stakeholder groups behave as they do?" Marshalling theories of collective action, resource dependence, game theory, and social identity, stakeholder researchers have explored this question in several steps, starting first with the question of why stakeholder groups mobilize and then advancing to the question of why, when they do mobilize, they choose the influence strategies that they do. A final step, as yet relatively unexplored, is what conditions determine whether or not these influence strategies actually succeed.

The question of stakeholder mobilization would, at first glance, seem simple enough. Stakeholders act when their interests are threatened. For many years, students of business and society argued some variant of this thesis, contending that stakeholder action resulted from some violation (real or perceived) of the stakeholder group's expectations. When they did not receive what they expected, they tended to strike, boycott, protest, or otherwise mobilize against the company. This was both an intuitive and, in many cases, entirely adequate explanation, but in many important cases, stakeholders mobilized around relatively small violations of their interests, and in many more instances, groups with clear interest did not mobilize or, at least, did not manage to do so in sufficient numbers to have much impact.

Efforts by Timothy Rowley and Mihnea Moldoveanu represent one attempt, premised on an identity-based account, to explain these phenomena. They argue that interests do play an important role in mobilization; so, too, does the collective identity of stakeholder group members. Groups (e.g., certain activist groups) that see protest as a fundamental piece of their group identity are more likely to mobilize. Moreover, structural conditions can strengthen or undermine a common sense of identity. People who are, for example, both parents and churchgoers may be much more likely to mobilize against television violence than those who occupy only one of those groups. Likewise, some groups will possess more or less of the resources necessary to overcome the considerable barriers to collective action for stakeholder groups. Here, again, previous experience with protest and overlapping identities play an important role. In sum, companies must attend to the constellation of interests and identity that surround them, lest they inaccurately assess the likelihood of stakeholder group mobilization.

A second important step in this stream of literature involves the study of why stakeholder groups, once mobilized, choose the strategies that they do to influence the company. Here, the work of Jeff Frooman, extending resource dependence theory to a stakeholder context, sheds some insight. Frooman maintains that a stakeholder's choice of influence strategy depends on just how dependent the stakeholder group is on the focal company for resources and on how dependent the company is on the stakeholder. Depending on how these conditions combine, stakeholders will choose to act either directly or indirectly and will choose either to coerce or compromise with the company. Subsequent empirical research on the subject suggests that there is much to these insights, though other institutional factors may be at play as well.

The final step in this area remains relatively unexplored: When do these influence strategies succeed or fail to change company policy? Here, as Rowley has argued in his earlier piece, a link can be forged back to the question of antecedents of stakeholder management, yet much works remain to make this connection explicit.

CONCLUSION

Stakeholder theory remains a high growth field of research in the study of business and society, with numerous articles and books being published each year. With students of business strategy and organization theory now showing renewed interest in studying this subject, this is likely to continue. This entry has only hinted at the complexities of this literature, yet it is hoped that it has shown important steps in our evolving understanding of the empirical and normative dimensions of company-stakeholder interaction.

—Michael E. Johnson-Cramer

Further Readings

Donaldson, T., & Preston, L. (1995). The stakeholder theory of the corporation: Concepts, evidence, and implications. *Academy of Management Review, 20*(1), 65–91.

Evan, W., & Freeman, R. E. (1993). A stakeholder theory of the modern corporation: Kantian capitalism. In T. Beauchamp & N. Bowie (Eds.), *Ethical theory and business* (pp. 97–106). Englewood Cliffs, NJ: Prentice Hall.

Freeman, R. E. (1984). *Strategic management: A stakeholder approach.* Boston: Pitman.

Johnson-Cramer, M., Berman, S. L., & Post, J. E. (2003). Reexamining the concept of "stakeholder management." In J. Andriof, S. Waddock, S. Rahman, & B. Husted (Eds.), *Unfolding stakeholder thinking* (Vol. 2., pp. 145–161). London: Greenleaf.

Jones, T. (1995). Instrumental stakeholder theory: A synthesis of ethics and economics. *Academy of Management Review, 20*(2), 404–437.

Phillips, R. (2003). *Stakeholder theory and organizational ethics.* San Francisco: Berrett-Koehler.

Rowley, T., & Moldoveanu, M. (2003). When do stakeholders act? An interest and identity-based model of stakeholder mobilization. *Academy of Management Review, 28*(2), 204–219.

Schilling, M. (2000). Decades ahead of her time: Advancing stakeholder theory through the ideas of Mary Parker Follett. *Journal of Management History, 6*(5), 224–243.

ETHICAL DECISION MAKING

E thical decision making is a cognitive process that considers various ethical principles, rules, and virtues or the maintenance of relationships to guide or judge individual or group decisions or intended actions. It helps one determine the right course of action or the right thing to do and also enables one to analyze whether another's decisions or actions are right or good. It seeks to answer questions about how one is supposed to act or live.

ETHICAL DECISION-MAKING PROCESS

Many ethics scholars have developed models of ethical decision making or provided us with specific procedural steps enabling one to reach an ethically supported decision or course of action. In the abstract, this process is a fairly rational and logical course. In reality, ethical decision making is filled with abstractness, illogic, and even whim. Nonetheless, the following is a synthesis of these models and procedures.

Step 1: Identify the Ethical Dimensions Embedded in the Problem

In the first step of the ethical decision-making process, the decision maker must be able to determine if an ethical analysis is required. The decision maker must determine if there is a possible violation of an important ethical principle, societal law, or organizational standard or policy or if there are potential consequences that should be sought or avoided that emanate from an action being considered to resolve the problem.

Step 2: Collect Relevant Information

The decision maker must collect the relevant facts to continue in the ethical decision-making process. Related to Step 1, if an ethical principle, such as an individual's right, is in jeopardy of being violated, the decision maker should seek to gather as much information as possible about which rights are being forsaken and to what degree. A consequential focus would prompt the decision maker to attempt to measure the type, degree, and amount of harm being inflicted or that will be inflicted on others.

Step 3: Evaluate the Information According to Ethical Guidelines

Once the information has been collected, the decision maker must apply some type of standard or assessment criterion to evaluate the situation. As described below, the decision maker might use one of the predominant ethics theories—utilitarianism, rights, or justice. Adherence to a societal law or organizational policy may be an appropriate evaluation criterion. Others may consider assessing the relevant information based on a value system where various ethical principles or beliefs are held in varying degrees of importance.

Step 4: Consider Possible Action Alternatives

The decision maker needs to generate a set of possible action alternatives, such as confronting another person's actions, seeking a higher authority, or stepping in and changing the direction of what is happening. This step is important since it is helpful to limit the number of actions that it may realistically be possible to respond to or that may be required to resolve the ethical situation.

Step 5: Make a Decision

In Step 5, the decision maker should seek the action alternative that is supported by the evaluation criteria used in Step 3. Sometimes there may be a conflict between the right courses of action indicated by different ethics theories, as shown later in the illustration provided. It might not be possible in all cases for a decision maker to select a course of action that is supported by all the ethics theories or other evaluation criteria used in the decision-making process.

Step 6: Act or Implement

Ethical decision making is not purely an intellectual exercise. The decision maker, if truly seeking to resolve the problem being considered, must take action. Therefore, once the action alternatives have been identified in Step 4 and the optimal response is selected in Step 5, the action is taken in Step 6.

Step 7: Review the Action, Modify if Necessary

Finally, once the action has been taken and the results are known, the decision maker should review the consequences of the action and whether the action upheld the ethical principles sought by the decision maker. If the optimal resolution to the problem is not achieved, the decision maker may need to modify the actions being taken or return to the beginning of the decision-making process to reevaluate the analysis of the facts leading to the action alternative selected.

APPLYING ETHICS THEORIES

The following is an illustration of Step 3 of the ethical decision-making process that applies three predominant ethics theories—utilitarianism, rights, and justice—to a common business problem: Should a company close an operating plant and lay off its workers?

When using a *utilitarian perspective*—where the decision maker considers the consequences or outcomes of an action and seeks to maximize the greatest good for the greatest number of those affected by the decision—it is critical for the decision maker to determine to the greatest extent possible who will be affected by the decision. In the example used here, those affected may include the company itself (since closing the plant may improve its bottom line by dramatically reducing plant overhead and employee payroll expenses); the company's investors, if a publicly held business (who may receive a greater return on their investment if the plant closes and employees are laid off); the company's employees (who will suffer if the plant closes and they are laid off from their jobs); and the local community where the plant is located (who will suffer a reduction in the municipal tax base as well as a loss of economic activity for businesses that relied on the plant and its employees).

One might argue that the greater good is served if some workers are immediately laid off and the plant is closed, ensuring the immediate financial viability of the company. Yet others might reason to an ethical solution that requests all employees to take a slight pay cut so that no workers are laid off and the plant remains open, thus achieving the greatest good for the greatest number of people affected.

A decision maker who considers a *rights perspective* would consider the entitlements of those affected by the decision. There are economic rights

31

affecting the displaced employees and the community surrounding the plant in question, as well as the rights of the laid-off employees to be informed of the potential plant closing. These rights may be in opposition to the managers' right to act freely in a way that could be understood as acting responsibly, by closing the plant and thus benefiting the remaining employees of the company and the company's investors.

A rights reasoner might provide ample notice to the workers of the layoffs so that they could seek other employment. Or the rights reasoner might consider the economic rights of the community and actively seek a buyer for the plant in the hope that it would remain open and continue to employ the workers. Finally, the rights of the company and its investors could persuade the decision maker to conclude that closing the plant and firing the workers is the right thing to do.

Finally, one who considers a *justice perspective* may focus on either the equitable distribution of the benefits and costs resulting from the plant closing and employee layoffs (distributive justice) or the maintenance of rules and standards (procedural justice). For the distributive justice reasoner, the ethical decision process would focus not only on the benefits incurred by the company and its investors through the plant closure and layoffs but also on the significant harms or costs imposed on those employees laid off from work and the local community and businesses negatively affected by the plant closing.

The procedural justice reasoner would focus on the preservation of the social contract that exists between the employer and employees or would seek to minimize the harm imposed on the powerless (the employees and the local community) by the powerful (the employer and investors). The procedural justice reasoner would argue that the employees, community officials, and local business leaders should have a voice in this decision since they are significantly affected by the decision.

The decision maker may decide that a more just action would require the company to assume greater financial responsibility by providing job training and outplacement services for the displaced employees. The company could consider making some type of economic contribution to the local community to soften the blow of a reduction in the tax base or economic activity in the area. Or the company could involve the employees and local community leaders in developing a system that results in the plant closure occurring over a longer period of time to spread out the eventual costs endured by the community.

CONCLUSION

People during their daily routine at work or in society are called on to make ethical decisions. Therefore, their ethical decision-making process may be a frequent, yet subconscious, cognitive process. Do you drive the speed limit or come to a complete stop at the intersection where a stop sign is posted? An individual can decide to act in the right way almost without thinking about it, but the decision maker is implicitly considering and processing the steps delineated above to reach the ethically supported decision to obey the speed limit or stop at the intersection in the road.

—James Weber

Further Readings

Beauchamp, T. L., & Bowie, N. E. (Eds.). (2004). *Ethical theory and business* (7th ed.). Upper Saddle River, NJ: Prentice Hall.

Darwall, S. (Ed.). (2003). *Virtue ethics*. Malden, MA: Blackwell.

Hartman, L. P. (1998). *Perspectives in business ethics*. Chicago: Irwin/McGraw-Hill.

Held, V. (Ed.). (1995). *Justice and care: Essential readings in feminist ethics*. Boulder, CO: Westview Press.

Velasquez, M. G. (2002). *Business ethics: Concepts and cases* (5th ed.). Upper Saddle River, NJ: Prentice Hall.

COMPETITION

competition is a process in which individuals strive to achieve mutually exclusive positions, such as the attainment of a single reward. Competitive processes may be among individuals within a single business, or it may be among businesses. Decision making in a competitive context tends to emphasize the efficient accomplishment of self-interested goals. Governments often intervene in competitive processes with laws and regulations to influence competitive processes and outcomes.

This entry discusses issues of efficiency, justice, human rights, and public policy associated with competition. The trade-offs and debates surrounding these issues are likely to intensify as the global economy becomes increasingly competitive and rival businesses seek to outdo each other by harnessing genomics and nanotechnology for their own advantage.

COMPETITIVE ALLOCATION OF RESOURCES

A key outcome of competition is the allocation of resources in a marketplace where supplies are limited or scarce. A business conducts its activities in an environment of scarcity—scarce supplies, scarce skills, and scarce channels to the customer—and it may confront other organizations dependent on access to the same scarce inputs. In this context, competition allocates scarce resources among businesses based on the relative advantages of each to create value for potential suppliers and customers.

Businesses that are lucky, skillful, or endowed with advantages in the competitive process expend less capital, time, and effort to operate their value-creating activities. Conversely, competitors with relative disadvantages in an environment of scarcity are not able to operate with comparable scale, scope, efficiency, and quality. In this way, competition between businesses is the conduct of interdependent organizations striving for mutually exclusive positions of advantage to create value so that the success of one comes at the expense of another.

One consequence of competition is that rivals may bid up the prices for valuable and scarce inputs they demand for their activities. In an economy that equilibrates supply and demand, more supply of these inputs is offered as their prices are bid up, and competitors are provided with more inputs to produce a greater quantity of valuable goods and services. The process seemed to Adam Smith as if an invisible hand guided productive resources for social progress.

Another consequence is that competitors strive for relative advantage in forming valuable relationships. For example, competition may cause a rival to invest in product innovation, extend warranty programs, develop new channels for convenient shopping and delivery, customize service, and enhance the postsales customer experience. In competition, a successful seller must remain alert to opportunities for strengthening the unique value it brings to a potential customer relationship.

Business competitors, each motivated by self-interest to capture profit, also strive to outdo each other to form and protect attractive relationships with suppliers. For example, a rival might offer to share proprietary technology with its suppliers, train suppliers' personnel at no cost, enter long-term contracts, or provide suppliers with development funds.

In these ways, competition appears as an intendedly efficient process of struggle for advantageous position to reduce scarcity and strengthen the creation and distribution of value in society. Business competitors, motivated by self-interest to capture profit, constantly strive to outdo rivals by forming and protecting increasingly attractive relationships with customers and suppliers.

PUBLIC POLICY ISSUES

At some times in some places unregulated competition may lead to unserved needs and unintended consequences. One function of government is to regulate the actions of business so that their competitive pursuit of advantage is not at the expense of the public good. Typical government regulatory controls on competitive action target the effects on the environment, safety, health, and property. For example, antitrust regulations limit consolidation within industries to encourage the social benefits of competition, commerce regulations govern the actions of competitors within industries to ensure fair trade, and some regulations may be used to raise or lower barriers against the entry of new competitors. In the United States, for example, broadband communications is subject to regulations restricting competitors in the cable industry from either consolidating or realizing exclusive advantage from their own investments in cable assets.

Barriers can be a factor in an industry's competitive structure. In this vein, licensing regulations are an example of a regulatory barrier to competition. In the United States, for example, there are more than 500 occupations that require licensing. Licensing may facilitate honest and fair exchange by monitoring and controlling quality and standards. Conversely, licensing may be a barrier that limits competition, economic opportunity, and wealth creation. For example, occupational licensing has sometimes limited the supply of hairstyling salons for minorities in some areas of the United States because the local certification requirements excluded the hair needs of the minority groups. This is an example of a regulatory limit on competition that affects the fair distribution of goods and services to all segments of the community.

Some businesses may seek to participate in the public-policy-making process to influence the scope and magnitude of the regulatory constraints on their competitive conduct. Mechanisms for their participation include organizing in trade associations and supporting autonomous advocacy groups for research, information dissemination, lobbying, and political donations. Though competitors in business, they may cooperate through these mechanisms to persuade legislators and regulators to pass laws and regulations that are favorable, and to defeat those that are unfavorable, to the special interests of the participating businesses.

Business participation in the public-policy-making process, motivated by the competitive struggle for advantage, may have both good and bad consequences. For example, participation that increases the use of reliable information in the process is likely to enable better policy decisions than could be expected from a relatively uninformed process. Conversely, the pursuit of self-interested advantage may motivate some competitors to corruptly "capture" governments by coercing or compelling the public policy decision makers to align with their special business interests against the interests of other public policy participants and citizens.

PROBLEMS OF GLOBAL COMPETITION

The dynamics of global competition compel business activities to locate in geographic areas where scarce supplies can be acquired and deployed most advantageously. As comparative advantages among geographic areas change and businesses relocate their activities, the changes in the quality of life in local communities may lead to calls for social protection. These dynamics highlight the temporal dimension of social welfare in those areas where competitors are engaged and the need for competitors to demonstrate responsibility in both the short and long terms as the process unfolds across multiple geographic areas.

When competing on a global scale, a significant challenge for managers is to effectively and fairly balance the interests of stakeholders in both the home and host societies. This situation has potential conflicts of interest, created when one individual has an explicit responsibility to one party and simultaneously has an incentive to serve inconsistent interests of another. The efficacy of competition as a process to create value and increase social welfare in this situation is put at risk. Calls for government regulation on business may become more frequent if competition disrupts traditional lifestyles and sustainability of communities.

OTHER SOCIAL CONCERNS

Competitive conduct arises from the decision making of competitors responding to their perceptions of opportunities to create value. Decision making that is misinformed, grounded in uncertainties, or unable to efficiently adjust to the information of the marketplace may lead to surpluses and shortages. Factors influencing these outcomes include the magnitude of profit that satisfies their motive for competitive conduct and their responsiveness to trade-offs between profit and commonly accepted definitions of basic human rights. The paragraphs below consider issues of just distribution, human rights, and social efforts to lessen the potential harms from competitive failures.

Competition and Distributional Justice

Cognitive constraints on competitive decision makers may, even without unjust intent, produce unjust distributions. For example, self-interested competitors may pursue a "cherry-picking" strategy in which they first rank-order potential customers based on their value and then serve the most valuable in the order until the capacity of the seller is exhausted. This strategy leads to underserving the least attractive segments of need.

Absent any regulatory constraints, for example, private health care providers in a community may compete, but still may leave unsatisfied a portion of the community's need for care (e.g., care for the uninsured) even while abundantly serving another portion (e.g., care for the insured). This situation, common in the United States, focuses attention on the strength of profit and the weakness of distributive justice as motivators of competition in free markets. Furthermore, this example illustrates that the principle of appropriable value embedded in unregulated competition may not consider all social costs in its accounting.

Article 25 of the United Nations' Universal Declaration of Human Rights lists access to health care as a basic human right. In this view, the inability of competition to produce a sufficient supply of health care to satisfy the entire need, including the need of those unable to pay a market price, points out a fundamental deficiency of competition. Related basic human rights include (but are not necessarily limited to) food, housing, clothing, education, information, and transportation. Those who view competition as conduct that does not fairly distribute the basic necessities of human rights often call for constraints on self-interested autonomy in business decision making. Socialism is an alternative system intended to introduce such constraints. There are many forms of socialism, ranging from fully centralized planning of production to more mixed economies, which attempt to blend the benefits of competition with public welfare interests.

Subsidies for Competition

Subsidies, financial assistance given by one person or government to another to serve some private or public purposes, can be one mechanism of a mixed economy to ensure broad participation in competitive processes likely to have beneficial social consequences. For example, a national government may subsidize private sector research and development to ensure the home country's ability to compete in high-technology global markets; or it may subsidize its domestic farm community so that it can compete in world food markets.

The recipient of a subsidy could apply it to reduce its internal cost of business or pass it along to its buyers in the form of lower prices. In markets that are not perfectly competitive, however, either approach may lead to a distortion of the competitive process for determining prices. This calls attention to the ethical issues related to fair bargaining and determining a just price in a marketplace that mixes competition with subsidies.

The justice with which costs and benefits are distributed is a consideration when evaluating government-subsidized competition. For example, a subsidy recipient may externalize environmental and public health impacts and fail to consider the fairness or justice associated with burdening third parties with these costs. Similarly, subsidies may go to businesses with large existing endowments and leave out small poorly endowed businesses that have no other means to enter the competitive arena; or a business may organize strictly to benefit itself by the amount of the subsidy rather than to establish the value-creating competitive activities that were the intended economic purpose of the subsidy.

Competition as Action: The Precautionary Principle

In the 21st century, business competition often takes the form of a race to commercialize innovative technology. Examples of these competitive races include the pursuit of opportunities created by rapid advances in sciences of genetics and nanotechnology to resolve great problems of scarcity in access to food, organ transplants, and pharmaceuticals. Many individuals and organizational stakeholders are concerned, however, that the pace of innovation in these areas exceeds our capabilities to determine the consequences prior to commercialization. There are risks to be first to commercialize innovations. Not only are there potential technical and market failures but also potential costs to litigate and resolve harms to health, safety, or the environment.

These concerns have led some to urge business to voluntarily restrain the pace of competitive action in their strategies for genetic commerce. This "better safe than sorry" approach to competition, called the precautionary principle, lets others try to prove novel approaches, and then quickly copies the ones proven safe, effective, and valuable. The principle, however, is highly contested by some business stakeholders. It has been called antiscientific, forcing business to offer proof against every allegation of harm. Many competitors argue that uncertainties will never be completely resolved, and it is the job of independent scientists to monitor human health and the environment for signs of harm. In competition, businesses strive for positions of advantage. One approach to capture advantage is to act before rivals—to be the innovator—and then to protect the position with patents and long-term contracts.

Advocates on both sides, however, recognize that the precautionary principle's key test will be in the regulatory context and economic incentives of competition. The rapid pace of scientific discovery makes the balance between commercializing innovations and the precautionary principle an increasingly important dimension of business competition.

Intra-Organizational Competition and Legal Compliance

Compliance with law and regulation is important in countries with developed and enforced legal systems governing competition. Competition within organizations also may be governed. For example, the integrity of internal competition for job promotions may need to demonstrate compliance with legal requirements such as equal opportunity rules in the United States. To ensure integrity of competition within a business, formal processes must address the honest reporting of information, fair and diligent analysis according to standard practice, and visibility for independent monitoring. When the intensity of competition within an organization may cause some to violate, or witness violations of, informal standards for integrity, then the desirable traits of trustworthiness and virtue become increasingly important values. Neutral ombudsmen, hotlines, recruiting, training, and codes of ethics are examples of mechanisms that organizations may use to increase alertness, monitoring, and appropriate resolution of threats to competitive integrity.

Competition, Cooperation, and Individual Decision Making

Attention to the competitive context, or "rules of the game," is useful to understand the ethics of strategic decision making in competition. Game theory, an approach for gaining insights into strategies of decision making constrained by rules, offers a widely known model of the context of competition—the prisoner's dilemma. The prisoner's dilemma illustrates that the outcomes of competition may depend on the instrumental ethics embedded in the rules of the competitive processes. These include trade-offs between social accounting and private interests in the governance of competition and competitors' reputations for honesty, integrity, fairness, and virtue.

In this competitive game, two prisoners not yet convicted are held by a judicial system in separate prison cells. They are not allowed to communicate with each other. The prosecutor wants convictions with minimal expense, and she or he offers a reduced sentence for the prisoner who confesses and testifies against the other. At the same time, the prosecutor promises an extremely long sentence for the prisoner who does not confess. If both confess, however, the testimony is not needed and will not be rewarded. The prisoners are given the sentences for each possible decision. The prisoners cannot change their decision once made and they cannot confer with each other.

The prisoners each see that the total time they will spend in prison is the least if they both do not confess (4 years for the first and 4 years for the second equals 8 years total). Prisoner 1 sees a risk of receiving a 15-year sentence if Prisoner 2 decides to confess. Without the benefit of additional communication, Prisoner 1 will receive a lower sentence by confessing no matter what Prisoner 2 decides (10 instead of 15 years for Prisoner 1 if Prisoner 2 confesses; 1 instead of 4 years if Prisoner 2 does not confess). Thus, Prisoner 1, competing for the lowest sentence, confesses.

Prisoner 2 sees the same logic from her or his cell. No matter what Prisoner 1 decides, Prisoner 2 gets a lighter sentence by confessing. Not so regrettably, perhaps, the logic of competition in this game leads both prisoners to confess. From the prosecutor's perspective, the cause of social justice could not have been better served—the criminals will be in prison for the longest combined sentences possible given the alternatives.

In addition to its suggestion of an interesting prosecutorial technique, the game offers two major insights into the ethical principles of self-interested decision making in a competitive context. These principles address the interest of society relative to that of the competitors and the value of reputations for reliable trustworthiness and, surprisingly, for vengeance. The first insight is that more social welfare is created (the longer combined sentences when they both confess) when competitors cannot communicate with one another. If they are permitted to communicate before they make their choice, they may arrange to collude with each other by agreeing "not to confess." Collusion earns the best outcome for the competitors under the circumstances, though it is to society's detriment.

The second insight is that competitors' (i.e., prisoners') mutual interests are best served when they may be trusted to forbear and trade fairly. One may be exploited, however, by a self-interested competitor willing to defect from the position of mutual forbearance. It follows, then, that there are advantages to be gained from cooperation when competitors have known reputations for reliability and trustworthiness.

CONCLUSION

Competition as a process to allocate scarce resources has been praised for its efficiency and criticized for its amoral focus on short-term self-interest. Some people believe social progress is best served when the smooth functioning and integrity of competition is supported by government institutions and regulation. Others prefer to use public policy and nongovernmental organizations to create alternatives to competition that they believe will better serve the needs of a fair and just society. This debate is likely to intensify as the global economy continues to affect the lives of more of the earth's people.

—Greg Young

Further Readings

Knight, F. H. (1923, August). The ethics of competition. *Quarterly Journal of Economics, 37,* 579–624.

Porter, M. E. (1998). *On competition.* Boston: Harvard Business School Press.

Prakash, S. S., & Sama, L. M. (1998, January). Ethical behavior as a strategic choice by large corporations: The interactive effect of marketplace competition, industry structure and firm resources. *Business Ethics Quarterly, 8*(1), 85–104.

STRATEGY AND ETHICS

Strategy is commonly understood to be a plan of action adopted by an organization to attain its goals, while ethics can be described as a system of moral values and principles that govern the conduct of an individual or a group. In a business enterprise, strategy reflects a company's pattern of decisions, commitments, and actions undertaken by the company to improve its competitiveness and generate profits for its owners. However, earning a profit is not the only goal of a business. It must provide quality products for its consumers, continued jobs for its employees, and taxes for its government. In the process of formulating and implementing strategies, potential conflicts arise in the goals of the company's various stakeholders such as stockholders, managers, employees, suppliers, government, and society at large. It is while dealing with these conflicting goals that managers face ethical dilemmas in prioritizing the demands of various constituents that form the core of the strategy-ethics interface, which we address in the following paragraphs.

Ethics in business strategy has gained renewed focus due to the scandals that have unfolded in recent years at several major corporations in the world including Enron, Arthur Andersen, Tyco, and Adelphia in the United States; Parmalat in Italy; and Livedoor in Japan. As a consequence of these business debacles, numerous employees lost jobs, shareholders lost wealth, governments lost taxes, and society as a whole suffered. To prevent future occurrences of such widespread harm, the U.S. government enacted the Sarbanes-Oxley Act in 2002 to ensure governance mechanisms to protect the interests of shareholders and other stakeholders of the firm. The U.S. Corporate Sentencing Guidelines also provide a strong incentive for businesses to promote ethics at work. Tort laws, contract law, intellectual property law, and securities law all govern business behavior. However, while the law can regulate the basic actions of the firm, it tends to be reactive in nature and contains several ambiguities that present opportunities for unethical practices. Therefore, merging company strategy with an ethical framework can guide managers in their task of strategy formulation and implementation. We briefly describe the concepts of strategy and ethics as commonly understood and then discuss the role managers play in the interface between the two.

STRATEGY

Companies try to pursue strategies that will help them remain competitive and earn superior returns. While formulating a strategy, a company thoroughly analyzes its external and internal environment. The external environment includes general or macroenvironmental conditions such as global trends, industry conditions, and competitive environment. The internal environment includes the company's internal resources and capabilities such as knowledge, technology, physical assets, manpower, and capital. Based on the perceptions of its environmental opportunities and threats, and internal strengths and weaknesses, a firm will consider different strategies and implementation approaches. A company achieves sustained success only if it has an astute, timely strategic game plan, revises its strategies according to changes in the environment and company situation, and implements the strategies with proficiency. Competitive success requires companies to position well in the existing market space, develop and use distinctive competencies to support their strategy, and design internal systems and practices to effectively implement the strategy. The industrial organization (I/O) model suggests that companies should first assess the external environment, select industries with high potential for superior returns, and then develop strategies as called for by the industry. I/O theory suggests that internal resources and capabilities should be developed as called for by the external environment. On the other hand, the resource-based view suggests that the primary basis for strategy and sustained advantage are internal resources and capabilities of the company. Companies, thus, need to develop resources that are valuable, rare, nonimitable, and nonsubstitutable and craft strategies that will help both exploit current resources and develop new resources. Strategy formulation, therefore, involves analysis of both external and internal aspects of a company and developing an appropriate course of action or strategy. Strategy implementation involves developing internal organizational structure, systems, and processes to execute the strategy and matching them to the strategy.

In a large company, strategies exist at multiple levels and, correspondingly, ethical issues also arise at multiple levels. Corporate-level strategy relates to the decisions and priorities of corporate managers of large diversified corporations (such as General Electric), which may include the choice of the mix of different types of businesses it will have under its corporate umbrella, that is, whether to acquire, merge, or sell off individual business units. Each of these decisions will have ethical implications such as should employees be laid off, or will the merger stifle competition? Functional strategies relate to the pattern of actions and priorities of various functional areas such as production, marketing, human resources, and finance. Again, ethical issues can arise in each functional strategy. Production of defective products can injure innocent people, toxic production processes pose a threat to the environment, misleading product information and deceptive advertising can misguide buying decisions, excessive monitoring can invade employee privacy, and so on.

ETHICS

To understand ethics and its relationship to strategy, it is important to briefly consider some philosophical underpinnings. The utilitarian approach espoused by John S. Mill and Jeremy Bentham in the 18th and 19th centuries evaluates action based on the following maxim: greatest good for the greatest number of people. Many businesses adopt this approach to evaluate a course of action by using a cost-benefit analysis. However, costs are often hidden. For example, damage to the environment cannot be readily quantified. Besides, utilitarianism as a framework does not consider the rights of all parties concerned and, therefore, can be unfair to the minority. A small number of employees may be laid off to garner greater profits for many investors, so while this action may be consistent with the utilitarian approach it may be unfair to those few employees affected by job loss. The Kantian or rights approach framework advocates that people be treated as ends and not as means and that basic individual rights of all should be respected. Moral theorists argue that fundamental human rights are the base of the moral compass managers navigate by when making decisions that have an ethical impact. However, the rights approach is not useful when the basic rights of two groups of individuals are in conflict. The justice approach propounded by John Rawls evaluates a strategy based on the impartial and equitable distribution of benefits and harm among stakeholders. This framework suggests that managers should weigh a course of action behind a *veil of ignorance* of the particular characteristics of the people involved, and economic goods and services should be so distributed as to be just and advantageous to the least advantaged groups in society. The virtue approach developed by Aristotle is based on virtues such as honesty, fairness, trust, and toughness. According to this framework, moral virtues and habits enable a person to live according to reason and, thus, make ethical decisions. Moral education aimed at improving moral reasoning and debate and the ability to summon courage to take a principled stand regardless of pressure or punishment are considered very important.

Viewed as a continuum, a business strategy can range from being egoist to altruistic, drawing again on the philosophical underpinnings of ethics. Ethical egoism suggests that each person ought to pursue his or her own self-interest, and an action is considered right when it serves one's personal goal. Ethical egoism does not forbid actions that may help others when interests of the self and others coincide. In contrast, altruism is devotion to the interests of others. It is "other directed" behavior at the cost of one's own self-interest. Altruism emphasizes loyalty, devotion, and the subordination of self to a cause, a person, or an ideal. Put in the context of business ethics and strategy, egoism suggests that a business should focus on its primary goal of providing returns to its owners, the challenge being, however, to find the path that aligns the interests of a firm and its managers with those of all stakeholders. An altruist strategy, on the other hand, would have the firm forgo some of its immediate gains and profits to benefit some constituent, say employees or even society, by investing resources in providing health care or education or in mitigating poverty.

STRATEGY-ETHICS INTERFACE AND ROLE OF MANAGERS

Strategy and business ethics are inseparable from each other. While the corporation is a separate entity for legal purposes, it cannot act on its own will. The behavior of the corporation is the result of decisions made by the managers and top executives of the firm. Managers act as agents of the shareholders, who are one set of the stakeholders of the firm. Agency theory postulates that managers, instead of acting in the interests of their principals (owners of the firm), will act opportunistically in their own interests when not properly monitored. Such managers are ethical egoists who focus on self-interest and self-promotion. Indeed, the recent scandals of fraud mentioned earlier have been attributed to the failure of adequate monitoring of executives entrusted with the task of making decisions for the benefit of the corporation. The managers put their own personal welfare ahead of others' welfare. In an alternative view, managers are perceived to be stewards of the distinct stakeholders of the firm, acting altruistically to promulgate ethical strategies that create value and meeting the needs of all constituents of the firm. Stewardship theory is based on the premise that managers will act in a manner consistent with the long-term interests of all stakeholders basing their decisions not on short-term gains for themselves but on corporate principles that enable their firm to be viable through actions that promote sustainable profitability. Sustained profitability of the firm requires long-term investments that may not bear immediate returns. High emphasis on short-term economic returns may be detrimental to the interests of several stakeholders and the society at large. Yet employees are evaluated every year, and companies need to meet stock market's quarterly performance expectations—both short-term horizons. While the notion of "performance" is multidimensional and includes social, environmental, and economic performance, the economic dimension generally supersedes others. Some argue that strategy is at odds with ethics primarily because of the overriding concern of strategy with instant economic performance and the inability of managers to find the point of equilibrium between long-term investment and short-term reward.

While the notions of egoism and altruism described above are the two ends of the continuum to evaluate strategy with the perspective of ethics, a practical "middle" perspective is often used to balance the needs of multiple stakeholders. The notions of corporate social responsibility, corporate citizenship behavior, and corporate accountability are more appropriate to explain the interface of strategy and business ethics. As corporations are members of society, they should engage in socially responsible actions in a manner consistent with fundamental social, moral, philosophical, and ethical principles. The corporation should play an active role in benefiting society, even helping solve problems such as environmental degradation. Even from the extreme economic perspective of strategy, enlightened self-interest dictates that pure business interests are best served by being intertwined with social interests. A company enhances its business when various stakeholders support it. Employees are likely to be more motivated and committed when they perceive their employers to be just, transparent, and doing the right thing; customers are likely to be loyal when the company has a reputation for fair dealing and providing safe products; suppliers are likely to be consistent and reliable when they are treated with consideration; lenders are likely to extend credit readily when they have confidence in the governance and accounts of the firm. In sum, the costs of doing business will be reduced for a firm that follows an ethical strategy that is responsive to the needs of all stakeholders, which eventually leads to better economic performance ensuring greater shareholder returns.

STRATEGY AND ETHICS IN THE GLOBAL CONTEXT

Modern corporations operate in several competitive environments, national boundaries, societies, and cultures. The notion of ethical standards varies across countries and cultures, and managers are faced with many ethical dilemmas globally. Practices that are illegal and certainly unethical in the United States may be acceptable in some other countries. While gift giving is common and might be expected in the Japanese, Oriental, and Middle-Eastern cultures, it is unacceptable in the United States as it can be construed as bribery. While labor laws in developed countries ensure a minimum level of ethical behavior toward employees, absence of such laws in developing nations have led multinational corporations to adopt sweatshop labor conditions, use of child labor, and unsafe working conditions to reap cost efficiencies. Countries that do not legislate or have environment protection laws find themselves dumping grounds for toxic or hazardous waste by corporations following a strict wealth maximization strategy for shareholders to the exclusion of other objectives. Corporations, thus, are confronted with a great number of strategies and contextual conditions that contribute to their facing ethical dilemmas.

Several international organizations such as Social Accountability 8000, Global Compact, International Labour Organization, and United Nations Commission on Transnational Corporations provide uniform guidelines and codes of conduct to multinational corporations. These guidelines are not mandatory laws and cannot be enforced. However, many companies have found that when they have swerved away from following an ethical strategy, they have become a target of negative media attention leading to loss of customers, as Nike did when their sweatshop labor practices in developing countries came to light.

STRATEGIZING ETHICALLY

As noted earlier, strategy and ethics are intertwined. Higher ethical standards and practices improve a firm's image and reputation, and this intangible resource is likely to provide a sustainable advantage to the firm. While violating basic ethical norms may provide temporary benefits and short-term economic gains, long-term financial performance is likely to improve when firms consider the interests of all stakeholders, which results in a positive image of the company. Even investors and shareholders seek out companies that implement ethical strategies that ensure profits by following principles, as evidenced by the growth and popularity of social investing in portfolios such as domini social investments.

Strategizing ethically would mean that businesses should deeply embed ethical principles and standards in their mission, strategies, and day-to-day practices. Managers need to set high ethical standards, need to be cognizant of ethical principles while formulating and implementing strategies, and need to recognize and reward employees who follow ethical standards and penalize those who do not. Statements about the long-term direction and strategy can include a company's philosophy and values, key corporate values can be incorporated in the company's mission statement and then translated into the employee code of conduct, and the code of conduct could be strictly followed and reinforced. Similarly, the design of the organization and formal reporting systems can ensure enforcement of ethical standards and practices at all levels and in all functional areas of operation. Besides formal mechanisms, informal mechanisms such as organization culture, shared norms, values, and beliefs can be very useful in fostering an ethical climate within an organization. Human resource practices, such as recruitment, compensation, training, and promotion decisions, can also be geared to explicitly value and emphasize ethical standards. A well-developed whistle-blowing policy that allows benign disobedience and encourages constructive criticism can also be instrumental in cultivating an ethical climate. Many firms have trained ethics officers whose job is to monitor ethical behavior and counsel managers when the need arises. Above all, managers as leaders could set an example by their own behavior and serve as referent models to employees throughout the organization.

—Devi R. Gnyawali and Manisha Singal

Further Readings

Boatright, J. R. (2003). *Ethics and the conduct of business.* Upper Saddle River, NJ: Prentice Hall.

Donaldson, T. (1996). Values in tension: Ethics away from home. *Harvard Business Review, September/October,* 48–62.

Donaldson, T., & Dunfee, T. W. (1999). *Ties that bind: A social contracts approach to business ethics.* Boston: Harvard Business School Press.

Freeman, R. E. (1984). *Strategic management: A stakeholder approach.* Marshfield, MA: Pitman.

Freeman, R. E., & Gilbert, D. R. (1988). *Corporate strategy and the search for ethics.* Englewood Cliffs, NJ: Prentice Hall.

Green, R. M. (1994). *The ethical manager: A new method for business ethics.* New York: Macmillan.

Hill, C., & Jones, G. (2004). *Strategic management: An integrated approach.* Boston: Houghton Mifflin.

Lawrence, A. T., Weber, J., & Post, J. E. (2005). *Business and society: Stakeholders, ethics, public policy.* New York: McGraw-Hill.

Porter, M. (1996). What is strategy? *Harvard Business Review, November/December,* 61–78.

Rachels, M. (2003). *The elements of moral philosophy.* New York: McGraw-Hill.

Solomon, R. C. (1993). *Ethics and excellence: Cooperation and integrity in business.* New York: Oxford University Press.

Werhane, P. H. (1999). *Moral imagination and management decision-making.* New York: Oxford University Press.

CORPORATE SOCIAL RESPONSIBILITY (CSR) AND CORPORATE SOCIAL PERFORMANCE (CSP)

The concept of corporate social responsibility (CSR) refers to the general belief held by many that modern businesses have a responsibility to society that extends beyond the stockholders or investors in the firm. That responsibility, of course, is to make money or profits for the owners. These other societal stakeholders typically include consumers, employees, the community at large, government, and the natural environment. The CSR concept applies to organizations of all sizes, but discussions tend to focus on large organizations because they tend to be more visible and have more power. And, as many have observed, with power comes responsibility.

A related concept is that of corporate social performance (CSP). For the most part, CSP is an extension of the concept of CSR that focuses on actual results achieved rather than the general notion of businesses' accountability or responsibility to society. Thus, CSP is a natural consequence or follow-on to CSR. In fact, it could well be argued that if CSR does not lead to CSP then it is vacuous or powerless. Interestingly, many advocates of CSR naturally assume that an assumption of responsibility will lead to results or outcomes. Thus, the distinction between the two is often a matter of semantics that is of more interest to academics than to practitioners. Most of our discussion will be focused on CSR with the general assumption that CSP is a vital and logical consequence.

DEVELOPMENT OF THE CSR CONCEPT

The concept of CSR has a long and varied history. It is possible to trace evidences of the business community's concern for society for centuries. Formal writings on CSR, or social responsibility (SR), however, are largely a product of the 20th century, especially the past 50 years. In addition, though it is possible to see footprints of CSR thought and practice throughout the world, mostly in developed countries, formal writings have been most evident in the United States, where a sizable body of literature has accumulated. In recent years, the continent of Europe has been captivated with CSR and has been strongly supporting the idea.

A significant challenge is to decide how far back in time we should go to begin discussing the concept of CSR. A good case could be made for about 50 years because so much has occurred during that time that has shaped theory, research, and practice. Using this as a general guideline, it should be noted that references to a concern for SR appeared earlier than this, and especially during the 1930s and 1940s. References from this earlier period worth noting included Chester Barnard's 1938 publication, *The Functions of the Executive,* J. M. Clark's *Social Control of Business* from 1939, and Theodore Kreps's *Measurement of the Social Performance of Business* from 1940, just to mention a few. From a more practical point of view, it should be noted that as far back as 1946 business executives (the literature called them businessmen in those days) were polled by *Fortune* magazine asking them about their social responsibilities.

In the early writings on CSR, the concept was referred to more often as just SR rather than CSR. This may have been because the age of the modern corporation's prominence and dominance in the business sector had not yet occurred or been noted. The 1953 publication by Howard R. Bowen of his landmark book *Social Responsibilities of the Businessman* is argued by many to mark the beginnings of the modern period of CSR. As the title of Bowen's book suggests, there apparently were no *businesswomen* during this period, or at least they were not acknowledged in formal writings.

Bowen's work proceeded from the belief that the several hundred largest businesses at that time were vital centers of power and decision making and that the actions of these firms touched the lives of citizens at many points. Among the many questions raised by Bowen, one is of special note here. Bowen asked, what responsibilities to society may businessmen reasonably be expected to assume? This question drove much subsequent thought and is still relevant today. Bowen's answer to the question was that businesspeople should assume the responsibility that is desirable in terms of the objectives and values of society. In other words, he was arguing that it is society's expectations that drive the idea of SR.

Bowen went on to argue that CSR or the "social consciousness" of managers implied that businesspeople were responsible for the consequences of their actions in a sphere somewhat wider than that covered by their profit-and-loss statements. It is fascinating to note that when Bowen referenced the *Fortune* article cited earlier, it reported that 93.5% of the businessmen agreed with this idea of a wider SR. Because of his early and seminal work, Bowen might be called the "father of corporate social responsibility."

If there was scant evidence of CSR definitions in the literature in the 1950s and before, the decade of the 1960s marked a significant growth in attempts to formalize or more accurately state what CSR means. One of the first and most prominent writers in this period to define CSR was Keith Davis, then a professor at Arizona State University, who later extensively wrote about the topic in his business and society textbook, later revisions, and articles. Davis argued that SR refers to the decisions and actions that businesspeople take for reasons that are at least partially beyond the direct economic or technical interest of the firm.

Davis argued that SR is a nebulous idea that needs to be seen in a managerial context. Furthermore, he asserted that some socially responsible business decisions can be justified by a long, complicated process of reasoning as having a good chance of bringing long-run economic gain to the firm, thus paying it back for its socially responsible outlook. This has often been referred to as the enlightened self-interest justification for CSR. This view became commonly accepted in the late 1970s and 1980s.

Davis became well known for his views on the relationship between SR and business power. He set forth his now-famous *Iron Law of Responsibility*, which held that the social responsibilities of businesspeople needed to be commensurate with their social power. Davis's contributions to early definitions of CSR were so significant that he could well be argued to be the runner-up to Bowen for the "father of CSR" designation.

The CSR concept became a favorite topic in management discussions during the 1970s. One reason for this is because the respected economist Milton Friedman came out against the concept. In a 1970 article for the *New York Times Magazine*, Friedman summarized his position well with its title—"The Social Responsibility of Business Is to Increase Its Profits." For many years since and continuing today, Friedman has maintained his position. In spite of Friedman's classic opposition, the CSR concept has continued to be accepted and has continued to grow.

A landmark contribution to the concept of CSR came from the Committee for Economic Development (CED) in its 1971 publication *Social Responsibilities of Business Corporations*. The CED got into this topic by observing that business functions by public consent, and its basic purpose is to serve constructively the needs of society to the satisfaction of society. The CED noted that the social contract between business and society was changing in substantial and important ways. It noted that business is being asked to assume broader responsibilities to society than ever before. Furthermore, the CED noted that business assumes a role in contributing to the quality of life and that this role is more than just providing goods and services. Noting that business, as an institution, exists to serve society, the future of business will be a direct result of how effectively managements of businesses respond to the expectations of the public, which are always changing. Public opinion polls taken during this early period by Opinion Research Corporation found that about two thirds of the respondents thought business had a moral obligation with respect to achieving social progress in society, even at the possible expense of profitability.

The CED went on to articulate a three-concentric-circles definition of SR that included an inner, an intermediate, and an outer circle. The *inner circle* focused on the basic responsibility business had for its economic function—that is, providing products, services, jobs, and economic growth. The *intermediate circle* focused on responsibilities business had to exercise its economic activities in a sensitive way by always being alert to society's changing social values and priorities. Some early arenas in which this sensitivity were to be expressed included environmental conservation; relationships with employees; and meeting the expectations of consumers for information, fair treatment, and protection from harm. The CED's *outer circle* referred to newly emerging and still ambiguous responsibilities that business should be involved in to help address problems in society, such as urban blight and poverty.

What made the CED's views on CSR especially noteworthy was that the CED was composed of businesspeople and educators and, thus, reflected an important practitioner view of the changing social contract between business and society and businesses' newly emerging social responsibilities. It is helpful to note that the CED may have been responding to the times in that the late 1960s and early 1970s was a period during which social movements with respect to the environment, worker safety, consumers, and employees were poised to transition from special interest status to government regulation. In the early 1970s, we saw the creation of the Environmental Protection Agency, the Consumer Product Safety Commission, and the Equal Employment Opportunity Commission. Thus, it can be seen that the major initiatives of government social regulation grew out of the changing climate with respect to CSR.

Another significant contributor to the development of CSR in the 1970s was George Steiner, then a professor at UCLA. In 1971, in the first edition of his textbook, *Business and Society,* Steiner wrote extensively on the subject. Steiner continued to emphasize that business is fundamentally an economic institution in society but that it does have responsibilities to help society achieve its basic goals. Thus, SR goes beyond just profit making. Steiner also noted that as companies became larger their social responsibilities grew as well. Steiner thought the assumption of social responsibilities was more of an attitude, of the way a manager approaches his or her decision-making task, than a great shift in the economics of decision making. He held that CSR was a philosophy that looks at the social interest and the enlightened self-interest of business over the long-run rather than just the old narrow, unrestrained short-run self-interest of the past.

Though Richard Eells and Clarence Walton addressed the CSR concept in the first edition of their book *Conceptual Foundations of Business* (1961), they elaborated on the concept at length in their third edition, which was published in 1974. In this book they dedicated a whole chapter to recent trends in corporate social responsibilities. Like Steiner, they did not focus on definitions, per se, but rather took a broader perspective on what CSR meant and how it evolved. Eels and Walton continued to argue that CSR is more concerned with the needs and goals of society and that these extend beyond the economic interest of the business firm. They believed that CSR was a concept that permits business to survive and function effectively in a free society and that the CSR movement is concerned with business's role in supporting and improving the social order.

In the 1970s, we initially found mention increasingly being made to CSP as well as CSR. One major writer to make this distinction was S. Prakash Sethi. In a classic 1975 article, Sethi identified what he called dimensions of CSP and, in the process, distinguished between corporate behavior that might be called social obligation, SR, or social responsiveness. In Sethi's schema, social obligation was corporate behavior in response to market forces or legal constraints. The criteria here were economic and legal only. SR, in contrast, went beyond social obligation. He argued that SR implied bringing corporate behavior up to a level where it is congruent with the prevailing social norms, values, and expectations of society. Sethi went on to say that while social obligation is proscriptive in nature, SR is prescriptive in nature. The third stage in Sethi's model was social responsiveness. He regarded this as the *adaptation* of corporate behavior to social needs. Thus, anticipatory and preventive action is implied.

Some of the earliest empirical research on CSR was published in the mid-1970s. First, in 1975, Bowman and Haire conducted a survey striving to understand CSR and to ascertain the extent to which companies were engaging in CSR. Though they never really defined CSR in the sense we have been discussing, the researchers chose to measure CSR by counting the proportion of lines devoted to SR in the annual reports of the companies they studied. While not providing a formal definition of CSR, they illustrated the kinds of topics that represented CSR as opposed to those that were strictly business in nature. The topics they used were usually subheads to sections in the annual report. Some of these subheads were as follows: corporate responsibility, SR, social action, public service, corporate citizenship, public responsibility, and social responsiveness. A review of their topical approach indicates that they had a good idea of what CSR generally meant, given the kinds of definitions we saw developing in the 1970s.

Another research study in the mid-1970s was conducted by Sandra Holmes in which she sought to determine executive perceptions of CSR. Like Bowman and Haire, Holmes had no clear definition of CSR. Rather, she chose to present executives with a set of statements about CSR, seeking to find out how many of them agreed or disagreed with the statements. Like the Bowman and Haire list of "topics," Holmes's statements addressed the issues that were generally believed to be what CSR was all about during this time period. For example, she sought executive opinions on businesses' responsibilities for making a profit, abiding by regulations, helping to solve social problems, and the short-run and long-run impacts on profits of such activities. Holmes further added to the body of knowledge about CSR by identifying the outcomes that executives expected from their firms' social involvement and the factors executives used in selecting areas of social involvement.

In 1979, Archie B. Carroll proposed a four-part definition of CSR, which was embedded in a conceptual model of CSP. Like Sethi's earlier article, Carroll sought to differentiate between CSR and CSP. His basic argument was that for managers or firms to engage in CSP they needed to have (1) a basic *definition* of CSR, (2) an understanding/enumeration of the *issues* for which a SR existed (or, in modern terms, stakeholders to whom the firm had a responsibility, relationship, or dependency), and (3) a specification of the *philosophy or pattern of responsiveness* to the issues.

At that time, Carroll noted that previous definitions had alluded to businesses' responsibility to make a profit, obey the law, and to go beyond these activities. Also, he observed that, to be complete, the concept of CSR had to embrace a full range of responsibilities of business to society. In addition, some clarification was needed regarding that component of CSR that extended beyond making a profit and obeying the law. Therefore, Carroll proposed that the SR of business encompassed the economic, legal, ethical, and discretionary expectations that society had of organizations at a given point in time.

A brief elaboration of this definition is useful. First, and foremost, Carroll argued that business has a responsibility that is *economic* in nature or kind. Before anything else, the business institution is the basic economic unit in society. As such it has a responsibility to produce goods and services that society wants and to sell them at a profit. All other business roles are predicated on this fundamental assumption. The economic component of the definition suggests that society *expects* business to produce goods and services and sell them at a profit. This is how the capitalistic economic system is designed and functions.

He also noted that just as society expects business to make a profit (as an incentive and reward) for its efficiency and effectiveness, society expects business to obey the law. The law, in its most rudimentary form, represents the basic rules of the game by which business is expected to function. Society expects business to fulfill its economic mission within the framework of legal requirements set forth by the society's legal system. Thus, the *legal* responsibility is the second part of Carroll's definition.

The next two responsibilities represented Carroll's attempt to specify the nature or character of the responsibilities that extended beyond obedience to the law. The *ethical* responsibility was claimed to represent the kinds of behaviors and ethical norms that society expected business to follow. These ethical responsibilities extended to actions, decisions, and practices that are beyond what is required by the law. Though they seem to be always expanding, they nevertheless exist as expectations over and beyond legal requirements.

Finally, he argued there are *discretionary* responsibilities. These represent voluntary roles and practices that business assumes but for which society does not provide as clear cut an expectation as in the ethical responsibility. These are left to individual managers' and corporations' judgment and choice; therefore, they were referred to as discretionary. Regardless of their voluntary nature, the expectation that business perform these was still held by society. This expectation was driven by social norms. The specific activities were guided by businesses' desire to engage in social roles not mandated, not required by law, and not expected of businesses in an ethical sense, but which were becoming increasingly strategic. Examples of these voluntary activities, during the time in which it was written, included making philanthropic contributions, conducting in-house programs for drug abusers, training the hard-core unemployed, or providing day care centers for working mothers. These discretionary activities were analogous to the CED's third circle (helping society). Later, Carroll began calling this fourth category *philanthropic*, because the best examples of it were charitable, humanistic activities business undertook to help society along with its own interests.

Though Carroll's 1979 definition included an economic responsibility, many today still think of the economic component as what the business firm *does for itself* and the legal, ethical, and discretionary (or philanthropic) components as what business *does for others*. While this distinction represents the more commonly held view of CSR, Carroll continued to argue that economic performance is something business does for society as well, though society seldom looks at it in this way.

CORPORATE SOCIAL PERFORMANCE

As suggested earlier, the concept of CSP is an extension of the CSR concept that places more of an emphasis on *results achieved*. The development of the CSP concept has occurred somewhat in parallel with the CSR concept, but with a slightly different emphasis. The *performance* focus in CSP is intended to suggest that what really matters is what companies are able to accomplish, that is, the results or outcomes of their CSR initiatives and the adoption of a responsiveness strategy or posture. Many of the writers on CSR would argue that results were implied in their concepts and discussions of CSR, but the literature added a branch in the 1970s when writers began emphasizing the "performance" aspect rather than the "responsibility" aspect. Obviously, the two go hand in hand.

Actually, many of the earlier discussions of CSR transitioned to an emphasis on corporate social *responsiveness* before the performance focus became common. Brief mention should be made of this in the discussion on CSP. William Frederick is often credited with best describing the difference between responsibility and responsiveness when he dubbed them CSR_1 and CSR_2. With CSR_1, he was referring to the concept of CSR that we discussed in the previous section. The emphasis there is on accountability. CSR_2, in contrast, was intended to reflect the emphasis on responsiveness, or action. In the responsiveness focus, attention turned to the mechanisms, procedures, arrangements, and patterns by which business actually responds to social expectations and pressures in society. The responsiveness focus, therefore, turned the attention from responsibility (business taking on accountability) to responsiveness (business actually responding to social expectations).

In many respects, the emphasis on performance in CSP continues to carry this line of thought forward. That is, the term implies the field has transitioned from *accountability* to *responding* to *results* achieved.

The concept of CSP began appearing in the literature in the mid-1970s. Writers such as Lee Preston, S. Prakash Sethi, and Archie Carroll were among the early authors to speak of the importance of CSP. As mentioned earlier, Carroll presented a conceptual "model" of CSP that motivated a series of improvements and refinements to the concept. Steven Wartick and Philip Cochran took Carroll's three dimensions and broadened them into more encompassing concepts. Wartick and Cochran proposed that the social issues dimension had matured into a new management field known as social issues in management. They extended the model further by proposing that the three dimensions be viewed as depicting *principles* (corporate social responsibilities, reflecting a *philosophical* orientation), *processes* (corporate social responsiveness, reflecting an *institutional* orientation), and *policies* (social issues management, reflecting an *organizational* dimension). In short, Wartick and Cochran updated and extended the three dimensions of the model.

The CSP model was further developed by Donna Wood in her reformulation of the model. Wood expanded and elaborated Carroll's model and Wartick and Cochran's extensions and set forth a reformulated model that went into further detail emphasizing the *outcomes* aspect of the model. Wood argued that CSP was a business organization's configuration of principles of SR; processes of social responsiveness; and policies, programs, and other observable outcomes related to the firm's relationship with society. More than previous conceptualizations, she emphasized the importance of the *outcomes* of corporate efforts.

Diane Swanson extended Wood's model by elaborating on the *dynamic nature* of the principles, processes, and outcomes reformulated by Wood. Relying on research from corporate culture, Swanson's reoriented model linked CSP to the personally held values and ethics of executive managers and other employees. She proposed that the executive's sense of morality highly influences such policies and programs of environmental assessment, stakeholder management, and issues management carried out by employees. One of Swanson's major contributions, therefore, was to integrate business ethics into the implementation of the CSP focus.

Other concepts have developed in recent years that have embraced a concern for CSR and CSP. They are mentioned here but not developed because they get somewhat outside the traditional boundaries of these concepts. *Corporate citizenship* is a concept that must be mentioned because in the minds of many it is synonymous with CSR/CSP. The entire *business ethics movement* of the past 20 years has significantly overlapped these topics. The *stakeholder concept* has fully embraced and expanded on these concepts. The concept of the "triple bottom line," a concern for economic, social, and environmental performance, has embraced the CSR/CSP literature. The concept of "sustainability" has also embraced CSR/CSP thinking. Corporate sustainability is the goal of the triple-bottom-line and CSR/CSP initiatives—to create long-term shareholder value by taking advantage of opportunities and managing risks related to economic, social, and environmental developments.

BUSINESS'S INTEREST IN CSR AND CSP

To this point, we have been discussing primarily the contributions of academics to the development of the concepts of CSR and CSR. To be sure, the business community has had a parallel development of its interest in the concepts as well. The business community, however, has been less interested in academic refinements of the concept and more interested in what all this means for them, in practice. Prominent business organizations have developed specialized awards for firms' social performance. One example of this would be *Fortune* magazine's "most admired" and "least admired" categories of performance. Among *Fortune*'s eight attributes of reputation, one will find the category of performance titled "social responsibility." The Conference Board is another organization that has developed an award for corporate leadership in the CSR realm. The Conference Board annually gives an award titled the "Ron Brown Award for Corporate Leadership" that recognizes companies for outstanding achievements in community and employee relations. Among the core principles for this award are that the company be committed to corporate citizenship, express corporate citizenship as a shared value visible at all levels, and it must be integrated into the company's corporate strategy.

For several years now, *Business Ethics* magazine has published its list of Annual Business Ethics and Corporate Citizenship Awards. In these awards, the magazine has highlighted companies that have made stellar achievements in CSR/CSP. One of the important criterion used by the magazine in making this award is that the company have programs or initiatives in SR that demonstrate sincerity and ongoing vibrancy that reaches deep into the company. The award criteria also stipulate that the company honored must be a standout in at least one area of SR, though the recipients need not be exemplary in all areas.

Though one will always find individual businesspeople who might reject or fight the idea of CSR/CSP, for the most part today, large companies have accepted the idea and internalized it. One of the best examples of this acceptance was the creation in 1992 of the association titled Business for Social Responsibility (BSR). BSR is a national business association that helps companies seeking to implement policies and practices that contribute to the companies' sustainability and responsible success. In its statement of purpose, BSR claims to be a global organization that helps its member companies achieve success in ways that respect ethical values, people, communities, and the environment. A goal of BSR is to make CSR an integral part of business operations and strategies. An illustrative list of BSR's more than 1,000 members includes such well-known companies as ABB Inc., AstraZeneca Plc., Coca-Cola, Johnson & Johnson, Nike Inc., Office Max, GE, GM, UPS, Procter & Gamble, Sony, Staples Inc., and Wal-Mart.

THE BUSINESS CASE FOR CSR AND CSP

After considering the pros and cons of CSR/CSP, most businesses today embrace the idea. In recent years, the "business case" for CSR/CSP has been unfolding. Before buying in to the idea of CSR, many business executives have wanted the "business case" for it further developed. The business case is simply the arguments or rationales as to why businesspeople believe these concepts bring distinct benefits or advantages to companies, specifically, and the business community, generally. Even the astute business guru Michael Porter, who for a long time has extolled the virtues of competitive advantage, has embraced the concept that corporate and social initiatives are intertwined. Porter has argued that companies today ought to invest in CSR as part of their business strategy to become more competitive. Of course, prior to Porter, many CSR academics had been presenting this same argument.

Simon Zadek, a European, has presented four different business rationales for being a civil corporation. These reasons form a composite justification for businesses adopting a CSR/CSP strategy. The first is the defensive approach. This approach is designed to alleviate pain. That is, companies should pursue CSR to avoid the pressures that create costs for them. The second is the cost-benefit approach. This traditional approach holds that firms will undertake those activities that yield a greater benefit than cost. The third is the strategic approach. In this approach, firms will recognize the changing environment and engage in CSR as a part of a deliberate corporate strategy. Finally, the innovation and learning approach is suggested. Here, an active engagement with CSR provides new opportunities to understand the marketplace and enhance organizational learning, which leads to competitive advantage. Most of these rationales have been around for years, but Zadek has presented them as an excellent set of business reasons for pursuing CSR.

Putting forth the business case for CSR requires a careful and comprehensive elucidation of the reasons why companies are seeing that CSR is in their best interests to pursue. Two particular studies have contributed toward building this case. One study by PricewaterhouseCoopers, presented in their 2002 Sustainability Survey Report, identifies the following top 10 reasons why companies are deciding to be more socially responsible:

1. Enhanced reputation

2. Competitive advantage

3. Cost savings

4. Industry trends

5. CEO/board commitment

6. Customer demand

7. SRI demand

8. Top-line growth

9. Shareholder demand

10. Access to capital

A survey conducted by the Aspen Institute, in their Business and Society Program, queried MBA student about attitudes regarding the question of how companies will benefit from fulfilling their social responsibilities. Their responses, in sequence of importance, included the following:

- A better public image/reputation
- Greater customer loyalty
- A more satisfied/productive workforce
- Fewer regulatory or legal problems
- Long-term viability in the marketplace
- A stronger/healthier community
- Increased revenues
- Lower cost of capital
- Easier access to foreign markets

Between these two lists, a comprehensive case for business interest in CSR/CSP is documented. It can be seen how CSR/CSP not only benefits society and stakeholders but also how it provides specific, business-related benefits for business.

EXAMPLES OF CSR IN PRACTICE

There are many ways in which companies may manifest their CSR in their communities and abroad. Most of these initiatives would fall in the category of discretionary, or philanthropic, activities, but some border on improving some ethical situation for the stakeholders with whom they come into contact. Common types of CSR initiatives include corporate contributions (or philanthropy), employee volunteerism, community relations, becoming an outstanding employer for specific employee groups (such as women, older workers, or minorities), making environmental improvements that exceed what is required by law, and so on.

Among the 100 Best Corporate Citizens identified in 2005 by *Business Ethics* magazine, a number of illuminating examples of CSR in practice are provided. Cummins, Inc., of Columbus, Indiana, has reduced diesel engine emissions by 90% and expects that within 10 years the company will be at zero or close to zero emissions. In addition, the engine maker underwrites the development of schools in China, is purchasing biodiverse forest land in

Mexico, and funds great architecture in its local community. Cummins also publishes a sustainability report that is available to the public.

Xerox Corporation, Stamford, Connecticut, is a multinational corporation that places high value on its communities. One of its most well-known community development traditions has been its Social Service Leave Program. Employees selected for the program may take a year off with full pay and work for a community nonprofit organization of their choice. The program was begun in 1971, and by 2005, more than 460 employees had been granted leave, translating into about half a million volunteer service hours for the program.

Green Mountain Coffee Roasters, Waterbury, Vermont, was a pioneer in an innovative program designed to help struggling coffee growers by paying them "fair trade" prices, which exceed regular market prices. The company has also been recognized for offering microloans to coffee-growing families and underwriting business ventures that diversify agricultural economies.

Another example of CSR in practice is the Chick-fil-A restaurant chain based in Atlanta, Georgia. Founder and CEO Truett Cathy has earned an outstanding reputation as a businessman deeply concerned with his employees and communities. Through the WinShape Centre Foundation, funded by Chick-fil-A, the company operates foster homes for more than 120 children, sponsors a summer camp, and has hosted more than 21,000 children since 1985. Chick-fil-A has also sponsored major charity golf tournaments.

In the immediate aftermath of Hurricane Katrina in 2005, judged to be the worst and most expensive ever in terms of destruction, hundreds of companies made significant contributions to the victims and to the cities of New Orleans, Biloxi, Gulfport, and the entire Gulf Coast. These CSR efforts have been noted as one of the important ways by which business can help people and communities in need.

As seen in the examples presented, there are a multitude of ways that companies have manifested their corporate social responsibilities with respect to communities, employees, consumers, competitors, and the natural environment.

CSR IN THE NEW MILLENNIUM

As we think about the importance of CSR/CSP in the new millennium, it is useful to review the results of the millennium poll on CSR that was sponsored by Environics, International, the Prince of Wales Business Leaders Forum, and the Conference Board. This poll included 1,000 persons in 23 countries on six continents. The results of the poll revealed how important citizens of the world now thought CSR really was. The poll found that in the 21st century, companies would be expected to do all the following: demonstrate their commitment to society's values on social, environmental, and economic goals through their actions; fully insulate society from the negative impacts of company actions; share the benefits of company activities with key stakeholders, as well as shareholders, and demonstrate that the company can be more profitable by doing the right thing. This "doing well by doing good" approach will reassure stakeholders that new behaviors will outlast good intentions. Finally, it was made clear that CSR/CSP is now a global expectation that now requires a comprehensive, strategic response.

—Archie B. Carroll

Further Readings

Ackerman, R. W. (1973). How companies respond to social demands. *Harvard Business Review, 51*(4), 88–98.

Ackerman, R. W., & Bauer, R. A. (1976). *Corporate social responsiveness.* Reston, VA: Reston.

Asmus, P. (2005). 100 Best corporate citizens. *Business Ethics,* Spring, 20–27.

Aupperle, K. E., Carroll, A. B., & Hatfield, J. D. (1985). An empirical investigation of the relationship between corporate social responsibility and profitability. *Academy of Management Journal, 28,* 446–463.

Backman, J. (Ed.). (1975). *Social responsibility and accountability.* New York: New York University Press.

Barnard, C. I. (1938). *The functions of the executive.* Cambridge, MA: Harvard University Press.

Bowen, H. R. (1953). *Social responsibilities of the businessman.* New York: Harper & Brothers.

Carroll, A. B. (1979). A three-dimensional conceptual model of corporate social performance. *Academy of Management Review, 4,* 497–505.

Carroll, A. B. (1991, July/August). The pyramid of corporate social responsibility: Toward the moral management of organizational stakeholders. *Business Horizons, 34,* 39–48.

Carroll, A. B. (1999). Corporate social responsibility: Evolution of a definitional construct. *Business & Society, 38*(3), 268–295.

Carroll, A. B., & Buchholtz, A. K. (2006). *Business and society: Ethics and stakeholder management* (6th ed.). Cincinnati, OH: South-Western/Thompson.

Committee for Economic Development (CED). (1971, June). *Social responsibilities of business corporations.* New York: Author.

Davis, K. (1960, Spring). Can business afford to ignore social responsibilities? *California Management Review, II*, 70–76.

Davis, K. (1973). The case for and against business assumption of social responsibilities. *Academy of Management Journal, 16*, 312–322.

Davis, K., & Blomstrom, R. L. (1966). *Business and its environment.* New York: McGraw-Hill.

Drucker, P. F. (1984). The new meaning of corporate social responsibility. *California Management Review, XXVI*, 53–63.

Eels, R., & Walton, C. (1974). *Conceptual foundations of business* (3rd ed.). Homewood, IL: Richard D. Irwin.

Epstein, E. M. (1987). The corporate social policy process: Beyond business ethics, corporate social responsibility, and corporate social responsiveness. *California Management Review, XXIX*, 99–114.

Frederick, W. C. (1960). The growing concern over business responsibility. *California Management Review, 2*, 54–61.

Frederick, W. C. (1978). *From CSR₁ to CSR₂: The maturing of business and society thought.* Working Paper No. 279, Graduate School of Business, University of Pittsburgh.

Friedman, M. (1962). *Capitalism and freedom.* Chicago: University of Chicago Press.

Griffin, J. J. (2000). Corporate social performance: Research directions for the 21st century. *Business & Society, 39*(4), 479–491.

Griffin, J. J., & Mahon, J. F. (1997). The corporate social performance and corporate financial performance debate: Twenty-five years of incomparable research. *Business & Society, 36*, 5–31.

Harrison, J. S., & Freeman, R. E. (1999, October). Stakeholders, social responsibility, and performance: Empirical evidence and theoretical perspectives. *Academy of Management Journal, 1999*, 479–485.

Husted, B. W. (2000). A contingency theory of corporate social performance. *Business & Society, 39*(1), 24–48.

Jones, T. M. (1980, Spring). Corporate social responsibility revisited, redefined. *California Management Review, 1980*, 59–67.

Manne, H. G., & Wallich, H. C. (1972). *The modern corporation and social responsibility.* Washington, DC: American Enterprise Institute for Public Policy Research.

McGuire, J. W. (1963). *Business and society.* New York: McGraw-Hill.

Parket, I. R., & Eilbirt, H. (1975, August). Social responsibility: The underlying factors. *Business Horizons, XVIII*, 5–10.

Preston, L. E. (1975). Corporation and society: The search for a paradigm. *Journal of Economic Literature, XIII*, 434–453.

Preston, L. E., & Post, J. E. (1975). *Private management and public policy: The principle of public responsibility.* Englewood Cliffs, NJ: Prentice Hall.

Rowley, T., & Berman, S. (2000). A brand new brand of corporate social performance. *Business & Society, 39*(4), 397–418.

Schwartz, M. S., & Carroll, A. B. (2003). Corporate social responsibility: A three domain approach. *Business Ethics Quarterly, 13*(4), 503–530.

Sethi, S. P. (1975, Spring). Dimensions of corporate social performance: An analytic framework. *California Management Review, XVII*, 58–64.

Steiner, G. A. (1971). *Business and society.* New York: Random House.

Swanson, D. L. (1995). Addressing a theoretical problem by reorienting the corporate social performance model. *Academy of Management Review, 20*, 43–64.

Wartick, S. L., & Cochran, P. L. (1985). The evolution of the corporate social performance model. *Academy of Management Review, 10*, 758–769.

Wood, D. J. (1991). Corporate social performance revisited. *Academy of Management Review, 16*, 691–718.

STRATEGIC CORPORATE SOCIAL RESPONSIBILITY

S trategic corporate social responsibility is the attempt by companies to link those largely discretionary activities explicitly intended to improve some aspect of society or the natural environment with their strategies and core business activities. While corporate social responsibility has historically referred to a firm's economic, legal, ethical, and discretionary responsibilities to society, strategic corporate social responsibility, in general, represents discretionary activities that form a company's community relations function or foundation, including corporate philanthropy, volunteerism, and multisector collaborations. Corporate social responsibility can be compared with the mere general concept of corporate responsibility, which is a company's complete set of responsibilities to its stakeholders, societies where it operates, and the natural environment, as manifested through its operating practices.

Corporate social responsibility represents the direct efforts by a company to improve aspects of society by the firm as compared with the integral responsibilities that every firm has with respect to primary stakeholders such as employees, customers, investors, and suppliers. The use of the term *strategic* implies that the discretionary socially oriented activities of the firm are intended to have direct or indirect benefits for the firm—that is, to somehow help the firm achieve its strategic and economic objectives. There is a wide range of ways in which companies can use corporate social responsibility activities strategically. These ways range from helping local schools improve so that, long term, the workforce will be better educated, to improving local conditions in the community so that it will be easier to recruit and retain employees, to improving the firm's reputation among customers so that they will continue to use the company's products and services, as well as numerous other examples.

Sometimes termed *enlightened self-interest*, strategic corporate social responsibility initiatives are closely linked to strategic philanthropy and cause marketing. They attempt to help achieve a company's core mission and strategies by providing a socially beneficial foundation for enhanced economic value added. This benefit to the firm happens through improved reputation from the social desirability that key stakeholders, such as customers and employees, feel for being affiliated in some way with a company perceived to be more socially responsible or, more directly, through increased use of the company's products and services that are tied to donations to specific charitable organizations.

Some observers object to strategic corporate social responsibility on the grounds that the company cannot or should not both be doing moral or social good while also profiting financially. Other observers see no necessary conflict in what is called doing well and doing good, because for companies that are under increasing pressure for good short-term results, strategic corporate social responsibility represents a way for them to attempt to meet the needs of multiple stakeholders, particularly investors and societal stakeholders, including customers, employees, and investors concerned with corporate responsibility, simultaneously.

There is significant and growing evidence from a large number of research studies that companies that are more socially responsible, or more responsible in general to all their stakeholders, perform at the same level or somewhat better than less responsible companies. This empirical evidence suggests that there are no necessary trade-offs between profitability in terms of financial performance and responsibility, even explicitly socially beneficial activities. Companies with good corporate social responsibility records, according to employee and consumer surveys, may find it easier to recruit and retain employees, attract and keep new customers, and even attract investors concerned about issues of corporate responsibility, also called socially responsible or ethical investors.

—Sandra Waddock

Further Readings

Gourville, J. T., & Kasturi Rangan, V. (2004). Valuing the cause marketing relationship. *Harvard Business Review, 47*(1), 38–57.

Lantos, G. P. (2001). The boundaries of strategic corporate social responsibility. *Journal of Consumer Marketing, 18*(7), 595–630.

Phillips, R. (2000). The corporate community builders: Using corporate strategic philanthropy for economic development. *Economic Development Review, Summer,* 7–11.

PART II

Ethics and the Marketing Mix

ETHICS OF MARKETING

Marketing ethics is the systematic study of how moral standards are applied to marketing decisions, behaviors, and institutions. Because marketing is a process inherent to most organizations, marketing ethics should be viewed as a subset of business ethics; thus, much of what is written about business ethics applies to marketing ethics as well. At the outset, it is also useful to distinguish between *positive* and *normative* marketing ethics. Positive marketing ethics looks at marketing practices from the standpoint of "what is." For example, specifying the percentage of organizations that have codes of ethical marketing practice or tracking the number of violations that deal with *deceptive advertising* would be examples of positive marketing ethics. In contrast, normative marketing ethics deals with how marketing *ought* to operate according to some moral standard or theory. The sort of moral standards (or theories) applied to marketing situations involve the usual moral frameworks commonly applied when evaluating business ethics (e.g., utilitarianism, duty-based theories, virtue ethics). When the words "marketing ethics" appear in the general media or business press, the reports typically describe a marketing strategy, tactic, or policy that some constituency feels is "unfair" or "exploitive" or "deceptive." Often, the subsequent discussion turns to how marketing practices might become more consumer-friendly, socially compatible, or put in philosophical terms, how marketing might be *normatively* improved.

Normative marketing practices might be defined as those that emphasize transparent, trustworthy, and responsible personal and/or organizational marketing policies and actions, and exhibit integrity as well as fairness to consumers and other stakeholders. In the true spirit of normative ethical standards, this definition provides certain virtues and values (e.g., trust, fairness) to which marketing practitioners ought to aspire. However, the definition also raises myriad questions. What do we mean by transparent? Does that mean no trade secrets are ever allowed? What is the essential nature of integrity? Does it mostly involve keeping organizational promises to customers or is it broader than that? What is the nature of fairness, and who decides what standard of fairness is to be applied? Should it be consumers, the company at focus, regulatory agencies, or a broader cross-section of society? What stakeholder interests should be taken into consideration, and how should they be weighted? As one can see from these questions, the area of normative marketing ethics is likely to generate considerable controversy because there are differing views among various parties about what constitutes "proper" behavior in marketing.

GENERAL PERSPECTIVES

Because marketing is the organizational process focused directly on exchange, ethical issues in marketing have existed since the inception of trade. The Roman philosopher Cicero counseled merchants to avoid raising prices too high in times of shortage, lest they alienate their customers, who might shun them when supplies were more abundant. However, the analysis of marketing ethics from a more systematic and analytical standpoint has only begun to develop in the past 40 years. Since the mid-1960s, the literature on marketing ethics has grown substantially. A 2005 ABI/Inform literature search using the term *marketing ethics* as its search query generated a list of more than 400 citations to the literature—all of which presumably addressed marketing ethics in some scholarly form or fashion. While cynics view the term *marketing ethics* as an oxymoron, no doubt due partly to the frequent questionable activities of some used car dealers, advertising copyrighters, and telemarketers, there exist clear and articulated standards of proper behavior that are "peer endorsed" by marketing practitioners. In other words, marketing managers themselves have expressed their opinions as to the ideal obligations inherent in the honest and forthright conduct of marketing. Perhaps the best known of these codes of conduct is the American Marketing Association's (AMA's) "Statement of Ethical Norms and Values for Marketers." This document— endorsed by the largest professional organization of marketing practitioners in the world—and available for review at www.marketpower.com (search: code of ethics) specifically states that marketers serve not only their company enterprises but also act as stewards of society in creating, facilitating, and executing the efficient and effective exchange transactions that are part of a greater economy. The AMA statement recognizes the duties that marketers have to all stakeholders (e.g., customers, employees, investors, channel members, regulators, and the host community) as they discharge their job responsibilities. This document explicitly warns that marketers must not knowingly do harm in executing their selling responsibilities, that marketers have a duty to foster trust in the marketing system, and that they should embrace basic marketplace values, including truth telling, genuine service to customers, avoidance of practices acclaimed to be unfair, and an adherence to honest and open communications with clients. Significantly, it states that marketing organizations have responsibilities of "citizenship" just as individuals do. Documents such as the AMA Statement represent hard evidence that there are bedrock ethical standards and values that have been agreed on by numerous marketing practitioners.

Of course, the extent of practitioner compliance with these values is another issue. Over the years, surveys of marketing managers report that the vast majority of practitioners discharge their job responsibilities in a lawful and meritorious manner. Nonetheless, every year brings its share of horrific and controversial marketing blunders. Current issues in the news involving marketing practices have to do with price-gouging when gasoline shortages occur (as they did in the wake of Hurricane Katrina) and stealth marketing techniques such as surreptitiously gathering information about consumer patterns when they surf shopping sites on the Web. In general, national opinion polls of the public suggest that marketers have plenty of room to improve their ethical performance before it conforms to public expectations. Perhaps the "truth" about marketing lies somewhere between the practitioners view that marketers are predominantly "good guys" and the public perception of marketers as suspect purveyors of sometimes dubious goods and services.

While the above-mentioned statement of AMA of "norms and values" is partly inspirational in nature, there has also been substantial effort expended by marketing academics and ethics scholars to develop pragmatic models of marketing behavior that delineate the factors that shape and affect ethical (or unethical) marketing decisions. An example of such a work (*positive* marketing ethics) would be the Hunt-Vitell model of marketing ethics—a framework that has been subjected to extensive empirical testing. This complex model takes into account various factors such as (1) environmental dimensions in industry and the organization influencing ethical actions, (2) the recognition by decision makers of an ethical problem and its likely consequences, (3) the teleological and deontological norms used by marketing decision makers that might affect their selection of various alternative choices, (4) the type of ethical judgments made in various situations, (5) the formation of any intentions attributable to the marketing practitioners at focus, and (6) a measure of the outcomes of actual behavior. The purpose of weighing the myriad factors involved in real-world marketing decisions associated with ethical questions is that it helps specify the gaps between what the actual behavior of marketing practitioners *is* versus how far managers need to go in order to be in conformance with various marketing ideals. Empirical studies, using models such as Hunt-Vitell, have suggested, for example, that the standards managers use to address ethical questions vary considerably (e.g., some are utilitarian; some derive their perspectives from religious traditions). Moreover, the response to ethical issues by managers depends on the issue being addressed. For instance, the majority of managers might be very concerned that clandestine competitive intelligence gathering is growing in their industry but most may not be bothered by "puffery" (advertising exaggeration). Yet both practices are subject to ethical debate in the public realm. It is in the conduct of such systematic *ethics research* that the positive and normative aspects of marketing come together because marketers can learn what to "fix" based on what is actually going on.

MARKETING PRACTICE

At the heart of marketing ethics are decisions that marketing practitioners make about ethical questions. Ethical questions most often arise in marketing when a stakeholder group or some segment of the public feels that the actions taken by some (or many) marketers might be judged to be morally inappropriate. Currently, for instance, many consumers feel that *spam* advertising over the Internet is far too prevalent and/or that product rebates have too often been intentionally made to be difficult to redeem. Similarly, other ethical questions occur when marketing managers believe that they might be compromising their own personal values in the quest for increased organizational profit. In such situations, marketers are often evaluating whether they should take *business* actions that they feel ought *not* to be done from the standpoint of *personal* ethics that they hold—the essence of an ethical dilemma. Most managers cannot avoid facing such tough issues because the majority of marketing professionals report confronting such ethical questions at some point in their careers. These "ethical" branch points can pertain to a host of marketing issues such as selling cigarettes to teenagers, the promotion of violence-oriented video games, pricing products at a level that exploits unsuspecting consumers, bluffing in negotiations with long-time suppliers, writing intentionally misleading ad copy, and so on. If the marketing actions that are taken happen to be in violation of the law, these are also typically characterized as unethical. However, our focus in this entry is particularly on actions that are *not* illegal but that are criticized as "improper" according to some ethical value or norm. Therefore, marketing ethics is mostly focused on marketing behaviors that are not prohibited by the law but perhaps should not be indulged due to certain moral considerations. And thus, marketing ethics is often concerned with actions that are currently legal but still might be judged improper according to some invoked moral standard. For instance, NASCAR has every legal right to have their automobiles sponsored by and festooned with the logos of brewers, distillers, and other alcoholic beverage makers. Whether it is ethical to link speeding race cars to alcohol beverages given the significant "driving while intoxicated" problem that exists in the United States is a matter for debate.

Most generic areas of marketing practice provoke substantial ethical comment and discussion. These areas include marketing segmentation, marketing research, product development, pricing, distribution, personal selling, and advertising. In the paragraphs below, a sampling of marketing issues, often suggesting ethical questions from these areas of marketing practice, is briefly reviewed to illustrate both the nature and the scope of marketing ethics in the conduct of business operations.

Market Segmentation

One of the basic strategies of marketing campaigns involves the division of the mass market into "segments" followed by the development of specific offerings to appeal to the selected "target market." Ethical questions especially surround the target marketing of segments that include potentially vulnerable populations such as children, the elderly, the impoverished, and marketing illiterates. The "ethical issue" at focus here centers on whether marketers have too much "power" over certain groups who are not prepared to independently participate in the marketplace.

For example, children are a $25+ billion market in the United States alone for products such as toys, sugared cereal, DVDs, and video games. One major ethical question involves the extent to which marketers can freely treat children as "consumers in training" (mini adults) subject to pretty much the same promotions as the rest of the (adult) market. For young children (less than 8 years old), there is the issue of whether they even understand the difference between (for instance) television advertising and the programming itself. For older kids, the ethical issues might focus more on the appropriateness of certain products (violent video games), or the degree to which young teenagers might be susceptible to particular kinds of provocative fashion or lifestyle advertising. The key issue involved in targeting children turns on whether marketers should be held to a higher standard care and caution when marketing to children. One illustration of emergent constraints when approaching children involves the passage of the Children's On-line Privacy Protection Act of 1998 that was promulgated because of significant parental concerns regarding the collection of market research information data over the Internet from children younger than 13. Essentially, this federal legislation, inspired by numerous ethical questions raised by the general public, prohibits the collection of any personal information by market researchers from "under 13s" without verifiable permission from parents allowing it.

Similar questions about vulnerability to marketing scams occur with regard to older consumers—especially those more than 80 years of age. Such seniors are living longer, and as they grow older, they become less confident in their decision-making ability and become potential targets for the fraudulent sales of financial services, vacation packages, insurance annuities, and prescription drug plans—to name only a few product categories. As the baby boomers grow older and make up a larger percentage of the population, the focus on the appropriateness of marketing practices to this senior segment will only increase in prominence. Various scams that exploit seniors (e.g., sweepstakes that promise winnings but are designed only to sell magazines) are reported in the press almost weekly.

Marketing Research

Since marketing decisions are often data driven, market research techniques and outputs are frequently used by marketing practitioners. Market researchers themselves often have considerable training in methodological and statistical techniques, and one might surmise that because of their greater education, they exhibit a higher degree of ethical professionalism than other marketing practitioners. Certainly, it is true that various professional organizations related to the practice of marketing research such as the Council for Survey Research, the Market Research Society and the European Society of Marketing and Opinion Research have developed detailed codes of ethics addressing common conflicts that occur in the execution of marketing research. These "conduct codes" of these professional organizations can be accessed at their Web sites and provide a modicum of guidance for marketing researchers when facing common situations that occur as part of the research process. These codes stress that tactics such as protecting respondent confidentiality when it is promised, not misrepresenting the identity of the research sponsor, properly disclosing research procedures, and many other professional practices should be adhered to.

Additional ethical issues arise owing to the fact that marketing research often involves contact with the general public, usually through the use of surveys that are increasingly being conducted online. Because marketing research activity relies heavily on publicly submitted information, some of which is personally sensitive, marketing research is ripe for ethical abuse or misuse. As survey research has become digitized, researchers have gathered substantial records about consumer product and service usage as well as their satisfaction. As a result, the issue of *consumer privacy* is at the forefront of marketing research ethics. It is hoped that the coming decade will yield definitive answers about the extent of privacy protection that consumers can expect when shopping online. Second, most marketing research is conducted by for-profit organizations to aid decision making within corporations. As a result, the profit motive may cause researchers or their clients to compromise the objectivity and precision of the research that is undertaken. Researchers inherently want to provide support for the outcomes their sponsors hope to find. Clients basically want the research they conduct to tell the best possible story about their company and their products. It should not be surprising then that marketers sometimes fall to the temptation of misusing market research information by manipulating or exaggerating the results.

Product Management Ethics

Ethical issues surrounding the management of products are central to marketing because the marketing process generally begins with a product (broadly defined to include goods, services, or ideas). The most common ethical concerns in this area pertain to the safety of products. Earlier, in the brief discussion concerning the AMA practitioner norms and values, the notion of "never knowingly doing harm" was introduced as a central ethical percept. Certainly, this prescription directly applies to the area of products.

That products are safe "for their use as intended" is a basic consumer expectation and is embodied in common law within the concept of "implied warranty." While the sale of safe products is a fundamental marketing expectation, many consumers remain skeptical as to whether they are likely to receive this protection. A 2005 Yankelovich/MONITOR poll of consumers found that 61% agreed that even long-established companies cannot be trusted to make safe, durable products without the government setting basic industry standards. Indeed, a minimal base line of consumer protection in this area is assured via regulation by the U.S. Consumer Product Safety Commission, which has the general mandate to oversee product safety in the United States. Other government agencies also oversee specialized areas of product category such as the U.S. Department of Agriculture, the Food and Drug Administration, and the U.S. Department of Justice, which has specific jurisdiction for alcohol, tobacco, and firearms.

Despite all these protections, perennial ethical questions about product safety continue to be asked: How safe should products be? How safe is safe enough? When products harm consumers in the course of normal usage, who should be held liable? Too often marketers fail the safety test. For example, each Christmas season various consumer advocacy groups identify and publicize toys that are potentially dangerous to young children unless used with extreme care and under adult supervision. And, exactly where to draw the line in automobile safety is a never-ending debate. Should SUVs, which American consumers both love and demand, roll over as often as they do? Should side air bags, which consumers generally are reluctant to pay for as "add-ons," be mandatory because they can prevent serious injuries?

Another growing area of concern is product counterfeiting. Product counterfeiting involves the unauthorized copy of patented products, inventions, and trademarks or the violation of registered copyrights (often for the purposes of making a particular product look like a more popular branded leader). Common examples of product counterfeiting include fake Rolex watches, knockoff Levi jeans, and illegally pirated video and audio tapes of popular movies and music. It is estimated that product counterfeiting costs American companies $450 billion in sales each year. Product counterfeiting is unethical and, in most markets around the world, illegal as well. Counterfeiting is unethical because it involves an attempt to unfairly capture the "goodwill" created by one company's brand equity and unfairly transfer it to a knockoff product without royalty payment to the originating party. Simply put, counterfeiting is a form of intellectual theft. Interestingly, the majority of college students in the United States find "downloading" music from the Internet without paying to be a mostly harmless and ethical practice. With the expansion of China's economy and the many knockoff products that seem to originate there, product counterfeiting will be a major ethical issue for organizations in the early part of the 21st century.

Another instance of common ethical concern involves products that create problems for the physical or natural environment. Examples would include product packaging that is not biodegradable; products that use inordinate scarce resources such as large sports utility vehicles (e.g., the Hummer) along with their unusually low fuel mileage; various chemicals and detergents that pollute the land, air, and groundwater when improperly disposed of; and medical wastes that are sometimes dumped into oceans or lakes because the proper disposal of such material is burdensome for the user. Contributing further to all this is an increasingly "disposable lifestyle" in many developed countries that generates waste-handling problems, a residue of the convenience-oriented mentality—fueled by marketing. For example, the average American generates approximately 4 pounds of garbage a day of which 30% represents product packaging. The fundamental ethical issue connecting all these ecological examples is that of *externalities*. Basically, externalities are costs that are imposed on the society as a whole that are not paid for by the original producer or consumer. To take an obvious example, when beer bottles and soft drink cans are littered in public parks or recreational areas, the cleanup of that packaging represents an "externality." As a response to all this, a "green marketing" movement has developed, which puts a premium on product marketing and programs being compatible with environmentally protective principles. To this end, some organizations have embraced the Coalition for Environmentally Responsible Economies (CERES) principles—some of which speak directly to marketing-connected issues. In general, these principles involve adhering to an environmental ethic of strong commitment to ecological excellence as well as human health and safety. The CERES principles, which can be accessed online, are yet another normative code of conduct to help guide marketing actions in particular areas of operations.

Pricing

Perhaps no area of managerial activity is more difficult to assess fairly and to prescribe normatively in terms of morality than the area of pricing. The given price of a product or service commonly results from the confluence of three factors: demand, competition, and cost. Each of these factors can be central to ethical questions about pricing fairness. For example, when high demand puts pressure on supply, such as the desperate need for construction materials after a natural disaster, there may be a temptation for sellers to price-gouge. Or in an attempt to gain dominant market share, strong competitors may use predatory pricing (below cost pricing) to drive economically challenged sellers from the marketplace. In a business-to-business setting, a vendor may simply mislead a client concerning what "actual costs" have been incurred especially if they are operating under a "cost plus" pricing contract. While there is agreement that sellers are entitled to some profit margin above their full cost, how high prices can be and still be "fair" has been debated since medieval times. According to theologians such as Thomas Aquinas, the "just price" was often conceived of as the (debatable) amount above cost that the merchant needed to charge in order to maintain his or her business and to provide for his or her family. Charging more than that was to commit the grievous sin of avarice.

There is presently considerable regulation that helps establish some minimum behaviors for "fair pricing" (e.g., *price-fixing* by sellers, sometimes called "collusion," is illegal; similarly, "price discrimination" to different distributors by sellers without economic justification is also contrary to commercial law). Nevertheless, the concept of ethical pricing seems destined for considerable future debate. One current practice in the news has to do with the pricing strategy engaged in by the so-called pay day loan stores (i.e., those lending businesses that provide instant cash advances in lieu of unpaid, but earned, wages). These operations charge extremely high interest rates mostly to the impoverished segment of the market. A second dubious pricing instance involves some forms of adjustable rate mortgages that can often trigger significantly higher repayment rates for a variety of dubious reasons. And, a third questionable pricing scheme centers on "rent-to-own" furniture/appliance stores whose cumulative rate schemes often translate to payment totals far in excess of the total cost of the items rented. In each of these instances, it is argued that the pricing is "exploitive" because the high rates take advantage of certain unwary or desperate consumers.

Distribution

The distribution element of marketing involves the entire supply chain from manufacturer through wholesalers and distributors (including retailers) on to the final consumer. At each point in the supply chain, because there are economic interactions between these various parties, the potential for ethical issues to occur is quite common. Perhaps the most overarching issue within the channel of distribution supply chain has to do with the question of power and responsibility within the channel itself. Often one organization within the channel has greater economic leverage than other channel members, and with that economic leadership comes a potential for ethical abuse. A current example of this situation might be the enormous economic power that Wal-Mart possesses over its suppliers. Due to their dependence on Wal-Mart's access to the market, suppliers must conform to Wal-Mart's various contract requests or face losing a distribution outlet that serves tens of millions of customers. One perhaps encouraging lesson of marketing history is that channel members who abuse their power eventually lose it, often through the enactment of new government regulations that restrict and constrain certain competitive practices.

Another common concern within channel relationships has to do with "gift giving" that sometimes mutates into bribery. A long-standing business custom is to entertain clients and to give modest gifts to business associates. Such practices can cement important economic relationships. The pervading ethical question, of course, is, "When does a gift become a bribe?" Historically, for example, pharmaceutical companies have offered medical doctors lavish entertainment and gifts. The drug companies have argued that these amenities are not being provided to influence physician prescription decisions, but rather simply to inform them of the availability of new branded drugs. Consumer advocates contend that such practices are forcing consumers away from less-expensive generic drug alternatives and contribute directly to escalating health care costs. Not surprisingly, one of the best ways for channel members to deal with such potential ethical questions is to develop clear guidelines that address some of the typically questioned practices that exist within their particular industry. For instance, some companies restrict their employees from giving or accepting anything worth more than $20 in a given year when dealing with a business partner. In this manner, managers are given at least minimal guidance as to what constitutes acceptable and nonacceptable gift-giving practices.

Personal Selling and Sales Management

Sales positions are among the most typical marketing jobs. Ethical conflicts and choices are inherent in the personal selling process because sales reps constantly try to balance the interests of the seller they represent with the buyers that they presumptively serve. Moreover, sales reps seldom have the luxury of thoughtfully contemplating the ethical propriety of their actions. This is because sales reps operate in relative isolation and in circumstances that are dynamic with their business transactions frequently conducted under great time pressures. Even when sales reps electronically submit real-time sales reports of their client calls, such "outcome-oriented" paper evaluations contribute to a perceived clinical distance between sales managers and their representatives. Business case history tells us that sales people seem to be most prone to acting unethically if one (or more) of the following circumstances exist: when competition is particularly intense; when economic times are difficult placing their vendor organization under revenue pressure; when sales representative compensation is based mostly on commission; when questionable dealings such as gifting or quasi-bribes are a common part of industry practice; when sales training is nonexistent or abbreviated; or when the sales rep has limited selling experience.

Sales managers in particular bear a special responsibility for questionable selling practices because they are in a position both to oversee their sales staff and to influence content and implementation of sales policies. Ethically enlightened sales managers should regularly review their sales literature before distribution to minimize the possibility that inflammatory (to competitors) material is inadvertently circulated. They should counsel their sales people not to repeat unconfirmed trade gossip. They should strive to maintain a sales environment free of sexual harassment. They ought to encourage their sales people never to make unfair or inaccurate comparisons about competitive products and avoid claiming the superiority of their own product/service offerings unless it is supported by scientific facts or statistical evidence documented or prepared by an independent research firm. Despite best efforts of marketers, the area of sales will continue to have its share of ethical controversies. Sales are the most common entry-level position into the field of marketing and also the job position in marketing about which the general public feels most suspicious.

Advertising

Advertising is a significant economic force in the world economy, with global ad spending projected to be well over $300 billion in calendar year 2005. The visibility and marketplace influence of advertising is so great that many consumers think of advertising as synonymous with marketing. Various critics charge that advertising is biased, needlessly provocative, intrusive, and often offensive. Yet most surveys suggest that the majority of consumers, on the balance, find advertising both entertaining and informative. While some types of advertising involve outright transgressions of the law (e.g., deceptive advertising containing intentional errors of fact), a great deal of advertising controversy involves practices that are perfectly legal but still raise moral questions. For example, promoting handguns in magazines with a substantial teenage readership, the featuring of bikini-clad Paris Hilton suggestively soaping down a car in an ad campaign for hamburgers, and implied health claims for products that may not be especially healthy (e.g., low-carb beer) are instances of controversial (but legal) advertising approaches. Over the years, many lists of citizen concerns about the ethics of advertising have been put together. Often included on those lists are questions about the appropriateness of tobacco and alcohol advertising, the use of stereotypical images in advertising (e.g., Hispanic gardeners, hysterical housewives), the increased amount of negative (i.e., attack) political advertising, and various attempts to exploit children as buyers. The last issue is particularly sensitive to the public and, since the early 1970s, the Children's Advertising Review Unit, established by the Better Business Bureau, has monitored advertising directed to children less than 12 years and has sought the modification or discontinuance of ads that were found to be inaccurate or unfair in some fashion.

One of the more curious features of ethics in advertising is that the involvement of several parties (i.e., ad sponsor, ad agency, and the media) in the creation of advertising has probably led to a *lower* ethical standard in the practice of advertising than one might expect. The presence of multiple parties, none of whom has full responsibility, has created the default position of "leaving it to the others" to articulate and enforce an appropriate ethical standard.

IMPLEMENTING MARKETING ETHICS

Of course, at the heart of marketing ethics is the issue of how to improve the ethical behaviors of organizations as they discharge their marketing tasks and responsibilities. There are several elements of successful implementation that have been regularly articulated in the business ethics literature and successfully applied to marketing. Good ethics begins with a chief marketing officer (CMO) who must not only publicly embrace core ethical values but also live them. It is often said that the organization is but a lengthened shadow of the person at the top; this is no less true of the marketing organization. Implied also, then, is that the CMO is supported in the endeavor to maintain strong ethical values in marketing operations by the chief executive officer (CEO) of the corporation. Put another way, a key role of the leadership of any company wanting to travel the high ethical road is to keep publicly voicing the importance of ethical conduct in the discharge of their business affairs. Such ethical exhortations involve espousing the core ethical values identified in the corporate mission statement. These values should be made operational in a code of conduct that addresses the specific ethical issues that are most common to a particular company or industry sector. For instance, the Internet sellers must explicitly address privacy policies for their shoppers, vintners should comment on the question of responsible drinking, and so forth. Furthermore, it is important that any such marketing code be dynamic and periodically revised. Caterpillar Corporation, a manufacturer of heavy construction equipment, has revised its code of conduct five times since the mid-1970s. Moreover, any organizational code or statement of norms must also be communicated well enough that all employees can verbalize its essential values. It is equally important that managerial and employee behavior in the organization be monitored, including that of the CMO, so that conformance to company values is checked on in a pragmatic way. One tool for doing this is the usage of a periodic *marketing ethics audit* to systematically check company compliance with ethics policies and procedures. When ethical violations occur, proportionate punishment must be meted out. Similarly, when organizational managers perform in an ethically exemplary fashion, appropriate rewards also should be provided. This last step testifies to something beyond financial results leading to recognition in the organization. Details of executing all these steps have been exhaustively treated in the business ethics literature and modified for a marketing context. Johnson & Johnson and Ford are examples of organizations that conduct audits of their social performance that includes the evaluation of multiple marketing dimensions.

CONCLUSION

At the end of the day, the most vexing ingredient in the recipe for better ethical behavior by marketers remains the force of will to always keep ethics at the heart of a company's purpose. The pressure on individual organizations to maintain and improve their profitability and to grow revenues is incessant. The nature of marketing management is to provide needed consumer goods and services by undertaking risk that, if calculated properly, is rewarded with financial profit. Ethical operations, at least in the short run, can be detrimental to that profitability because they often include some economic cost. Keeping ethical marketing at the forefront of operations is an exceedingly difficult challenge given the constant pressures on marketing managers to remain financially successful and growing.

—Gene Laczniak

Further Readings

Brenkert, G. C. (1997). Marketing trust: Barriers and bridges. *Business and Professional Ethics Journal, 16*(1–3), 77–98.

Cohen, D. (1995). *Legal issues in marketing decision making.* Cincinnati, OH: South-Western College Publishing.

Davidson, K. (1996). *Selling sin: The marketing of socially unacceptable products.* Westport, CT: Quorum Books.

Ferrell, O. C., & Gresham, L. G. (1985). A contingency framework for understanding ethical decision making in marketing. *Journal of Marketing, 49,* 87–96.

Hunt, S. D., & Vitell, S. J. (1986, Spring). A general theory of marketing ethics. *Journal of Macromarketing, 6,* 5–16.

Karpatkin, R. H. (1999, Spring). Toward a fair and just marketplace for all consumers: The responsibilities of marketing professionals. *Journal of Public Policy and Marketing, 18*(1), 118–122.

Laczniak, G. R. (1983, Spring). Frameworks for analyzing marketing ethics. *Journal of Macromarketing, 3,* 7–18.

Laczniak, G. R. (1999, Fall). Distributive justice, Catholic social teaching and the morality of marketers. *Journal of Public Policy Marketing, 18*(1), 125–129.

Mascarenhas, O. A. J. (1995, April). Exonerating unethical marketing executive behaviors: A diagnostic framework. *Journal of Marketing, 59,* 43–57.

Murphy, P. E., Laczniak, G. R., Bowie, N. F., & Klein, T. A. (2005). *Ethical marketing.* Upper Saddle River, NJ: Pearson Education.

Murphy, P. E., & Pridgen, M. D. (1991). Ethical and legal issues in marketing. *Advances in Marketing and Public Policy, 2,* 185–244.

Robin, D. P., & Reidenbach, E. R. (1987, January). Social responsibility: Ethics and marketing strategy: Closing the gap between concept and application. *Journal of Marketing, 51*(1), 44–58.

Schlegelmilch, B. (1998). *Marketing ethics: An international perspective.* Boston: International Thomson Business Press.

Smith, N. C. (1995). Marketing strategies for the ethics era. *Sloan Management Review, 36*(Summer), 85–97.

Williams, O. F., & Murphy, P. E. (1990). The ethics of virtue: A moral theory for marketing. *Journal of Macromarketing, 10*(1), 19–29.

CONSUMER RIGHTS

The subject of consumer rights historically covers two related areas: issues related to the actual products and services that a company sells to consumers and corporate business practices that directly affect consumers. As part of the evolution of consumer rights and concerns, a third area, spawned in large part by the growth in information processing industries and integrated computing networks, has emerged. This area concerns the use of information *about* the consumer, including privacy and security of that information. While there is little legislation establishing actual rights of consumers, there is a large body of law dealing with a range of consumer issues, which taken together are often referred to as "consumer protection."

At its core, a discussion of consumer rights implies that the interactions between consumers and corporations will naturally tend to be to the advantage of the corporation (due not only to size but also due to political, economic, and social influence) and so legal and political means should be used to equalize any imbalance of power. (More bluntly, many laws passed to protect consumers assume that the consumer is either unable or incapable of protecting himself or herself, due to the complex nature of business or products, and must be protected in the most basic sense of the word.) The key assumption of most consumer rights initiatives is that, absent any restraining influences, corporations will make decisions that ignore the welfare of consumers and maximize the assumed advantages of the supplier. A secondary assumption is that the consumer will (1) usually have less information than a business and (2) will be more easily confused by business complexities and, therefore, must be protected from businesses that will take advantage of these informational or experiential asymmetries. (Note that the advent of the Internet has greatly reduced the information disparity between consumers and suppliers, as well as offering a significant increase in resources that consumers can use to defend their rights. Consumer rights advocates believe information is power and that information transparency is critical to producing informed consumers.)

Most of the societal and legislative initiatives over the years either prohibit what is considered to be anticonsumer behavior or provide tools to consumers by which they may force companies to address individual (or sometimes group) grievances related to products or business practices. Anticonsumer behavior has historically included clear-cut examples such as price-fixing and price-gouging, deceptive marketing and sales practices, production and distribution of dangerous products (including pharmaceuticals and medical devices), and failure to deliver promised products or services. Less obvious but no less critical to the consumer are more recent developments in the consumer-business relationship, such as information privacy (especially in health care matters), unsolicited sales and marketing, and refusal to provide services or nondiscriminatory prices to a particular class of consumer.

While there is a case to be made that the Hippocratic Oath (the traditional oath that physicians take that binds them to keep the best interests of the patient uppermost in their considerations) embodied the first consumer protection principles in history, arguably the first U.S. legislation intended to protect the consumer was the Sherman Antitrust Act, signed by President Benjamin Harrison in 1890. The act declared that "Every contract, combination in the form of trust or otherwise, or conspiracy, in restraint of trade or commerce among the several States, or with foreign nations, is declared to be illegal." Often assumed to restrict monopolies, the act was targeted not at the size or form of corporations or trusts but at "restraint of trade," which would ultimately lead to artificially high prices for the consumer. Free markets were deemed better for the consumer; anything that prevented free markets was, therefore, bad and should be outlawed.

Following the enactment of the Sherman Antitrust Act, just what was allowed and forbidden by the law remained open to interpretation, as the U.S. economy evolved and the size of corporations allowed greater market control by a few companies or individuals. Such questions were debated and refined over the ensuing 24 years, particularly during President Theodore Roosevelt's administration. Roosevelt believed the solution lay in a commission that would regulate business practices and established the Bureau of Corporations in 1903. In 1914, Woodrow Wilson signed the Federal Trade Commission and Clayton acts. These acts established the Federal Trade Commission (FTC) as an investigative and enforcement body, creating the first government agency with the power to protect consumers, and explicitly outlawed monopolies, respectively. Since 1914, Congress has continued to expand the reach and powers of the FTC, allowing the FTC to address consumer issues as diverse as defining deceptive or unfair practices, establishing rules for granting credit, and regulating telemarketing practices.

The modern era of consumer rights traces to March 15, 1962, when President John F. Kennedy sent a special message to Congress containing his statement of the four basic consumer rights that the government should work to protect and promote:

1. *The right to safety:* protection against hazardous goods

2. *The right to be informed:* the right to access information the consumer needs to make an informed choice and protection against fraud and deceit

3. *The right to choose:* access to a variety of products and fair prices and protection against business practices that reduce competition

4. *The right to be heard:* the guarantee that consumer concerns will be heard and fully considered by the government

Since Kennedy's message, these rights have been added to by various groups worldwide, most notably the United Nations, to include the following:

- *The right to consumer education:* early and lifelong education about the consumer marketplace and the laws supporting consumer rights
- *The right to consumer redress:* the right to be compensated for misrepresented or unacceptable goods and services and the responsibility to actively pursue such redress
- *The right to a healthy and sustainable environment:* the right to live and work in a safe and healthy environment that supports a life of dignity
- *The right to basic needs:* access to goods and services necessary for survival throughout societies
- *The right to access:* fair and equitable distribution of goods and services throughout society

Kennedy's main point was clear and has been echoed by many others: From an ethical perspective, consumers have certain rights that exist outside of government policy and law, and it is the government's job to ensure these rights are not infringed on in the marketplace. In the ensuing years, the federal government and state legislatures worked to implement laws and policies that institutionalized those rights.

Inherent in Kennedy's message is a more subtle requirement that the consumer, and the public as a whole, have a responsibility to *proactively* use consumer information, education, and rights to not only make informed decisions but also to actively work to be sure that government and industry act in the consumer's interest. The classic example of citizen responsibility in this regard is Ralph Nader and his group of young activists known as Nader's Raiders. Arguably the beginning of the modern consumer rights movement, Nader began in 1965 by taking on the auto industry over the alleged safety problems of GM's Corvair automobile. His activities soon expanded to include waste in government, including monitoring and exposing government agencies who were failing to effectively perform their duties to protect consumers.

While there are many laws at the federal and state levels aimed at protecting consumers by legislating against harmful business practices, a few are worthy of special note as examples of the philosophy of the government's role in protecting consumers. The Truth in Lending Act was originally enacted in 1968 and revised in 1980. It requires complete disclosure to consumers of all costs involved during the life of a credit transaction, including loans and leases, and demands explicit and clear statement of the conditions under which credit is granted. In addition, the law provides legal recourse for consumers against lenders who violate the terms of the act. The act was in response to predatory lending and leasing arrangements, deceptive credit marketing, and discriminatory practices in granting credit based on nonfinancial factors.

The Fair Credit Reporting Act (FCRA) passed in 1970 regulates the way that consumer credit information is collected, distributed, and reported. Prior to the passage of this law, major credit bureaus operated largely independently of oversight or even cursory review as regards to accuracy, privacy, security, use, and dissemination of consumer's credit information. Consumers for their part had no recourse against incorrect information provided by credit unions or the resulting burdens on their financial dealings. In the most egregious cases, consumers could be denied credit based on credit reports to which they had no access and were not even aware were the basis for the denial. In response to growing evidence of incorrect credit reporting, information and privacy abuses, and pressure from consumer advocates, Congress passed the FCRA to provide tools to consumers for dealing with credit reporting issues and to legislate how credit bureaus would conduct their businesses relative to consumers. The FCRA requires credit bureaus to provide consumers with the information in their files and to take all reasonable steps to be sure the information is complete and accurate. It also requires that credit bureaus undertake "reasonable investigations" of any information disputed by a consumer and inform the consumer of the disposition of that dispute.

In 2003, the FCRA was updated through the Fair and Accurate Credit Transaction Act (FACTA). As part of the FACTA, consumers are entitled to a free credit report every 12 months, from each of the three major credit reporting agencies (Equifax, Experian, and Transunion), available through an FTC Web site established for that purpose. In addition, consumers are entitled to notification when credit is denied based on negative information in a credit report and at that point are also entitled to a free credit report. FACTA also required the FTC create a "Summary of Rights for Consumers," which would be supplied with any credit report provided to a consumer, detailing the specific consumer rights and credit bureau responsibilities provided by FACTA.

Combined with the FCRA, the Fair Debt Collection Practices Act (FDCPA) provides the major portion of consumer credit rights. Passed in 1978, the FDCPA was in response to serious abuses by the debt collection industry that included home and workplace harassment by phone, misrepresentation, threats of arrest or legal action that are outside the scope of debt collection and therefore not credible, and reporting false information to credit bureaus. The FDCPA regulates the means by which third-party debt collectors may do business, details the rights of consumers when dealing with such agencies, and provides legal recourse for consumers against abusive or non-FDCPA-compliant debt collectors.

The Telephone Consumer Protection Act of 1991 was passed to limit the number of unsolicited phone calls consumers receive at their homes. Congress recognized that as well as being a nuisance to consumers, such calls were often the vehicle by which unscrupulous business operators and fraudsters preyed on the public. The act limits the entities that may call a consumer's house to those with which the consumer has an existing business relationship (although "existing" is loosely defined) and also prohibits calls from entities with an existing business relationship whom the consumer has specifically asked to cease calling. The act also required the FTC and the Federal Communications Commission to establish a National Do-Not-Call registry, containing the numbers of all consumers who do not wish to be subject to uninvited telephone solicitations. The registry requires consumers to proactively register phone numbers and is one of the laws that provides the tools for consumers to use to protect themselves.

The Health Insurance Portability and Accountability Act of 1996 (HIPAA) is intended to do for a consumer's health information what other laws have done for financial information.

HIPAA specifies a set of "patient rights" regarding access and dissemination of medical and health information and, in many ways, parallels the protections of financial data provided by the FCRA and the FACTA. As with the other laws, it also provides for consumer redress in cases where the law is violated.

HIPAA also signaled a fundamental shift in how personal data of all kinds, not just financial data, is to be considered by businesses. HIPAA established the rights of people to control access to information about themselves and placed the burden of information security and protecting confidentiality of personal information clearly on those who store and access it. Personal information is now a "thing," associated with a person, to be protected rather than information to be collected and used for the benefit of the business.

All these laws serve to protect consumers by leveling the playing field in complementary ways. It is clearly the intent of the government to force businesses to become more transparent in their dealings with consumers, as well as allowing consumers to dictate how they will interact with businesses. In addition, the government has chosen to specify what kinds of information must be given to the consumer, how it is to be presented, and how information about the consumer may or may not be disseminated. Perhaps most critically, these laws provide specific redress for the consumer when businesses violate the laws. Again, the assumption is that information is power, if put in the hands of the consumer, and short of being forced to act in a fair manner, businesses will withhold, misuse, or misrepresent information. The new assumption in these laws, though, is that given the proper tools, consumers can protect themselves, as well as other consumers, through penalties and processes specified by these laws.

While the aforementioned laws deal with protecting consumers from harmful business practices, there is also a "right" or expectation that businesses will not sell *products* that are harmful to consumers. Toward this end, Congress established the Consumer Product Safety Commission (CPSC) by passing the Consumer Product Safety Act of 1972. Again, Congress posited a fundamental inability of the consumer to understand the implications of using a product, finding that "complexities of consumer products and the diverse nature and abilities of consumers using them frequently result in an inability of users to anticipate risks and to safeguard themselves adequately." In the language of the act, the CPSC exists

1. to protect the public against unreasonable risks of injury associated with consumer products;

2. to assist consumers in evaluating the comparative safety of consumer products;

3. to develop uniform safety standards for consumer products and to minimize conflicting state and local regulations; and

4. to promote research and investigation into the causes and prevention of product-related deaths, illnesses, and injuries.

The other laws mentioned previously are somewhat passive in their protections, establishing guidelines for businesses and providing tools for consumers. The CPSC, however, was established as an active agency, charged with "protecting the public," "assisting consumers," and "investigating causes and prevention of injuries." When commerce and business practices are concerned, the consumer is given assistance in protecting his or her "rights." When injury and death are possible, the government is expected to not only assist but also to proactively work to protect the consumer.

—Tom Bugnitz

Further Readings

Krohn, L. (1995). *Consumer protection and the law: A dictionary.* Santa Barbara, CA: ABC-CLIO.
Meier, K. J., Garman, E. T., & Keiser, L. R. (1998). *Regulation and consumer protection: Politics, bureaucracy and economics.* Houston, TX: Dame.

PRODUCT LIABILITY

Product liability refers to the responsibility of manufacturers to compensate for injuries brought about through the use of their products. Legal and moral accounts of product liability seek to determine the conditions under which businesses can be held responsible for such harms. Since the risk of injury in the use of consumer products can never be completely eliminated, the notion of product liability raises important legal and philosophical questions about who should bear the burden of costs for such injuries. Determining the answer to these questions raises deontological issues of fairness and justice as well as utilitarian considerations as to how society can best prevent and recompense such harms. The wide publicity of famous cases of product liability, such as those involving McDonald's coffee, the Ford Pinto, Dow Corning breast implants, Firestone tires, and asbestos products, has particularly amplified such legal and moral questions.

HISTORICAL BACKGROUND

The Anglo-American law of liability until the end of the 19th century was largely governed by the doctrine of privity. Under the law of privity, injured persons could not legally collect compensation from parties with whom they did not have an explicit contractual relationship. Thus, since manufacturers who sold their products through retailers did not have a direct contractual relation with the final purchaser of those products, they were effectively immune from lawsuits for injuries to consumers brought about by those products. As such, the privity barrier essentially made it impossible for most victims of product-related injuries to recover damages from a manufacturer of a defective product unless they had purchased the product directly from the manufacturer. While the law of privity may have made sense when most products were bought directly from the persons who made them, its legitimacy began to come into question as retail distribution was becoming a hallmark of the modern economy.

In the United States, the landmark 1916 case of *MacPherson v. Buick Motor Car* more or less abolished the barrier of privity. In that case, a New

York court rejected Buick's argument that it could not be held responsible for an accident due to a defective wheel that it had used in the production of its automobile simply because it had no direct contractual relationship with the person injured. The court ruled that Buick should have detected the wheel defect while the automobile was being assembled and that Buick had a reasonable duty to provide consumers with safe and reliable products.

The *MacPherson* ruling was soon adopted in most U.S. jurisdictions, and it ushered in a new theory of "due care" in product liability law. Under the due care theory, companies are held responsible for taking reasonable precautions to produce products that are free from potentially harmful defects. Generally speaking, under the theory of due care, a person could recover damages for an injury if it could be proved both that the product that caused those injuries was defective and that the defect in question was the result of negligence on the part of the manufacturer of the product. Demonstrating negligence involved showing that the manufacturer was at fault for the defect in failing to adopt reasonable standards in the design or production of the defective product.

While the doctrine of due care in liability provided injured consumers with a greater ability to recover for damages caused by defective products, the burden was still on the injured party to prove negligence on the part of the manufacturer. A series of court decisions in the mid-20th century, including *Escola v. Coca Cola Bottling*, *Henningson v. Bloomfield Motors*, and *Greenman v. Yurba Power Products*, eventually eroded even this requirement. In each of these cases, the courts awarded damages to consumers without requiring proof of negligence on the part of the manufacturers, ushering in the era of strict liability in torts. Under the rule of strict liability, manufacturers can be held legally liable for injuries caused by the defective nature of a product even if they were not negligent in producing that product. In certain contexts, distributors, assemblers, retailers, and any other party involved in placing a defective product on the market can also be held strictly liable for injuries caused by that product. Although injured parties can still bring legal action under negligence, the doctrine of strict liability is presently recognized, to some degree, in nearly all U.S. jurisdictions.

FORMS OF DEFECT AND COMPENSATION

While the theory of strict liability does not require proving negligence, it still requires that the injury in question be caused by the defective nature of the product. Thus, under both negligence and strict liability, proving liability involves demonstrating the defective nature of the product. Since there is some risk associated with the use of any product, this issue is of moral and legal significance as well. In general, products may be defective in manufacturing, design, or warning. Manufacturing defects occur when a product does not conform to the manufacturer's own specifications, as when a food product becomes contaminated during processing or a tool leaves the production line missing a screw. Defects in design occur when a product line is designed in a manner that is deemed to be unreasonably dangerous, as when the design of a ladder makes it likely to fail under anticipated weights. Finally, defects in warning occur when consumers fail to receive proper instructions as to the safe use of a product, as when a pharmaceutical company fails to inform consumers of a drug of possible dangerous interactions with other common medications.

Since no manufacturer can anticipate or prevent every possible risk involved in the use of a product, the determination that a product is defective in any form concerns judgments as to the reasonableness of the risk presented. To constitute a defect, most theories accept that the condition must constitute an unreasonable danger to the consumer. In this regard, the reasonable person standard is often appealed to in determining the existence of a defect. The reasonable person standard holds that a product is sold in a defective condition when it presents dangers to ordinary consumers in its expected use that would not be reasonably foreseen by them. However, some courts have lowered the standard for determining defectiveness by holding that manufacturers should also anticipate the unreasonable ways in which people might put their products to use in producing them. It should be noted that some products—for instance, many pharmaceuticals—have inherent dangers associated with them. In cases of such unavoidably unsafe products, a standard of social risk/utility is often used to adjudicate questions of manufacturers' responsibility. A social risk/ utility standard holds that if the dangers inherent in the use of the product are outweighed by the potential benefits of its use, and there is no other means of obtaining those benefits or making the product safer given current technology, then the product should not be considered unreasonably dangerous as long as information concerning the risks is provided to consumers.

In seeking restitution for injuries caused by defective products, plaintiffs can request both compensatory and punitive awards. Since product liability cases generally fall under civil law, and not criminal law, such awards are usually measured in monetary terms. Compensatory awards are meant to compensate injured parties for the losses they incur as a result of their injuries.

These losses can include medical expenses incurred as a result of the injury as well as lost earnings, both past and future, due to the injury. They can also include awards for the pain and suffering and other intangible harms associated with the injury. Finally, juries can award punitive damages to victims for the purpose of punishing the defendant, though this is more usually restricted to cases of negligence. The last two forms of compensation have been made particularly contentious because of the well-reported examples of extremely large jury awards to victims, as in the case of the nearly $3 million award originally issued by the jury to the woman burned in the McDonald's hot coffee case. As a result, tort reform in some jurisdictions has involved placing monetary limits on awards for noneconomic and punitive damages.

SOCIAL AND ETHICAL ISSUES

There is a good deal of debate surrounding product liability law, particularly with regard to the rule of strict liability. These moral concerns are generally divided into questions of fairness and justice and those of social and economic utility. Both proponents and opponents of the theory of strict liability appeal to such concerns in making their cases. For instance, many critics of the rule of strict liability hold that it is inherently unfair to manufacturers, since it holds them responsible for defects even when they have fully exercised reasonable precautions in producing the defective products. As such, they claim that it is unjust to hold manufacturers responsible for harms if they were not at fault in bringing about such harms. Such critics are often particularly opposed to what they see as the unfairness of much mass tort litigation, such as asbestos and tobacco suits, since this litigation often involves holding a current business responsible for harms that originated long ago and under the control of different persons. For all these reasons, many opponents of the rule of strict liability argue for a return to standards of negligence or comparative negligence in liability cases.

Proponents of strict liability also appeal to considerations of justice and fairness, though. They argue that if companies are not held responsible for harms caused by defective products, then injured persons will go uncompensated. Since the injured person is not at fault for an injury caused by a defective product, it is just as unfair, they maintain, to deny that person the ability to seek recourse for the damages caused by such defective products. Indeed, they argue that since someone has to bear the costs involved in injuries caused by defective products, it is most fair that the party that profits from their production should do so. In this vein, some proponents of strict liability have even argued that since businesses can only profitably operate within a specific underlying social and economic system, they should also help bear the cost of the harms produced with that system, even when they are not directly at fault.

Both proponents and opponents of strict liability also appeal to utilitarian considerations in their arguments. Proponents of strict liability maintain that the doctrine of strict liability provides businesses with the incentive to be as careful as possible in producing safe and reliable products. They also argue that businesses can build the costs of such liability back into their products and thus efficiently spread the cost to all consumers of those products. Opponents of strict liability, on the other hand, argue that the litigation and insurance costs associated with strict liability place an increasingly unbearable cost on businesses that is stifling to the economy and hurts the competitiveness of businesses in the United States with their international competition. Critics of strict liability have also argued that the doctrine discourages companies from introducing new or innovative products, particularly those, such as pharmaceuticals, that are unavoidably unsafe. As the utilitarian arguments, both for and against strict liability, appeal to long-term social and economic benefits and costs that are difficult to measure precisely, determining the overall utility of the strict liability approach is likely to remain a contentious matter in the foreseeable future.

—Daniel E. Palmer

Further Readings

Fletcher, G. (1972). Fairness and utility in tort theory. *Harvard Law Review, 85,* 537–573.

Jasper, M. C. (1996). *The law of product liability.* Dobbs Ferry, NY: Oceana.

McCall, J. (2005). Fairness, strict liability, and public policy. In J. DesJardins & J. McCall (Eds.), *Contemporary issues in business ethics* (pp. 305–307). Belmont, CA: Wadsworth.

Moore, M. J., & Viscusi, W. K. (2001). *Product liability entering the twenty-first century: The U.S. perspective.* Washington, DC: AEI-Brookings Joint Center for Regulatory Studies.

Owen, D., Madden, M. S., & Davis, M. (2000). *Madden & Owen on products liability.* St. Paul, MN: WestGroup.

Piker, A. (1998). Strict product liability and the unfairness objection. *Journal of Business Ethics, 17,* 885–893.

Smith, M. (1979). The morality of strict liability in tort. *Business and Professional Ethics, 3,* 3–5.

ETHICAL ISSUES IN PRICING

Pricing, one of the four functions of marketing (along with product, place, and promotion), is a dynamic process by which buyers and sellers determine what, and how many, units of wealth should be exchanged for a needed product or service. Buyers and sellers have differing goals in this exchange process. Usually, buyers are interested in obtaining needed products and services at the lowest possible price, while sellers tend to concern themselves with maximizing their profits.

Price affects both the supply of, and the demand for, a particular item. Generally, higher prices encourage sellers to produce more of an item but discourage buyers from purchasing large quantities of the item. Contrariwise, low prices tend to whet buyer demand for an item while discouraging sellers from producing. There is a price point, called *price equilibrium*, at which the supply of and demand for an item are equal. At price equilibrium, buyers purchase as many units of production as sellers make available.

The ethical issues in pricing are similar to those governing other aspects of business and deal primarily with fairness—fair competition and fair treatment of buyers and sellers. Generally, any pricing practice that maintains the competitive nature of the market and is fair to market players is ethical; practices that hamper free competition or unfairly treat specific constituencies of buyers or sellers are likely to be unethical.

ANTICOMPETITIVE PRICING

Anticompetitive pricing practices impede the natural dynamism of a free market. Some anticompetitive pricing practices are illegal, in addition to being unethical. In *price discrimination*, the seller offers identical products or services at different prices. There are three types of price discrimination. Price may vary by customer, when the value of the product or service is subjective or demand is highly elastic. Price may vary by quantity sold, which allows the buyer to enjoy scale economies on large purchases. Price may vary by location or customer segment, which allows both the seller and the buyer to enjoy economies of location. From the seller's perspective, perfect price discrimination would allow the seller to charge each buyer the maximum price the buyer is willing to pay; this form of price discrimination would create an infinite number of points along the demand curve at which the maximum price could be attained from various buyers, each involving a different quantity sold. In theory, perfect price discrimination could be attained at any level of seller output at which there is at least one buyer willing to pay the asking price for the good.

Many forms of price discrimination are ethical. For example, many restaurants offer a children's or senior citizen's menu. Supermarkets offer discounts to customers who use coupons or become price club members. Cinemas may have lower-priced tickets for matinees or for children. Price discrimination may occur even when the seller does not have a monopoly. In this instance, sellers operate in competitive markets but enjoy some degree of discretion in pricing due to brand loyalty, special product characteristics, or market segmentation.

Price discrimination may be predatory in nature, such as when prices are set below cost for certain preferred customers or with the intention of driving smaller competitors out of the market. *Predatory price discrimination* may violate specific laws, such as the Robinson-Patman Act, antitrust legislation, and Federal Trade Commission regulations. Determination of the legality or ethicality of pricing discrimination must be done on a case-by-case basis.

Price-fixing is the process by which a number of sellers agree to sell their commodity for a specified price in a specific market. While all sellers in a market may indeed sell their wares for the same price, this situation is price-fixing only when the sellers agree to do so in advance. In most states, seller collusion to set prices at a certain level is illegal. There is often tacit collusion to fix prices when some sellers' pricing strategy is to match, but not exceed, the price of an industry leader. The Federal Trade Commission has decided in many instances of tacit collusion that the circumstances did not meet the definition of price-fixing because the sellers did not agree among themselves in advance to charge the same price. Tacit collusion can only be considered price-fixing as defined by the Federal Trade Commission when the sellers have advance knowledge of each other's pricing actions and agree to behave similarly. Many states also have "below-sales-costs" laws, which make it illegal to sell goods or services below costs if the purpose of such a strategy is to force competitors out of the market to create a monopoly. Price-fixing is sometimes a form of *predatory pricing* and may be determined as such on a case-by-case basis.

Another anticompetitive pricing practice, *resale price maintenance*, occurs when producers make rules that govern the pricing behaviors of wholesalers or retailers of their products. This is done to limit free competition among sellers and keep all sellers reasonably profitable. Resale price maintenance also helps maintain a premium image for some products and might be used to support after-sales customer service. While resale price maintenance is not strictly illegal, it does inhibit free trade.

UNFAIR PRICING

Unfair pricing practices are also unethical. Unfair pricing techniques are those that involve fraud or manipulation or violate the requirement that fair market exchanges be informed and voluntary. Unfair pricing also exploits buyers in cases of significant time pressure beyond the buyer's control, emotional distress, and lack of information or experience or where the buyer's normal bargaining power is diluted in a situation of emergent need. *Price-gouging* is a form of unfair pricing that is often considered unethical and is sometimes illegal. It occurs when sellers raise the price of scarce goods to the highest price the market will bear regardless of the cost associated with the production of the goods being sold. Price-gouging is often targeted in areas where substitute goods are not readily available. Frequently, price-gouging is also practiced for items in temporary shortage, such as ice during a power outage or temporary lodging after a natural disaster. Generally, sellers who are able to price-gouge enjoy at least temporary monopoly status in the market in which the price-gouging takes place. Many communities have outlawed price increases during emergency situations unless the seller can show demonstrable cause for the price increase.

Deceptive pricing is another form of unethical pricing and occurs when a seller intentionally misrepresents the total cost of an item, makes incorrect comparisons between the seller's price and the prices offered by competitors, or significantly and artificially inflates the asking price of a product or service with the intention of offering a deep discount for the item. In such a case, the bargain received by the purchaser is a false one, unless the original price is one at which the product was offered for a reasonably substantial period of time or a significant number of items were sold for the original price. In another form of deceptive pricing, products or services are sold as a set; buyers are not given an opportunity to purchase each item independently or decline those items for which they have no desire. The buyer ends up paying for items not needed or wanted.

Hidden costs are another type of deceptive pricing, in which the costs of the item are not readily apparent on examination of the item or the accompanying documentation. Undisclosed shipping or handling costs, finance charges, or maintenance fees are some examples of hidden costs. Failure to disclose such costs is illegal in many states and may violate some Federal Trade Commission regulations. In short, deceptive pricing occurs anytime the price of a product or service is misrepresented, is incorrectly compared with the price of a competitor's product, or includes items the buyer does want but is not given the right to refuse or when all costs are not revealed and made explicit to the buyer at the time of purchase.

Manipulative pricing is another form of unethical pricing, in which price points are set to make buyers think the actual price of an item is lower than it really is. Odd-even pricing is one kind of manipulative pricing, wherein an item is priced in such a way that buyers think the item costs less than it really does. For example, a seller might price an item at $9.99 to lead buyers to believe that the price of the item is significantly less than $10.00. In another form of manipulative pricing, sellers allow buyers to purchase goods and make payments over time, in an attempt to make buyers believe the item costs less than it would if paid for in one lump sum. For example, an item might be sold for $50.00, or for five payments of $9.99. The five-payment scheme might confuse buyers into believing that paying for the item in increments is a significant savings over making just one payment. Another form of manipulative pricing involves setting the price of an item and then offering a seeming discount for volume purchases. The seller might price a particular item for $5.00 or two for $9.99. Again, this form of pricing may confuse buyers into thinking purchasing two of the item results in savings, when it really does not.

THE CONCEPT OF A "JUST PRICE"

Many discussions of the ethics of pricing decisions stem from the idea of the *just price*, an economic concept originated in the 16th century by Dominican theologians at the School of Salamanca. The theory of just price uses concepts of natural law philosophy as the foundation of economic thinking. The just price of an item is the sum of material costs necessary to produce the item plus a reasonable wage that would allow the seller to maintain a lifestyle appropriate to his or her station in life. The just price, therefore, represents the inherent value of the good or service. Just price theory predates capitalist economic thought. Its origins in Spain in the 1500s mean that just price theory is based on certain assumptions about culture and commerce that do not hold true in a free market economy.

First, just price theory assumes that the household, rather than the firm, is the owner of the tools of production and that human labor is the chief source of wealth. Therefore, a just price must compensate the seller for the cost of materials and labor expended in the production of goods. Fair exchange is based on the value of the labor of the seller, which may increase only if the seller's station in life improves. Since this was unlikely in medieval times, the established price for an item rarely changed.

Second, just price theory assumes that people in similar occupations do not trade goods or services with each other and that the value of labor and raw materials does not change due to factors external to the naturally established price.

Third, profit is not a factor in the computation of a just price; in circumstances where production or labor costs decrease, sellers are expected to pass those savings along to buyers.

Finally, the theory of just price has as an underlying principle the assumption that virtuous human conduct is characterized by restraint from extreme action. Thus, a merchant's most virtuous conduct would be to take a moderate stance by holding to the naturally established price for an item.

The four assumptions underlying the just price theory create the following practical implications for its implementation:

1. Sellers may not sell their wares for more than the naturally established exchange price.

2. Sellers may not raise prices to recoup losses due to business downturn or inventory shrinkage.

3. Sellers may not raise prices in times of natural disaster.

4. Sellers may not raise their price for a commodity once it has been established.

While just price theory may have worked in medieval Europe, the degree to which it would be successful in a secular, capitalist economy is unclear. The limitations on seller behavior imposed by just price theory are incongruent with the demands of a free market and would probably impede the efficient allocation of goods. In addition, the inability to earn a reasonable profit would most likely retard long-term economic growth as it would hinder expansion and discourage new competitors from entering the market.

The question of ethics in pricing is best answered by considering the seller's motivation for choosing a particular strategy and the impact the strategy has on stakeholder constituencies. If it is a seller's intention to use pricing as a means of profit maximization regardless of its impact on those who need the product or service, if the intention is to use price to limit the availability of products needed to sustain life, or if pricing is used as a means of forcing competitors out of the market, such motives are likely to be unethical. If, however, the seller's intention is to make needed products and services available to all who need them, and to make a fair living in the process, this would likely be an ethical approach in pricing. Thus, it is not the strategy itself that is ethical or unethical; it is the reasons for choosing a particular strategy and its impact on the market that determine the ethics of the particular pricing approach.

—Cheryl Crozier Garcia

Further Readings

Baldwin, J. (1959). The medieval theories of the just price: Romanists, canonists, and theologians in the twelfth and thirteenth centuries. In *The evolution of capitalism: Pre-capitalist economic thought*. Philadelphia: American Philosophical Society.

Berry, L. (2001). The old pillars of new retailing. *Harvard Business Review, 79,* 4 [Electronic version]. Retrieved May 18, 2006, from http://hgswk.edu/item.jhtml?id=2282&t=marketing

Boatright, J. (2007). *Ethics and the conduct of business* (5th ed.). Upper Saddle River, NJ: Prentice Hall.

Federal Trade Commission. (1997). *FTC guides against deceptive pricing*. Retrieved May 18, 2006, from www.ftc.gov/bcp/guides/deceptprc.htm

Federal Trade Commission, Division of Special Projects, Bureau of Consumer Protection. (1975). *Funeral industry practices: Proposed trade regulation rule and staff memorandum*. Retrieved May 18, 2006, from www.ftc.gov/bcp/fulemaking/funeral/proprule.pdf

Gilbert, M. (1968). *The gold-dollar system: Conditions of equilibrium and the price of gold*. Princeton, NJ: Princeton University, Department of Economics, International Finance Section.

How to price a product. (n.d.). Retrieved March 21, 2005, from www.ineed2know.org/ProductPricing.htm

Lustgarten, S. (1984). *Productivity and prices: The consequences of industrial concentration.* Washington, DC: American Enterprise Institute for Public Policy Research.

Mandy, D. (2003). *Dynamic pricing and investment from static pricing models.* Washington, DC: Federal Communications Commission, Office of Strategic Planning and Policy Analysis. Retrieved May 4, 2006, from http://hraunfoss.fcc .gov/edocs%SFpublic/attachmatch/DOC-238934A2.pdf

Norman, G., & La Manna, M. (1992). *The new industrial economics: Recent developments in industrial organization, oligopoly, and game theory.* Aldershot, UK: Edward Elgar.

Phlips, L. (1983). *The economics of price discrimination.* New York: Cambridge University Press.

Price discrimination. (n.d.). Retrieved May 3, 2006, from www.ftc.gov/bc/compguide/ discrim.htm

Seeley, R. (1986). *Equilibrium price solution of net trade models using elasticities.* Washington, DC: U.S. Department of Agriculture, Economic Research Service, International Economics Division.

U.S. Congress, House Committee on the Judiciary, Subcommittee on Monopolies and Commercial Law. (1987). *Clarification of the evidentiary and substantive antitrust rules governing resale price maintenance: Hearing before the Subcommittee on Monopolies and Commercial Law of the Committee on the Judiciary.* In One-Hundredth Congress, first session, on HR 585, Freedom From Vertical Price Fixing Act of 1987, April 2, 1987. Washington, DC: Government Printing Office.

PRICE-FIXING

Price-fixing is any agreement between competitors ("horizontal") or between manufacturers, wholesalers, and retailers ("vertical") to raise, fix, or otherwise maintain prices. Many, though not all, price-fixing agreements are illegal under antitrust or competition law. Illegal actions may be prosecuted by government criminal or civil enforcement officials or by private parties who have suffered economic damages as a result of the conduct.

HORIZONTAL PRICE-FIXING

Examples of horizontal price-fixing agreements include agreements to adhere to a price schedule or range; to set minimum or maximum prices; to advertise prices cooperatively or to restrict price advertising; to standardize terms of sale such as credits, markups, trade-ins, rebates, or discounts; or to standardize the package of goods and services included in a given price. All such agreements are per se illegal under United States antitrust law; that is, the court will assume that any such agreement is anticompetitive and will not hear arguments to the effect that the agreement actually enhances quality, competition, or consumer welfare in a particular case. Horizontal price-fixing agreements are also illegal under European Union (EU) competition law, where they are similarly subject to so-called hard-core restrictions.

There is nothing illegal about competitors actually setting the same prices as one another or even about them doing so consciously. (Indeed, in a perfectly competitive market, we would expect retailers to sell their goods at the same prices.) The offense lies in their *entering into an agreement with one another* to set or raise or maintain prices. (Section 1 of the U.S. Sherman Act, for example, prohibits any "contract, combination or conspiracy" that restrains trade.) The agreement, to be a violation, need not set a particular price; the law frowns on any agreement that interferes with competitors' ability to set their own prices with complete freedom. Thus, agreements that set price ranges, establish formulae for rates of change in prices, or supply guidelines for competitors' responses to changes in their cost structures are all violations, even though they neither establish a precise common price nor eliminate all possible price competition. Not every competitor in the market need participate in the agreement. Even an agreement between two tiny competitors in an enormous, busy, and otherwise competitive market will be a violation.

ANALYSIS OF HORIZONTAL PRICE-FIXING

Economists generally agree that horizontal price-fixing agreements are bad for consumers. Competition normally drives prices down, as competitors seek to lure away one another's customers. In a competitive market, therefore, the consumer realizes the greatest possible amount of *consumer surplus*—the value to the consumer of the good in excess of what the consumer actually has to pay for it. Price-fixing agreements, since they reduce competitors' ability to respond freely and swiftly to one another's prices, diminish consumer surplus by interfering with the competitive marketplace's ability to keep prices low. More important, horizontal agreements among competitors may facilitate their joint acquisition of *market power*—the ability to sustain higher prices than free competition would allow, without losing customers. A wide enough agreement could permit competitors to act as de facto monopolists, raising prices and cutting back on production to the detriment of consumer welfare. Moreover, they could do this without gaining any of the efficiency benefits of an actual merger or consolidation.

There are some critics of horizontal price-fixing policy, however. Some conservative economists argue that it is scarcely worth policing horizontal price-fixing arrangements, since they are economically unstable. Each member of a horizontal price-fixing agreement has a strong incentive to defect, secretly offering lower prices to attract a greater share of customers. In addition, any market with inflated prices induced by a horizontal agreement will rapidly attract new entrants, and they can easily restore prices to the competitive level. Finally, many economists are skeptical of courts' and prosecutors' abilities to distinguish real price-fixing arrangements from other complex arrangements with legitimate, procompetitive purposes.

In addition, there have been some concerns about the per se prohibition of horizontal price-fixing agreements in contexts where it is difficult for consumers to judge the quality of goods or services on their own. Take medical care, for example: Patients are often unable to judge for themselves whether the care they receive is of high or low quality. (High-quality care does not guarantee good outcomes, and patients who have received care of poor quality may nonetheless get better.) If high-quality care is both expensive to provide and hard for consumers to detect, the argument goes, then vigorous price competition will drive high-quality care off the market. Patients will not pay more for a difference in care they can't detect or verify. On the other hand, if price competition is minimized through horizontal agreements, then the pressure to cut costs by cutting quality will be reduced.

A third argument against the prohibition of horizontal price-fixing agreements involves the social desirability of cross-subsidization of services for the poor. Physicians, lawyers, and institutional health care providers have frequently argued that a reduction in price competition among them can give them the cushion necessary to supply necessary services at a reduced price or at no cost to poorer consumers. (Another, perhaps more intuitive, way to put this is that vigorous price competition reduces margins, and reduced margins result in cutbacks in charity care and pro bono work.) While competition law has not accepted these arguments, a number of state and local legislatures and regulators have created schemes under which competing health care providers, for example, can apply for permission to fix their prices under close state supervision in order to subsidize low-cost care for the poor. These schemes shield the providers from prosecution by extending the state's immunity from antitrust enforcement to cover their private actions.

VERTICAL PRICE-FIXING

Vertical price-fixing arrangements include agreements by manufacturers to set minimum or maximum resale prices for their products. Minimum resale price-fixing is often termed *resale price maintenance*. Direct agreements to maintain resale prices are per se illegal in the United States and subject to "hard-core restriction" in Europe. In both places, however, it is possible for manufacturers to achieve de facto resale price maintenance through indirect means—for example, by refusing to deal with retailers who discount their goods or by offering rebate programs that gear rebate amounts to pricing levels. These indirect means are especially difficult for courts to sort out when the vertical pricing arrangements are combined with other vertical restraints, such as geographic exclusivity deals, service and parts agreements, promotional agreements, and so on.

Maximum vertical price-fixing is at least prima facie procompetitive, since it appears designed to keep prices to consumers low. It is therefore generally judged on a case-by-case basis, with the court balancing the pro- and anticompetitive effects of the agreement in question against each other. (This case-by-case standard of evaluation is known in U.S. law as the *Rule of Reason*; it contrasts with the per se standard, which permits no such balancing.)

State-mandated and -supervised vertical pricing schemes—such as state price controls on auto insurance or on hospital charges—are immune from federal antitrust prosecution under U.S. law. In contrast, EU member states enjoy no such broad "state action immunity" from European competition law. Government-sponsored price-fixing schemes at the U.S. federal or EU-wide level (e.g., agricultural price supports) do not violate domestic antitrust laws but may be challenged as protectionist by other countries through the World Trade Organization.

ANALYSIS OF VERTICAL PRICE-FIXING

The economic effects of vertical price-fixing are complex, but economists are generally agreed that at least some prohibited vertical price-fixing could be efficient and procompetitive. Consider, for example, a resale price maintenance program put in place by the manufacturer of a certain brand-name appliance. The program guarantees adequate profit margins for the brand's retailers and lets them attempt to capture market share from one another via nonprice competition. Such nonprice competition might include the provision of excellent and attentive service by sales staff in well-stocked retail showrooms, armed with informative promotional brochures. The price maintenance program's limits on *intra*brand price competition have the long-term effect of enhancing the brand's reputation for quality and service; this, in turn, would enhance *inter*brand competition. Without price maintenance in place, however, low-service discount retailers can free ride on the costly services provided by others. Consumers could get their information from the salesman in the comfortable showroom but then actually purchase their appliances from the free-riding low-service discount warehouses. In the long run, without price support, excellent service will be driven out of the market, and the brand's ability to compete with other brands on quality and service will be diminished. Resale price maintenance might also serve to secure margins for small-volume retailers who, without some such guarantee, would be disinclined to devote shelf space to the product. Here, again, intrabrand competition is curtailed to secure distribution channels that facilitate more vigorous interbrand competition. Where the prospect of enhanced interbrand competition is minimal, however—as in the case of a manufacturer with market power in the product being sold—the anticompetitive effects of resale price maintenance may dominate.

Maximum price-fixing keeps costs to consumers down. While it may impose burdens on retailers, those burdens may not be injurious to competition, since retailers who find the maximum resale price burdensome can in many cases simply switch to a different supplier. Moreover, in situations where manufacturers grant geographically exclusive distribution rights to retailers (perhaps to retain control over the secondary markets for parts, service, and repairs), maximum price-fixing can prevent the "local monopolists" from gouging consumers. Finally, maximum price-fixing can limit the total damage to consumers from the repeated markups that occur when all levels of the distribution chain—manufacturer, wholesaler, and retailer—are in the hands of firms with significant market power.

INTERNATIONAL PRICE-FIXING

Internationally, price-fixing has been common through the ages. OPEC, for example, is a well-known decades-old cartel of oil-producing nations that sets its production levels cooperatively, with an eye toward keeping oil prices high. OPEC is protected from prosecution under other nations' antitrust laws, both by the international legal doctrine of sovereign immunity and by Austrian law governing service-of-process (OPEC is headquartered in Vienna). Recently, however, the argument has been made that OPEC's price-fixing practices could be attacked through the World Trade Organization, to which the OPEC member nations belong.

In the last decade of the 20th century, an unusual number of global price-fixing cartels surfaced. Among those prosecuted criminally were cartels fixing prices on lysine, vitamins, graphite electrodes, sorbates, sodium gluconate, construction, computer memory chips, marine construction, and citric acid. These cartels inflicted billions of dollars of losses on consumers, raising prices from 30% to 100% during the course of the conspiracies. The cartels were prosecuted vigorously in several countries. Criminal fines paid by companies in half a dozen of the cases exceeded U.S. $100 million; to these were added billions of dollars in payments of private claims to customers alleging economic damages. Executives from Germany, Belgium, the Netherlands, England, France, Switzerland, Italy, Canada, Mexico, Japan, and Korea have been convicted, fined, and in some cases jailed for price-fixing violations.

—Stephen R. Latham

Further Readings

American Antitrust Institute [Web site]. Retrieved from www.antitrustinstitute.org
American Bar Association Section of Antitrust Law [Web site]. Retrieved from www .abanet.org/antitrust/home.html
European Commission Competition [Web site]. Retrieved from http://europa.eu.int/ comm/competition/index_en.html
Fox, E. M. (2002). *Cases and materials on the Competition law of the European Union.* St. Paul, MN: West Group.
International Competition Network [Web site]. Retrieved from www.international competitionnetwork.org
Posner, R. A. (2001). *Antitrust law* (2nd ed.). Chicago: University of Chicago Press.
U.S. Department of Justice Antitrust Division [Web site]. Retrieved from www.usdoj .gov/atr
U.S. Federal Trade Commission Bureau of Competition [Web site]. Retrieved from www.ftc.gov/bc/index.shtml
Viscusi, W. K., Harrington, J. E., Jr., & Vernon, J. M. (2005). *The economics of regulation and antitrust* (4th ed.). Cambridge: MIT Press.

Price-Fixing

PREDATORY PRICING
AND TRADING

Predatory pricing is an anticompetitive measure employed by a dominant company to protect market share from new or existing competitors. It generally involves temporarily pricing a product low enough to end a competitive threat. Thus, the two major parameters under consideration are costs and the intent of the firm. Costs are usually easy to define yet there is a debate on the appropriate ones to use. Intent, on the other hand, is easier to comprehend yet most difficult to prove.

The exact legal (statutory) conditions for predatory pricing vary across the globe. In the United States, pricing below a dominant average variable cost (the *Areeda Turner* test) was last used by the Supreme Court in 1993 as a criterion for this practice in deciding *Brooke Group Ltd. v. Brown & Williamson Tobacco Corp.* According to the Court, this practice arises when a business rival prices its products in an unfair manner in an attempt to eliminate competition and exercise control over prices in the market. While the law should protect price competition, it should distinguish unfair pricing practices that would eliminate competition. The basic antitrust dilemma is to distinguish price predation from hard competition.

Generally, the following conditions must exist to constitute predatory pricing:

- The predator must have the market power to unilaterally increase its prices.
- The predator must charge prices that fall below a predatory price standard (which varies from country to country).
- The predator should be able to recoup its losses after the competitors have been driven out of the market.

The predatory pricing argument is as follows. The predatory firm initially lowers its price until it is below the average cost of its competitors. The competitors are then forced to lower their prices below average cost, thereby incurring losses on every unit sold. They are then faced with a difficult situation: If they opt not to drop their prices, they are bound to lose their entire market share and their profitability in the long run; on the other hand, if they do cut their prices, they will also lose a lot of money. After forcing competitors out of the market, the predatory firm raises prices and recoups its losses in the short run and increases its profits in the long run.

Researchers over the past four decades have yet to provide a clear-cut example of a monopoly created by predatory pricing. Some contend that competitors who are unable or unwilling to cut prices make these claims. In most cases, the courts have wrestled with how to characterize price predation. So far, three tests have been used: (1) predatory intent, (2) below-cost pricing, and (3) likelihood of recoupment of costs. In most cases, they have considered a combination of these three cases.

HISTORY AND CASES OF PREDATORY PRICING

The notion of predatory pricing can be traced back to the dawn of the industrial era. Notable examples include John D. Rockefeller's Standard Oil Company, which was accused of using low prices to drive away competitors in the late 19th century. AT&T spent $100 million per year in the 1970s defending against claims of predatory pricing.

American Airlines in the Mid-1990s

Between 1995 and 1997, three small carriers—Vanguard, Sun Jet International, and Western Pacific—entered the Dallas market by offering low-priced service to midwestern cities. American responded by matching their fares and increasing service on these routes. For example, American's one-way fare from Dallas to Kansas City was $108 before the low-cost start-ups entered the market in 1995. American promptly cut fares to $80 and almost doubled the number of flights to 14. All three start-ups subsequently abandoned Dallas Airport. Soon after, American raised its prices to $147 and scaled back the number of flights. None of the start-ups remain in business today.

The airline industry typically operates with very high fixed costs (e.g., equipment) and low marginal costs. On the other hand, as noted earlier, to win predatory pricing cases, one has to prove that the firm sold products or services for less than its average variable cost. The U.S. Congress enacted the

Airline Competition Preservation Act in 2001, putting the airline industry on notice that it planned to monitor anticompetitive and "predatory" practices. The act issue guidelines to prevent large carriers from eradicating the start-ups. One such suggestion was to force the dominant carrier to continue offering the low fares for 2 years if they respond to a low-fare service by a new entrant. The proposal also gives the Transportation Department the authority to investigate whether or not an airline is charging an average fare on a route that is unreasonably high.

Microsoft in the Late 1990s

In 1996, Microsoft began giving away its Web browser, Internet Explorer, as well as free software and marketing assistance to use its products. This enabled the company to successfully overcome the marketing dominance of its archrival Netscape Communications in the mid-1990s. In addition, to gain supremacy in the software industry, the company repeatedly gave away software that other companies were selling, thus hurting other firms such as Stac, Symantec, Novell, and Oracle.

Microsoft has aggressively defended these giveaways, arguing that lower prices are good for consumers. Moreover, bundling several types of software packages into an affordable unit is driven by customer needs. The courts have sided with Microsoft to date, and the company has stayed out of further controversy by refraining from raising the prices of its products, coupled with a strong public relations campaign involving several corporate social responsibility programs.

Wal-Mart in 2000

In 2000, government officials in Wisconsin, Oklahoma, and Germany accused Wal-Mart of pricing goods below cost with the intent of driving competitors out of the market. The Wisconsin Department of Agriculture, Trade and Consumer Protection filed a complaint against the giant retailer for violating the state's antitrust law by selling butter, milk, laundry detergent, and other staple goods below cost in stores in many cities and towns, thereby forcing other local stores out of business, gaining a monopoly, and ultimately increasing its prices.

In Oklahoma, Crest Foods, a three-store supermarket chain, filed a predatory pricing suit against Wal-Mart, contending that the latter regularly sent employees to visit their store to monitor prices and subsequently targeted price cuts, often dipping well below their own costs, so as to undermine them.

Similarly, in Germany, the Federal Cartel office accused the retailer of predatory tactics using "corner product" items such as milk and vegetable oil. German law prohibits below-cost pricing because the practice decimates small businesses and independent shops.

SUPPORT FOR THE RATIONALE FOR PREDATORY PRICING

Many economic models based on game theory and the theory of imperfect competition have shown that predatory pricing can be rational and profitable under specific circumstances. For example, by using "low-cost signaling"— that is, by increasing production and simultaneously lowering costs below the price—a firm may hoodwink its competitors into believing that it has a lower cost of production than the rest, thereby persuading them to leave the market as it would not be profitable for them to compete. Aggressive pricing also enables predators to acquire the reputation of being "tough," which may deter many potential entrants in the future. A final reason for predatory pricing is that aggressive pricing strategies will ensure more loyal customers from whom the company can make a profit in the future.

SKEPTICISM REGARDING THE THEORY OF PREDATORY PRICING

Many question the justification for the theory of predatory pricing since it is an irrational practice and the laws designed to prevent the practice only discourage competition. The Federal Trade Commission has not successfully prosecuted any firm for this practice in over two decades, and there are no empirical examples illustrating demonstrated predatory pricing by a firm. Such practices can be very costly for a larger firm (usually the predator), and a price war is an extremely risky venture given the uncertainty of how long it is likely to last. In addition, the competition may temporarily shut down its operations and resume when the price wars are over. Critics further argue that there has been no case when predatory pricing has led to monopoly. Conversely, there is strong evidence of the practice having failed repeatedly.

It is interesting to note that when Ford introduced the Model T in the early 1900s, it actually lost money and market share to Buick, Oldsmobile, and other competitors. By 1910, the auto industry was booming, yet Ford decided to cut its price by 20%, to $780, which was below the average total cost. On the contrary, General Motors, Ford's major competitor, had decided to increase its prices. Ford may have "preyed" on its competitors, yet few would argue against the fact that the customers were the ultimate beneficiaries. However, it does make one wonder whether such actions would have been allowed in today's environment.

ISSUES FOR FURTHER RESEARCH

There are many issues that are yet unresolved regarding the effects of predatory pricing on marketing decisions and strategies. For example, it is not clear what the long-term effects of predatory pricing on customer behavior are. As noted before, consumers benefit by paying less in the short run, yet the impact of higher prices set by the predatory firm after the demise of competition is not clear. Are consumers aware of predatory practices, and if so, how, and does it cause any backlash? Research is also needed to identify product-, company-, and industry-based factors that contribute to the occurrence of predatory pricing practices.

Another issue relevant in international trade pertains to the circumstances under which dumping may be considered predatory marketing. Dumping occurs when a foreign firm sells a product in a host country at a price below the cost or at a price below that at which the firm sells the same product in its domestic market. This is not the same as predatory pricing as firms often sell in free markets for nonpredatory reasons as well, such as during recessions or when the company's sale price remains high enough to cover the variable cost as well as part of the fixed costs they would continue to incur even if they stopped selling. Although the U.S. antidumping law and policy do not specifically prohibit predatory pricing, it is worth investigating the relationship between dumping and predatory pricing in other markets throughout the world and the necessary conditions under which one is considered to be the other.

—Abhijit Roy

Further Readings

Brady, S. P., & Cunnigham, W. A. (2001). Exploring predatory pricing in the airline industry. *Transportation Journal, 41*(1), 5–15.

Campbell, T., & Sandman, N. (2004). A new test for predation: Targeting. *UCLA Law Review, 52*(2), 365–412.

DiLorenzo, T. J. (1992). *The myth of predatory pricing* (Cato Policy Analysis No. 169). Retrieved from www.cato.org/pubs/pas/pa-169es.html

Does predatory pricing make Microsoft a predator? (1998, November 23). *Business Week*.

Eckert, A. (2002). Predatory pricing and the speed of antitrust enforcement. *Review of Industrial Organization, 20,* 375–383.

Facey, B. A., & Ware, R. (2003). Predatory pricing in Canada, the United States and Europe: Crouching tiger or hidden dragon. *World Competition, 26*(4), 625–650.

Gilder, G. (1984). *The spirit of the enterprise.* New York: Simon & Schuster.

Guiltinan, J. P., & Gundlach, G. T. (1996). Aggressive and predatory pricing: A framework for analysis. *Journal of Marketing, 60,* 87–102.

Gundlach, G. T. (1990). Predatory pricing in competitive interactions: Legal limits and antitrust considerations. *Journal of Public Policy and Marketing, 9,* 129–153.

Gundlach, G. T., & Guiltinan, J. P. (1998). A marketing perspective on predatory pricing. *Antitrust Bulletin, 43,* 883–916.

Helgeson, J. G., & Gorger, E. G. (2003). The price weapon: Developments in U.S. predatory pricing law. *Journal of Business to Business Marketing, 10*(2), 3–22.

Lindsey, R., & West, D. S. (2003). Predatory pricing in differentiated products retail markets. *International Journal of Industrial Organization, 21*(4), 551–592.

Ten Kate, A., & Niels, G. (2002). On the rationality of predatory pricing: The debate between Chicago and post-Chicago. *Antitrust Bulletin, 47,* 1–24.

TRANSFER PRICING

The American Marketing Association defines transfer pricing as "the pricing of goods and services that are sold to controlled entities of the same organization, for example, movements of goods and services within a multinational or global corporation." Transfer pricing is an *intra*firm transaction that affects costs and profitability at the subsidiary level and overall after-tax profitability for the firm at the corporate level. How the firm accounts for its various intrafirm transactions is therefore of interest to host governments, who would understandably want to investigate any suspicions of tax evasion through transfer pricing practices.

Host governments are naturally concerned to ensure that multinationals are not using creative accounting to avoid paying taxes. As a result, host governments may impose restrictions and enact laws that curtail such practices if the intent is to avoid taxation. While different governments may have different laws prescribing how transfer pricing is to be accounted for, in general the principle of "arm's-length" transaction is the approach least likely to violate legal requirements. By *arm's-length transaction*, it is meant that a "fair" price is charged between subsidiaries as though these subsidiaries were unrelated. We should note, however, that such fair prices are often allowed to contain additional charges for technology transfer, R&D, other overhead expense allocations, and the like. The upshot is that even arm's length is not necessarily clear-cut or straightforward. For instance, the IRS's *Treasury Regulations Section 1.482,* which is one of their publications pertaining to transfer pricing (among other things), runs to 103 pages.

If multinational or global corporations were few in number and minimal in economic impact, the issue of transfer pricing would be of only passing interest to most. However, multinational companies (MNCs) are becoming more and more pervasive, and mergers and acquisitions serve to make them even more powerful and omnipresent than ever before. Consequently, what these companies do to avoid taxes is of major import to most national treasuries and by extension to the economies of those societies. Corporations have always tried to minimize their tax obligations, and few would question any entity's (individual or otherwise) attempt to legitimately reduce its tax burdens. However, transfer pricing as an instrument to reduce or eliminate a multinational's taxes sometimes resembles "creative accounting" and corporate malfeasance. Especially in situations where an MNC is operating in a developing country and uses transfer pricing as a means to minimize its taxes payable to that country, such practices may be criticized as a blatant attempt to exploit a developing country's resources.

Global or multinational companies can manipulate transfer pricing to their advantage in at least two common ways—by adjusting the prices being charged intracompany, and by deciding what and how much of intrafirm goods and services will be bought. In an MNC, a lot of purchasing and selling takes place within the boundaries of the firm itself. For example, say the Singapore subsidiary of XYZ Oil Company sells its lubricants to the Australian subsidiary for resale in Australia. The price that Singapore charges is the cost that Australia pays. Yet in the final analysis the funds stay within the firm. If not for taxation, the price being charged by Singapore (the transfer price) does not have an impact on the overall profitability of XYZ Corporation worldwide.

Contrast this with a scenario where multinationals do not exist. The "same" transaction is undertaken by an independent Singaporean company selling to an independent Australian entity. The funds change hands in this new scenario. Price matters here, regardless of tax implications.

It is obvious that transfer pricing decisions within the firm can have significant income tax consequences for the corporation as a whole. Consider a simple illustration, where the firm only has two international subsidiaries, A and B. If A has lower income tax rates than does B, then it makes sense for the company to make more profits in A (and pay less taxes) than in B. One way to do this is through transfer pricing, in which case the company would want A to charge higher prices (and make more profits), which adds to B's costs (and thus lower profits). In so doing, the company minimizes the amount of taxes it has to pay.

The multinational firm can also manipulate transfer pricing to its advantage by deciding to buy more (or less) of certain intrafirm products and services. Even if the price itself was based on an arm's-length evaluation, the fact remains that subsidiary A may be buying something from subsidiary B that it does not really need, but which it still has to pay for. The following example illustrates this point.

Exxon in 2002 sold its Disputada de las Condes copper mine operations in Chile to Anglo American for U.S. $1.3 billion. In the mid-1970s, Exxon had bought the mine for U.S. $80 million. Since that time, Exxon reported operating the mine at a loss every year, never paid taxes in Chile, and even accumulated gross tax credits of more than U.S. $0.5 billion. Further, to avoid paying Chilean taxes on capital gains from the sale, the sale was to be consummated in a foreign country.

Questions arose over the nature of these losses that Exxon suffered over the 23-year period of ownership. Apparently, Exxon's Disputada subsidiary borrowed heavily from Exxon's Bermuda-based financing arm and other Exxon entities, and the interest payments on these loans caused Disputada to tax. Exxon was able to withdraw funds from Disputada not in the form of profits (taxable at a 35% rate) but as interest payments (taxable at a maximum rate of 4%). Furthermore, since a large share of the interest payments went to Bermuda, where the financing arm was located, Exxon paid no income tax on those profits either.

The subsequent public outcry and Chilean government investigations resulted in an agreement by Exxon to pay the Chilean government U.S. $27 million in taxes (a relatively small amount relative to the magnitude of the operations and the sale). Partly because of incidents such as this, moreover, the Chilean government subsequently passed a law requiring large mining companies to pay a 3% royalty on copper sales regardless of profitability. Transfer pricing is, and will continue to be, an issue that various governments have to wrestle with as MNCs get even bigger and more numerous.

—Ed Chung

Further Readings

American Marketing Association. (n.d.). *Dictionary of marketing terms.* Retrieved from www.marketingpower.com

Fatehi, K. (1996). *International management.* Upper Saddle River, NJ: Prentice Hall.

Fazio, H. (2001). *La Transnacionalización de la Economía Chilena. Mapa de la Extrema Riqueza al 2000.* Santiago, Chile: Arcis, CENDA and LOM.

Lavandero, J. (2003). *Royalty, Regalía o Renta Minera; lo que sólo Chile no Cobra.* Santiago, Chile: Lafken Ltda.

Madura, J. (2000). *International financial management* (6th ed.). Cincinnati, OH: South-Western College.

UN Conference on Trade and Development (UNCTAD). *Corporate social responsibility.* www.natural-resources.org/minerals/csr/index.htm

PART III

Ethics and the Promotional Mix

ADVERTISING ETHICS

In a modern capitalist society, ads are ubiquitous; criticisms of advertising are nearly as common. Some ethical criticisms concern advertising as a social practice, while others attack specific ads or advertising practices. Central to ethical criticisms are concerns that ads subvert rational decision making and threaten human autonomy by creating needs, by creating false needs, by developing one-sided narrowly focused needs that can only be satisfied by buying material products and services, and/or by appealing to genuine and deeply rooted human needs in a manipulative way. A second sort of criticism is that ads harm human welfare by keeping everyone dissatisfied. At a minimum, ads try to make us dissatisfied with not currently having the product, but many ads also aim at keeping us permanently dissatisfied with our social positions, our looks, our bodies, and ourselves. Advertising has been blamed for people today being neurotic, insecure, and stressed.

Business ethicists have traditionally either considered advertising in general or divided ads into information ads, which are ethical as long as they are honest, and persuasive ads, which are always problematic. However, recent literature on advertising ethics considers the division of ads into informative and persuasive to be entirely inadequate because it fails to consider separately the various persuasive techniques that ads use.

ECONOMIC CRITICISMS AND THE FUNCTION OF ADVERTISING

One economic criticism of advertising in general is that advertising is a wasteful and inefficient business tool; our standard of living would be higher without it. This criticism fails to understand that economies of scale for mass-produced goods can often more than offset advertising costs, making advertised products cheaper in the end. It is also suggested that advertising causes people to spend money they do not have and that advertising combined with credit cards creates a debt-ridden society, which causes stress and unhappiness. Furthermore, it is claimed that advertising encourages a society based on immediate gratification, which discourages savings and the accumulation of capital needed for a thriving capitalist economy. Granted that American society may currently be deeply in debt, this cannot be blamed on advertising because there are numerous societies that are inundated with ads but have positive savings rates and fiscal surpluses. Canada is one, and there are others in Europe and Asia.

There are also economic defenses of advertising. It has been argued that the creation of consumer demand is an integral part of the capitalist system; capitalism needs advertising since capitalism has an inherent tendency toward overproduction. And capitalism is an economic system that has made us the richest, longest lived, healthiest society in human history; even the poor in consumer societies are better off than most people in the Third World. Surely such well-being makes advertising ethically justified.

INFORMATION ADS

Many ads are simple information ads. Consider, for example, the flyers left on your doorstep that say that certain products are on sale at a certain price at a store in your neighborhood. Such ads are generally considered ethical provided they are honest. Problems arise if they make claims that are false, misleading, or exaggerated. Making false claims is a form of lying and, hence, clearly unethical. A claim is misleading if it is literally true, but is understood by most consumers in a way that includes a false claim. The ad is misleading whether or not the advertiser intends the misunderstanding. Generally, the honesty of ads should be judged not on their literal truth, but on how consumers understand the ad; this is because companies have, or can easily get, this understanding of the ad from focus groups and other marketing research techniques. Exaggeration, or puffery, in ads is thought acceptable by many people on the grounds that consumers can be expected to discount claims in ads. This is true except for vulnerable groups such as young children.

Normally, withholding information in advertising does not raise ethical issues. Car ads, for example, do not often print crash and repair reports; such information is readily and inexpensively available, and obtaining it is rightly viewed as the customer's responsibility. However, ethical constraints on exaggeration, withholding information, and misleading advertising become much more severe in cases where the customer cannot obtain accurate information, or cannot obtain it at reasonable cost, and the information is important to the customer's physical or financial well-being. Drug advertising by pharmaceutical companies is often criticized for failure to meet these more stringent standards, even though regulations in many countries try to control this for prescription drugs by requiring details on possible side effects, contraindications, and so on. This is a clear case of the information not being available since drug trial results are often confidential to the corporation, and the implications for the user's well-being are clear. This situation is not helped by press coverage of new drugs; such coverage tends to emphasize benefits over risks.

IMPACT OF PERSUASIVE ADS ON INDIVIDUALS

Discussion of the ethical issues surrounding persuasive advertising must consider separately various persuasive techniques such as benefit advertising, emotional manipulation, symbol creation, and so on.

Benefit ads emphasis a product's benefits to the user rather than product features. Typically, benefit ads show an enthusiastic, often exuberant, person enjoying the results of using the product; for example, a housewife is shown as jubilant that her laundry detergent got her sheets whiter than her neighbors'. In benefit ads, users tend to appear like real people and are not overly idealized; their emotions, however, are greatly exaggerated. Most benefit ads are ethically harmless if we allow for consumer discounting of exaggeration. Some critics, however, question the hidden premise that the consumer ought to want the benefit. Why should a person care if their wash is whiter, their car is faster, their hair is bouncier? Though a consumer's ability to deal with this form of persuasion may be made more difficult by the fact that a benefit ad assumes but does not state its premises, most of these ads are not a serious threat to human autonomy. However, there are some cases for concern. Consider, for example, ads placed by pharmaceutical companies for mood-changing drugs; life's little hassles become stress, sadness becomes depression, tranquility becomes listlessness, and contentment becomes apathy. Normalcy is not stated but assumed to be a medical condition requiring prescription pills. We are encouraged to be constantly dissatisfied with our most personal emotions. There are ethical problems with the intentions of the advertisers in this case, regardless of the actual effect on people's autonomy.

Ads try to manipulate many human emotions; fear ads are only one example, but they make clear the ethical issues. Fear ads tend to become more common during economic recessions, and they reached a crescendo during the 1930s. A Johnson & Johnson ad for bandages from 1936, for example, shows a boy with his right arm amputated because a cut without Johnson & Johnson bandages became infected. More recently, American Express used a print ad in eerie gold and black colors showing a distraught mother frantically phoning while her feverish daughter lies in the background. The solution offered is that American Express keeps lists of English-speaking physicians in most large cities. Critics maintain that appeals to emotions undermine rational decision-making processes and threaten our autonomy. Defenders point out that the fears portrayed (of infection before penicillin, communication problems with foreign doctors) are real even if dramatized, and the product offers a legitimate solution for the problem.

Advertising can persuade by turning a product into a symbol of something entirely different from itself. Chanel is a symbol of Parisian sophistication, Calvin Klein a symbol of sex, DeBeers diamonds symbolize love, and Mercedes Benz is a status symbol. We often do not buy products for what they are, but what they mean to us, and, just as importantly, what they mean to others. Critics claim this undermines human rationality by preventing us from assessing products based on their intrinsic worth; symbolic meaning of the product invariably biases our judgments. But, in fact, it is not irrational for people to buy a symbol if they want to express something meaningful. There is nothing irrational, for example, with buying and waving your country's flag. If you want to project high economic status, a Mercedes does indeed do so. Symbolic ads are not false or misleading for the simple reason that they do in fact work; products and logos do come to have symbolic meaning for us. To give a diamond is to give an object useless in itself, but the symbolic meaning, largely created by decades of DeBeers advertising, can give the gift life-changing significance. Symbolic meaning can add to the price you pay for a product (consider designer labels, for example), but there is nothing irrational in paying a price for a symbol that you want. Indeed, advertising provides a useful social service by creating symbols that allow consumers to communicate various meanings to those around them.

A self-identity image ad turns the product into a symbol of a particular self-image; the product then allows the buyer to express to themselves or others what sort of person they are. For example, Marlboro cigarette ads for decades featured the Marlboro man, a symbol of rugged independence and masculine individuality. Marlboros were very popular with teenage males, not because they thought the product would turn them into cowboys, but because they wanted to conceive of themselves as ruggedly masculine and because they wanted their peers to see them like that.

The more unnecessary a product type is, the more likely it will be promoted with self-identity image ads; they are a common type of ad for perfumes and colognes, cigarettes, beer, and expensive designer labels. One of the ethical objections to self-identity ads is that they manipulate our fundamental conceptions of ourselves to sell us dangerous (as in the case of Marlboro cigarettes mentioned above) or useless products. In response, it can be argued that these ads do not manipulate us without our active participation; we have to play the image game for these ads to have any affect, and experimenting with one's self-image is voluntary. Perhaps concern should only be for vulnerable groups or individuals, such as insecure teenagers under peer pressure; but then, images available through logos may help teenagers feel more secure if they can afford the product with the label. There have been stories of people who have committed violent crimes to obtain footwear with the right logo, but advertising cannot be held responsible for poverty or the resulting violence. Ads that specifically target the poor may be unethical because they target a vulnerable group; ads for "power" beer that target inner-city neighborhoods have been criticized for this.

Self-identity image ads cannot be criticized for being false or misleading because they do not work by giving information or making promises. They mostly appeal to our fantasies, and fantasies as fantasies are not false. A woman, for example, does not buy a perfume because she thinks it will transform her into the slim, beautiful, chic young woman in the ad. Consumers are not that gullible. She buys the perfume because associating herself with that image in her own mind makes her feel good about herself. The resulting self-confidence may, in fact, make her more attractive. If we actively buy into the identity images of ads, there may be an element of self-fulfillment. None of this threatens human autonomy since active participation is required and is voluntary.

Even if self-identity image advertising is considered generally an ethical technique, there may still be ethical objections to specific images. For example, the images of women in ads have raised many ethical complaints. The most serious complaints concern the unremitting presentation as beautiful of an ideal body that is excessively thin or even anorexic looking, is extremely tall and long legged, and has a poreless, wrinkleless, perfectly smooth china-like complexion. That this body image dominates ads for women's beauty and fashion products is true, though recently there has been an increase in ads using more realistic body types. The tall thin image extends to fashion models, who now average more than 6 feet in height and are generally underweight.

This body type is impossible for most women to achieve even with dieting and plastic surgery. In fact, the images in ads often have their hair and complexions airbrushed and their legs stretched using computer techniques; the result is a distorted body image that no woman, not even the models in the photos, have or can ever obtain.

The purpose of this idealization and distortion is to make women dissatisfied with their own bodies; this leads them to purchase the "beauty" product in the hope of looking and feeling better. But since the ideal is so extreme and unachievable, dissatisfaction quickly returns, and the woman is ready to buy more beauty products. Constant dissatisfaction with one's own body is the objective.

Ethical objections to these beauty ads include claims that they undermine women's self-confidence; that they cause anorexia and other serious eating disorders; that they distract women from family, careers, and other serious aspects of life; that the "beauty myth" drains women of energy and locks them into a stereotype that belittles the serious contributions they make; and that all this is a male power move that oppresses women. There is much debate about how many of these criticisms are true, but the fact that many women react so strongly against body image ads seems by itself to indicate that there is at least some problem. Some advertisers have listened to women and other critics, and other more realistic body types have become more common in advertising over the past few years. The accusation that such body image ads are unfair to women is mitigated by the fact that in the past 15 years or so more and more body image ads have been targeted at men. How men will be affected by this in the long run will not be clear for a generation. This trend may mitigate the gender fairness issue, but the other ethical issues are made twice as extensive. Of course, the idealized body image is different for men, but it is nearly as hard to attain; we may soon be seeing excessive steroid use for fashion reasons as the male equivalent of anorexia.

Self-identity image ads also raise the problem of false consciousness. Image ads try to create a consumer who desires products as symbols of his or her self-image. The individual is seen by defenders of advertising as a free and autonomous self who chooses to play the image game and chooses which self-image to project. But the autonomous self may be an illusion: The reality is (according to some) that people are not defined by consumption; they are defined by their role in the system of production. That the individual can choose a self-image is an illusion that would be shattered by the consciousness of the person's true alienated relationship to themselves and others. A young male may choose Marlboros, for example, as a symbol of ruggedness and independence, but reality is earning the money for the Marlboros by working in a fast-food franchise where he humbly takes orders from both his boss and the customers, adapts his every movement to a predefined time-and-motion system, and is forced to fake a smile on cue. The real self is his role as worker; the consumer self is an illusion created by the capitalist system through advertising precisely to prevent consciousness of reality. Defenders of advertising can reply that people's consumer self-image is just as real to them as the self-image they derive from their job. Though the consumer image game is pleasant, why should we assume it blinds people to their role in production? They may be well aware of it.

IMPACT OF ADS ON SOCIETY

Besides concerns about how ads affect individuals, critics have raised ethical issues about how advertising affects society. For example, J. K. Galbraith argued that advertising creates the desires that the production of consumer goods then satisfies. This dependence effect, in which consumer desires for goods depend on the process of creating the goods, undermines the usual ethical justification of capitalism based on consumer freedom of choice and the value of supplying people with the goods that they want. Others accuse advertising of creating a materialistic society full of people who think that happiness lies in owning things and who are obsessed with buying consumer goods. These critics think we are creating a society in which private goods are plentiful but in which public goods, which are seldom advertised, are ignored—a society rich in private cars but whose highways and streets are disintegrating. Ads drive selfish consumption at the expense of friendship, community, art, and truth. Furthermore, advertising allows the system to "buy off" politically unsatisfied people with promises and consumer goods, leading to political apathy and the undermining of democracy.

However, there are many who think these sorts of criticisms exaggerate the impact of ads on society. Schudson, for example, claims that advertising does not have much impact on society because it does not increase product-type usage; it only leads to brand switching and functions primarily as reminders to people who are already heavy users of a product-type. Major social changes are not caused by advertising; ads follow social trends, they do not create them.

This debate centers on two perhaps unresolvable issues. First, there is the empirical question of how much impact advertising has on society; this is difficult to answer because the effect of ads cannot be separated from other social forces, and because it is hard to determine whether ads cause or follow social trends. Second, there is the ethical question of whether the purported effects, such as materialism, are morally objectionable. Perhaps it is more helpful to look at specific issues rather than the social impact of advertising in general.

LIFESTYLE ADS: SEX AND VIOLENCE IN ADS

Some people object to ads that encourage sex, gambling, smoking, the consumption of alcohol, and other "vices." Even people who are not much concerned about such vices are still concerned that ads encourage *underaged* sex, gambling, smoking, the consumption of alcohol, and other vices. They believe that ads present bad role models. Advertising, some critics say, contributes to the moral breakdown of society because it presents ubiquitous images of unconstrained hedonism.

Ethical concerns about ads for gambling, tobacco, and alcohol are often legitimate. Products that are harmful and sometimes addictive raise ethical issues in themselves; encouraging the use of such products is even more questionable. Many countries and states limit, control, or even ban ads for some or all these products.

Violence in advertising would be ethically objectionable if there was much of it, but it is rare. The main exceptions are ads for films and video games, but objections in these cases should be aimed at the violence in the products, not just in the ads. The exposure of unsuspecting people and children to such ads is an issue that should be, and in many jurisdictions is, controlled by regulations on the placement of the ads.

Sex in advertising is a much bigger issue because there is so much of it. The ethical issues can be best seen if we separate consideration of sex in ads for products that are connected to sex from consideration of sex in ads where it is gratuitous and has no or only a tenuous connection with the product.

Ads for condoms and sex clubs, of course, emphasize sex. Except for puritans, the only ethical issue about these ads is making sure young children are not exposed. Other products, such as fashions, jeans, underwear, perfume, and chocolate, are related to sex, and advertising is often used to associate a product or logo with sex. Calvin Klein, for example, has built his business on making his clothes and perfumes sexy. Raising ethical objections to this is difficult unless one objects ethically to current sexual mores in most developed countries. Advertising did not cause our liberal attitudes toward sex; the sexual revolution was caused by the pill, penicillin, and other social forces. Any decrease of sex in advertising would probably not change society's sexual attitudes, so there is no ethical problem with Calvin Klein jeans, underwear, and perfume being thought sexy.

Sex is also used gratuitously in ads for products that have nothing directly to do with sex. We are all familiar with scantily clad women in ads for beer, cigarettes, cars, trucks, and vacation beaches. Note that for the most part these ads are aimed at straight males and use the stereotypical sexy woman—sexy, that is, in the minds and fantasies of straight males. Consider, for example, a two-page ad from a men's magazine that shows on the first page a woman with huge breasts, clad only in a bikini and posed in a sexually suggestive fashion. The copy asks if her measurements get the reader's heart racing. Turn the page and there is a pickup truck and the reader is asked to look at the truck's measurements. Horsepower, torque, and so on are listed. How do such ads work? Their ubiquity in men's magazines certainly suggests that they do sell cars, trucks, and beer. Such ads seem to say, "If you are a straight male attracted to big breasted women, you can prove it to yourself and others by buying our 'masculine' product." This interpretation presupposes that many straight males are very insecure about their sexual orientation and need to have their masculinity constantly confirmed by buying products with a masculine image. Is this manipulation of insecurities unethical? Perhaps not; straight males are generally capable of freely choosing to buy or not buy these products.

A more serious ethical objection to such ads is the attitude toward women that they imply and encourage. Women in these ads are being used as sex objects. One does not have to be a radical feminist to be concerned about the effects that exposure to thousands of such ads might have on straight men. It does not encourage them to see women as intelligent, productive, and competent individuals. Perhaps the vast majority of straight males are not greatly affected individually, but it does set a social tone about what are acceptable attitudes toward women. And the few men who take the objectification of women as sex objects seriously sometimes commit extremely unethical actions.

ADVERTISING AND CULTURE: CLUTTER, APPROPRIATION, AND IMPERIALISM

Some critics of advertising are deeply concerned about the impact of advertising on our culture. Many of these criticisms are not so much about ethics as they are about aesthetics and taste, but some raise genuine ethical concerns.

Ads clutter our culture. Outdoor ads are unsightly, commercials interrupt television programs and sports, jingles jam the airwaves, and magazines seem to be nothing but ads. And ads are creeping everywhere. Clutter and ad creep raise two issues: general concerns about the ubiquity of ads and concerns about ads creeping into specific places such as public schools.

The ubiquity of ads certainly raises aesthetic issues, but in itself is not an ethical problem. Most ads are placed in media that people can choose to use or not. Magazines, newspapers, television, and radio can be avoided if a person wishes, and there are ad free news sources and alternatives to most media. Outdoor ads cannot be avoided, but their unsightliness is and should be a matter for local bylaws. Ad creep will not increase the impact of advertising on the consumer or society. The psychological wall we all have that blocks out ads is only made stronger by more ads. In terms of advertising impact, more is less. It is the lack of impact of advertising that is forcing advertisers to place more and more ads.

There are, however, specific places that many feel should be ad free. These include religious institutions, government buildings, and schools. The first is a private matter for the institution. Policy on placing ads on government property should be decided democratically. Ads in schools, on the other hand, raise ethical issues. School attendance is compulsory and so the audience for the ads is trapped; school pupils are children or adolescents so they may be vulnerable; the ads are shown in an educational environment so children may find it hard to discount their message; and finally, the peer pressure and groupthink inevitable in classrooms may dramatically increase the impact of ads. However, as long as schools are underfunded, schools will be tempted to accept advertising. Any solution to the ethical concerns about ads in schools will have to be enacted democratically.

Ads appropriate images from cultures and history, using them for the private gain of the advertiser. For example, perfume ads have used images of the beautiful "Indian princes"; motorcycles and cigarettes have used the "Indian brave" with feathers or a headdress as a symbol of masculinity. Is it ethical to use cultural symbols and images such as this? If an ad does use such a symbol, do they have any obligation to historical accuracy, or are faux simulacra acceptable? The peoples who created these symbols and images in the first place are generally not able to trademark or copyright them. Asking permission is often not an option; it is frequently not possible to identify whom to ask. One possibility that would minimize the ethical concerns would be to refrain from using cultural symbols if people from the relevant culture object. Images that do not receive complaints could be used; the Scots, for example, seem to like the kilted curmudgeon who sells malt whiskey. This approach requires a certain amount of cultural sensitivity on the part of corporations and a willingness to pull ads if they offend, even if those offended are not consumers of the product advertised.

Some critics complain that advertising is a form of American cultural imperialism. It is true that American advertising images such as Ronald McDonald and Coca-Cola are a large part of globalization, but European and Japanese corporations advertise worldwide too, and Chinese, Indian, and other cultures will be playing much larger roles in the future. Also, the dominance of American images is partly caused by the desire of many people for these images; Coca-Cola is advertised in many countries because the people there are eager to buy the product. In fact, it is this local popularity of American symbols and products that make some people in other cultures feel threatened. Some Italians and French may think that liking McDonald's food shows bad taste compared with liking their traditional foods, but the fact that McDonald's offends some people does not make it unethical to promote a popular symbol or product. Interfering with people's free choice by, for example, occupying or destroying restaurants raises more ethical issues than does advertising foreign products.

ADVERTISING TO VULNERABLE GROUPS

Children and some people in the Third World are especially vulnerable to manipulation by advertising. Furthermore, we are all vulnerable to subliminal techniques if subliminal advertising works.

Children are vulnerable to advertising because they do not understand the purpose of ads; cannot tell ads from the rest of their environment; cannot separate fantasy from reality; find it difficult to control their emotions; do not understand finances, takeoffs, and deferred gratification; and do not have the psychological wall that blocks most ads in adults. Some people defend ads aimed at children by pointing out that young children cannot themselves buy most of the products advertised; they have to ask their parents who can and should make rational decisions on the child's behalf. But this defense leaves out advertising's intentional and conscious use of the "nag factor." Ads are designed (with verification using focus groups) to get children to whine and nag their parents for the advertised products. This technique tends to undermine the rationality of parental decisions, and it causes unhappiness in both parents and children, which is unethical on utilitarian grounds.

Some jurisdictions, such as Quebec and some European countries, ban altogether television or other advertising aimed at children. Many others ban only images that might be traumatic to children, such as sex and violence, or try to control the use of fantasy by insisting ads be realistic. Some people advocate also banning ads for products that might harm a child, calling, for example, for bans on junk food ads during children's programs. Ethically, corporations ought at least to stay within the law, but should also consider the impact of their ads on children's happiness and welfare.

Advertising to people in those Third World countries in which advertising is not a traditional part of their culture and who are not used to advertising yet can raise special ethical issues. These issues can be aggravated if the population targeted by the ads is illiterate, uneducated, and lacking in freedom and empowerment. A good example is the advertising campaigns Nestlé used in Africa that featured images of Caucasian "doctors" and "nurses" advocating the use of Nestlé baby formula in place of breast-feeding. The ads exploited the target market's illiteracy and lack of familiarity with advertising and its purpose, but the ethical issues in this case went beyond this; the ads were deceptive in that Western medical opinion did not support the use of formula feeding in the Third World. But the most serious ethical problems arose because of the consequences of the use of baby formula; it exposed the infants to malnutrition, disease, and contaminated water. International agencies claimed many babies died as a result. This case makes clear that using advertising to exploit people's vulnerabilities puts an ethical obligation on the advertiser to ensure that no harm results.

Subliminal ads are ads that the target market cannot see, hear, or otherwise be aware of. For example, if a movie theater flashes "Drink Brand X Soda" on the screen so fast no one can perceive it, this is an attempt to manipulate people below their level of consciousness; as such, it tries to subvert rational decision making and so is unethical. Key's book titled *Subliminal Seduction: Ad Media's Manipulation of a Not So Innocent America,* popular in the 1970s, claimed that this technique was common and that large numbers of people were being brainwashed by it. Since then, experiments have failed to show that subliminal advertising works, and it is unlikely that it was ever widely used. Notwithstanding that, many legal jurisdictions have banned it.

Subliminal ads should not be confused with suggestive ads. As an example of a suggestive ad, consider a magazine ad that shows a couple passionately embracing in the background; in the foreground is a long cylindrical bottle of men's cologne obviously suggestive of a phallus. This is not subliminal; the viewer can clearly see what is going on. (In case the viewer needs confirmation, the letters "man's co...." disappear strategically around the side of the bottle.) Suggestive advertising is not inherently unethical since there is no evidence that it manipulates below our level of awareness or that it subverts rationality.

ADVERTISING AND THE NATURAL ENVIRONMENT

Advertising affects the natural environment in three ways: ads use resources; some ads encourage destructive activities; and ads always encourage consumption, never nonconsumption.

Although radio ads and television commercials use a minimum of natural resources, print ads such as newspaper ads and inserts, flyers, and direct marketing mailings use vast amounts of paper. However, pulpwood for paper is a renewable resource if forests are harvested sustainably, and paper can be recycled, so reduced usage may not be ethically required. What is required is a sustainable paper industry, but is this the ethical responsibility of the advertisers? If advertisers insist on print media using sustainable paper supplies, the pulp industry would be hugely affected in a positive way. But the grounds for saying this is that the advertiser's ethical responsibility are not clear unless, of course, the advertiser claims to be an environmentally friendly company.

Some ads encourage activities destructive to the environment, such as the multitude of SUV ads that idealize off-road driving. Ethically, it is questionable whether advertisers should use such images. Sometimes, a negative environmental impact is inherent in the product advertised; for example, flying to the Caribbean on a vacation package uses petroleum, a nonrenewable and polluting natural resource. In such cases, environmental concerns should concentrate on the product, not just the advertising. What actions should be taken about such products is greatly debated, but the ads do not interfere with environmentalists who choose, for example, to vacation nearer home. Nor do they interfere with such environmentalists advocating this course of action to others.

Finally, critics of ads point out that consumer advertising always promotes consumption; reduced consumption is never advertised except occasionally by some advocacy groups that never have the money to compete with large corporations. Even government advocacy ads tend to emphasize recycling rather than reduced consumption; reduced consumption threatens jobs, taxes, and the economy. Environmentalists argue that, ethically, the developed countries ought to reduce their level of consumer consumption. Perhaps this is true, but the ethical responsibility cannot lie with the individual advertisers because they would be at a potentially fatal competitive disadvantage if they stopped advertising. This is a social and cultural problem that should only be changed by citizens through democratic processes and changes of their own behavior.

CORPORATE CONTROL OF THE MEDIA

Advertising critics claim that advertising gives corporate advertisers too much control of the programming and editorial content of the media; advertising biases mass media news coverage, and as a result, the media in North America only present what is in the interests of corporations for people to believe. For example, cigarette advertisers for decades threatened to and did pull their ads from any magazine or newspaper that carried articles on the health risks of cigarettes. Most magazine advertisers ask for advanced information on articles in the issues their ads will appear in; their ads are pulled if any article might create negative associations with their products.

Defenders of advertising do not deny that corporations sometimes withdraw ads or threaten to; they argue that corporations have a right to select where they advertise, and a fiduciary duty to shareholders and other stakeholders not to jeopardize the image of the corporation or its products. It can also be pointed out that newspapers and magazines that do not rely on corporate advertising are available to those who choose them; their subscription price is, of course, much higher (compare, e.g., the subscription prices of *Time* or *Newsweek* with the *Guardian Weekly*), but if people choose to be free of corporate influence they cannot expect to benefit from the subsidy that advertising gives much of the media.

IN DEFENSE OF ADVERTISING

The volume of criticism of advertising can make us lose sight of possible ethical defenses. Besides the economic role of advertising mentioned above, it can also be pointed out that advertising gives us information, introduces us to new products, presents us with images we can enjoy, creates symbols that allow us to express ourselves, subsidizes our media, and promotes human freedom by presenting to us vast numbers of products from which we can freely choose what we want to buy. Those who want to ban or strictly regulate all advertising should remember that advertising is a form of expression and that freedom of expression is a basic human right recognized in the UN Declaration of Human Rights and most national constitutions. However, that should not prevent the regulation of ad techniques or placements that cause specific harms. Those who worry about advertising should consider Schudson's point that ads are targeted primarily at people who are already heavy uses of a product-type and that the purpose of most advertising is not increase product-type usage, only brand switching. Ethical objections to ads have to make a case about specific ads on grounds of harm, viewer vulnerability, subversion of rationality, or plain dishonesty.

—John Douglas Bishop

Further Readings

Bishop, J. D. (2000). Is self-identity image advertising ethical? *Business Ethics Quarterly, 10*(2), 371–398.

Brenkert, G. (1998). Marketing to inner-city blacks: Powermaster and moral responsibility. *Business Ethics Quarterly, 8*(1), 1–18.

Goodrum, C., & Dalrymple, H. (1990). *Advertising in America: The first two hundred years.* New York: Harry N. Abrams.

Leiss, W., Kline, S., & Jhally, S. (1986). Social communication in advertising: Persons, products and images of well–being. New York: Methuen.

Mikkelson, B., & Mikkelson, D. P. (2002, August 18). *Subliminal advertising.* Retrieved October 21, 2005, from www.snopes.com/business/hidden/popcorn.asp

Schudson, M. (1984). Advertising, the uneasy persuasion: Its dubious impact on American society. New York: Basic Books.

Shields, V. R. (2002). *Measuring up: How advertising affects self-image.* Philadelphia: University of Pennsylvania Press.

Twitchell, J. B. (2000). *Twenty ads that shook the world.* New York: Three Rivers Press.

Williamson, J. (1978). Decoding advertisements: Ideology and meaning in advertising. London: Marion Books.

Wolf, N. (1990). *The beauty myth.* Toronto: Random House.

DECEPTIVE ADVERTISING

As it is used by regulators, the courts, and social scientists, *deceptive advertising* is a technical, legal term: A deceptive advertisement is one that involves a representation, omission, or practice likely to mislead a reasonable consumer. To be regulable under the law, however, a further condition must be met: The deception must be "material," which is to say that it must be likely to detrimentally affect the consumer's purchasing decisions. While injurious effects on consumers account for much of what is objectionable about deceptive advertising from a moral and ethical point of view, deceptive advertising also harms competitors and generally weakens trust in the marketplace.

The above legal definition agrees with the one operative in European Union (EU) countries in essential respects, although the means by which many EU countries regulate deceptive advertising differs from the United States. In the United States, the Federal Trade Commission (FTC) has primary federal responsibility for preventing deceptive advertising in both broadcast and print forms, although consumer protection agencies of the various states have authority over local advertisements. The major source of industry self-regulation is the National Advertising Division (NAD) of the Council of Better Business Bureaus. Some enforcement also occurs through private lawsuits, most commonly those brought by competitors under the Lanham Trademark Act. Nonetheless, many deceptive advertisements that meet the legal standard for deception persist, either because they have not been challenged or because government agencies have limited resources. In general, the greater the amount of potential physical and economic injury to consumers, the greater is the incentive for regulators to act.

"DECEPTION" IN ITS ORDINARY AND LEGAL SENSES

Setting the issue of materiality aside, the sense of "deception" found in the legal notion of deceptive advertising can be usefully contrasted with our "ordinary" concept of deception in two respects. First, at least insofar as issues of moral concern are raised, the ordinary concept of deception, like that of lying, applies only to acts done intentionally and purposefully. For regulatory and legal purposes, however, an advertisement need not be *intentionally* deceptive. Rather, the legal notion focuses exclusively on false consumer beliefs caused by the advertisement. Second, deception in the ordinary sense requires a measure of success; there cannot be a deception without at least someone who is actually deceived or misled. Deception differs from lying in this respect, as one can be lied to without being taken in by the lie. The legal notion of deception is also outcome oriented, but in a special way. Since a deceptive advertisement must be likely to mislead a consumer acting reasonably under the circumstances, strictly speaking, the law does not require that anyone has actually been deceived. Consequently, one might say that the legal definition focuses on deceptiveness rather than deception—the likelihood that an advertisement will cause false beliefs rather than whether it in fact has done so.

In terms of actual regulatory practice, however, the issue is somewhat more complicated. The likelihood that an advertisement will mislead a consumer depends not only on the advertisement itself but also on the background knowledge and sophistication possessed by the consumer. For a time, backed by decisions of the U.S. Supreme Court, the FTC applied an ignorant person standard according to which an advertisement need only mislead the most gullible consumers in order to be deceptive. Invoking this criterion, the FTC once found deceptive Clairol's claim that its hair coloring would color hair permanently on the grounds that some (particularly naïve) consumers might interpret this to mean, falsely, that Clairol would color all the hair to be grown in a user's lifetime. More recently, however, the FTC has adopted a more lenient approach. Since advertisers typically dispute FTC allegations that their claims are likely to mislead, the agency often relies on extrinsic evidence, usually in the form of consumer surveys, to show that a significant percentage of consumers have formed materially false beliefs as a result of exposure to particular advertisements. Typically, the threshold percentage for FTC prohibition is in the range of 20% to 25%. In this way, regulators can be seen as attempting to strike a balance between the costs of suppressing informative claims and the benefits of suppressing deceptive claims.

In both its ordinary and legal senses, however, deception is a much broader concept than either that of lying or falsity. One can deceive without lying, because while lying necessarily involves an explicit statement by the speaker, deception can occur by variously distorting, withholding, or manipulating the truth. Deceptive advertising is, thus, often quite different from false advertising, if by "false advertising" we simply mean advertising that makes false statements, even though the two expressions are often treated colloquially as synonyms. Advertisements can be deceptive without explicit falsity, such as when they mislead by omitting crucial facts or by taking advantage of consumer ignorance. They can also make false claims without being deceptive, such as when what is literally claimed is so improbable or ridiculous that no one is likely to be deceived by it. Exxon gasoline's once-famous claim to put a tiger in your tank is a case in point.

THE VARIETY OF DECEPTIVE ADVERTISEMENTS

FTC cases have involved a wide range of practices that the agency has found deceptive in particular instances, including false written and oral representations, misleading price claims, sales of dangerous or defective products without adequate disclosures, the use of bait-and-switch techniques, failure to disclose information pertaining to pyramid sales, and a failure to meet warranty obligations.

The most straightforward cases involve explicit misrepresentation of a product or service, which thanks to regulatory efforts are now relatively rare. The more common and controversial cases, however, involve claims that advertisers imply but do not explicitly state. The pain reliever Efficin, for example, was claimed to contain no aspirin. Although literally true, the FTC found this advertisement deceptive on the grounds that consumers would naturally interpret this to mean that Efficin lacked many of the side effects caused by aspirin. This implied claim was false, however, since Efficin and aspirin are chemically very similar. A different sort of implication was involved in the famous Volvo advertisement that depicted a big-wheeled "monster truck" rolling over a line of cars, crushing all of them except the Volvo. The spot failed to disclose the fact that both the Volvo and the other cars had been specially rigged to produce this result. The implication that only a Volvo can withstand a monster truck intact was thus false. Advertisers are as responsible for the message consumers draw from an advertisement as they are for what is actually stated or shown.

A special kind of implication is addressed by the FTC's advertising substantiation doctrine, according to which advertising claims that do not have a reasonable basis are deceptive if the ad implies that such a basis exists. When

Bayer claimed its children's aspirin to be superior to any other children's aspirin in terms of its therapeutic effect, the FTC held that Bayer implied a factual basis for this claim which the company lacked. Interestingly, even if such a claim is ultimately proven to be true, the advertisement making it can still be prohibited if the advertiser lacks a reasonable basis for the claim when it is originally made. In another case, advertisements for Promise margarine used the slogan "Get Heart Smart" and showed heart-shaped pats of the product on food items. The FTC found these advertisements deceptive because the manufacturer could not adequately substantiate the implied claim that using Promise helped diminish the risk of heart disease.

Comparative advertising raises especially thorny questions of implication. While relatively rare in Europe, comparative advertising has flourished in the United States since restrictions on it were lifted in the 1970s and 1980s. One kind of issue arises in incomplete comparisons. Suppose it is claimed of Brand X pain reliever that Brand X relieves pain faster—faster than what? Another kind of problem is raised by implied superiority claims. Suppose that Brand X is advertised with the line that no other pain reliever works faster. If Brand X relieves pain faster than some competitors but only as fast as others, is the advertisement deceptive? A further issue results if Brand X is claimed to both relieve pain faster than Brand Y and be long-lasting. Consumers may infer that Brand X is longer-lasting than Brand Y, which may be false.

This last issue arose in connection with Kraft's advertisements of its Singles line of cheese products. After years of losing market share to lower-priced imitation slices, Kraft began advertising the fact that Singles were made from five ounces of milk per slice versus hardly any for the imitation slices. Although these claims were true, the FTC objected to the fact that the same ads touted the calcium content of milk. As it turns out, much of the calcium contained in milk is lost during the cheese-making process, and many brands of imitation slices actually had more calcium than Kraft's Singles. Without knowing these details, however, consumers would likely infer that the calcium content of the Kraft product was higher than that of imitation slices.

Deceptive advertising in its various forms should be distinguished from mere puffery, which has long been treated permissively by regulators and the courts. A *puff* is an evaluative claim used by an advertiser, such as when a product is described as "the best," "best tasting," "the freshest," or "amazing."

Strictly speaking, a puff cannot be legally deceptive. This is partly because the law regards such claims as mere subjective opinions that cannot be disproved. It is difficult, for example, to pin down the precise meaning of Tony the Tiger's exclamation that Frosted Flakes are great. Regulators also tend to assume that puffs are forms of hype and exaggeration that customers do not take seriously. This point is sometimes questioned, however; were it really true that customers do not believe puffed claims, advertisers would stop using them. Particular examples sometimes raise difficult questions as to the distinction between evaluative and factual statements. If, for instance, the claim that a certain brand of beer has more flavor than competitors is taken to imply that a majority of consumers agree, the implied claim is factual and not purely evaluative. In general, the more vague and imprecise the puff, the less likely it is to be found legally actionable.

Advertisements directed at children are also a special case. It is widely acknowledged that children are particularly vulnerable to advertisers' enticements, and the FTC has accepted special responsibilities in this regard. Still, many authors complain that regulators have not done enough to curb abuses, especially since in much programming aimed at children the lines between commercials and entertainment have become blurred.

Product placements and the so-called stealth advertising are increasingly common forms of advertising that also seem at least potentially deceptive. A product placement occurs when an advertiser pays producers of a television show or movie to integrate its product into the story. The potential deceptiveness of the practice is that viewers may not be aware that the product has been included only because a fee has been paid. Stealth advertising is a practice whereby people are paid to tout a product under the guise of doing something else. For example, a camera company might hire representatives to pose as tourists, standing on street corners in a large city and asking passersby to photograph them with a new camera the company is marketing. Those who agree to the request end up holding and using the new camera—the purpose of the ruse, from the company's perspective—although the passersby may quite naturally believe that they are merely doing a stranger a favor. Thus far, however, both these practices have escaped serious regulatory attention. As advertisers invent new methods of pitching their products, however, further questions about deceptive advertising can be expected to arise in the future.

—Samuel V. Bruton

Further Readings

Attas, D. (1999). What's wrong with "deceptive" advertising? *Journal of Business Ethics, 21,* 49–59.

Carson, T. L., Wokutch, R. E., & Cox, J. E., Jr. (1985). An ethical analysis of deception in advertising. *Journal of Business Ethics, 4,* 93–104.

Federal Trade Commission. (1983). *FTC policy statement on deception.* Retrieved from www.ftc.gov/bcp/policystmt/ad-decept.htm

Petty, R. D. (1997). Advertising law in the United States and the European Union. *Journal of Public Policy & Marketing, 16,* 2–13.

Preston, I. (1994). *The tangled web they weave: Truth, falsity and advertisers.* Madison: University of Wisconsin Press.

Richards, J. I. (1990). *Deceptive advertising: Behavioral study of a legal concept.* Hillsdale, NJ: Lawrence Erlbaum.

PUBLIC RELATIONS

Public relations is a business function that can have any number of names—namely, corporate communications, corporate affairs, public affairs, or external affairs. The senior public relations officer usually reports to the chief executive officer, although sometimes the function reports to a second-level senior officer (e.g., chief administrative officer or, occasionally, the general counsel).

No matter what the name, the function will have a core mission of ensuring good relations with important constituencies, particularly the media. In many instances, the function will include a government relations component, manage corporate charitable contributions, handle relationships with the local community (and sometimes plant communities), and maintain relationships with important activist and interest groups involved with issues affecting the company's business. The same function is also likely to manage internal communications with employees and may have an important role in communications to the financial community—for example, it may produce annual reports and organize annual meetings.

EVOLUTION OF THE FUNCTION: THE FIRST DECADES

Public relations has grown and evolved as a business function from its earliest days at the beginning of the 20th century. Ivy Lee is often credited with being the "founder" of the field when he began to advise John D. Rockefeller about ways to improve his public image, through philanthropy, policies toward workers, selection of plant sites, and so on.

While the press agency aspect of public relations was—and remains—a core activity, Ivy Lee's determination to go beyond simply issuing press releases laid the groundwork for a much broader business function that would provide input to basic business decisions. Rockefeller at first resisted the advice but eventually gave in to the notion that public reaction had to be a factor in his business decisions.

Later, when Edward Bernays, another "founder" of the public relations profession, wrote the first book on the profession, titled *Crystallizing Public Opinion*, he too went beyond press relations. A student of Freud, he discussed the critical roles that events, third-party opinions, and social trends played in forming public opinion. He argued that public relations professionals had to be able to manipulate these elements if they were to be truly successful.

The early founders of the public relations function focused on image making. Given the historical period in which they were operating, which included the influence of F. W. Taylor's scientific management and the development of sophisticated mass marketing, Bernays and others worked to develop a scientific patina for public relations that ultimately came close to being a glorification of propaganda. Indeed, Bernays's second book was titled *Propaganda*. In it, he argued that in a complex democratic society, propaganda provided the means through which consensus could be reached, and he posited that those who knew how to manipulate public opinion were, in essence, the true ruling power in society.

While public relations professionals learned to shy away from promoting themselves in such terms during the 1930s, 1940s, and 1950s, the focus remained on image making. The corporate public relations function was grounded in press relations activity—sending out press releases, maintaining good contacts with reporters, holding press conferences—but also included speech writing and the development of corporate brochures and films and, occasionally, systematic "speaker's bureaus" that would send out representatives to make speeches and presentations to schools and community groups. Ronald Reagan, for example, spent many years doing the speech circuit for General Electric.

Companies such as AT&T (then a national telephone monopoly), DuPont ("Better Things for Better Living Through Chemistry"), and General Motors were practitioners of very sophisticated image efforts, as were many smaller companies and some industries. Several also worked with the emerging field of public opinion research to develop public opinion tracking surveys to monitor their image and report back to management on how they were doing.

EVOLUTION OF THE FUNCTION: INTO THE MAELSTROM

Rachel Carson's *Silent Spring* and Ralph Nader's *Unsafe at Any Speed* ushered in a new era for public relations. Suddenly, the companies and industries that had felt confident about their image-making abilities found their reputations collapsing under a barrage of new questions about corporate behavior—environmental impacts, workplace discrimination, safety, operations in South Africa, and so on. The age of issue management had begun.

The term *issue management* is credited to Howard Chase, who coined it in 1976, describing a process of how issues emerge through a mixture of events, media, and activist groups: how issues grow and how they eventually lead to regulation—as they did in the early 1970s, in a panoply of new federal regulatory agencies, including the Occupational Safety and Health Administration, the Environmental Protection Agency, the Consumer Product Safety Commission, the Equal Employment Opportunity Commission, and so on. Like Bernays and Ivy, Chase argued that smart business management disciplines could be applied to the world of public opinion if a company or industry acted quickly during the early stages of issue development to reduce the underlying problem, to show that the perceived problem was not really a problem, or to offer other solutions besides regulation.

The public relations function—both within companies and in the agency world—expanded exponentially to deal with the new issue-laden environment, becoming more focused on public affairs activities. New lobbying offices were opened, not just in Washington but also in state capitals and in many European nations (and ultimately in Brussels). Public affairs experts emerged to offer new services, such as ally development (i.e., finding or creating third parties to communicate points of view), constituency mobilizations (e.g., letter-writing campaigns), and issue advertising (a technique pioneered by Mobil Oil during the energy crisis of the 1970s because of what it viewed as biased media coverage of energy issues).

Drawing on the evolving techniques used in political campaigns, public relations practitioners began to target their audiences through psychographic profiling, becoming more sophisticated at identifying and then mobilizing political forces. No longer was public relations concerned about a generalized public opinion; now the question was who were the opinion leaders on particular issues and who were the mobilizable publics who needed to be reached through direct mail, telemarketing, or targeted media campaigns.

The field of marketing offered other new possibilities, such as focus group message testing to determine the right mobilizing messages. One of the most visible and successful issue-driven campaigns was probably that launched by insurance companies, pharmaceutical companies, and others to stymie President Bill Clinton's health care reform in the early 1990s. The message was crafted around protecting the right of health care consumers to choose their own providers. Through television and print advertising, targeted mobilization of letter writing, ally development, and other techniques, the Clinton plan was stopped in its tracks.

Parallel to these developments was the emergence of television as the dominant medium both in the United States and elsewhere. Until the 1960s, the public relations function had been mostly focused on print media—the leading local newspapers, the wire services that fed them, and major national magazines. Following the Kennedy assassination, television stations and the three nationally dominant networks (NBC, CBS, and ABC) vastly expanded news coverage and created new programs that covered issues of the day (e.g., *60 Minutes*, the morning news and talk shows). Then came CNN, followed in later decades by CNBC, MSNBC, Fox News, and so on.

Television became—as it continues to be—the most powerful force in defining and prioritizing public concerns. And it changed the timetable of the news cycle, which used to define the day in terms of the deadlines for going to press or the nightly news shows. Now there was no cycle—only endless news coverage.

Public relations professionals developed new skills and techniques to respond, taking advantage of the technological changes. An early innovation was media training for executives appearing on television, a medium where physicality is often as important as the words spoken and where message delivery strategies can differ depending on whether an interview is live or on tape.

In the 1980s, public relations agencies invented the video news release (VNR) and Radio Actualities, which were electronic versions of the traditional press release. They also developed "B-roll," which is a collection of video snippets with or without audio components that TV producers can use in developing a news segment. They learned how to create press conference environments that played first and foremost to television and only secondarily to the print media.

As satellite technology developed, both VNRs and B-roll could be distributed electronically and instantaneously. Equally important, companies and agencies discovered that they could have their own broadcast studios on the premises, offering a business executive live for an interview with a TV news host thousands of miles away. By the 1990s, "satellite media tours" allowed a spokesperson to sit in a small studio for a few hours and make sequential appearances on multiple local TV shows, answering local reporters. Then, with the advent of the Internet, "sound bite" sequences could be stored centrally for any reporter to pull down on demand.

These technological innovations became particularly useful for crisis communications, yet another emerging specialty in public relations. Starting with the nuclear accident at Three Mile Island in 1979, the Tylenol cyanide poisonings in 1982, and the chemical plant disaster in Bhopal, India, in 1984, companies began to realize that rapid and appropriate communications were critical in a fast-moving crisis environment. Various crisis communications experts began to outline procedures for managing communications in a crisis, and companies developed crisis communications manuals. Crisis preparedness planning became part of normal business practice. Companies in industries susceptible to large accidents (oil, chemicals, airlines) established technology-laden crisis communications centers on their premises, and many companies began to engage in crisis simulation exercises, in which press inquiries and press management were critical factors.

Another new field that developed was litigation communications. More and more companies under legal fire began to realize that battles were fought in the court of public opinion long before they were engaged in the court of law. With the investment community concerned about the potential costs of litigation and customers and employees worried about corporate or product reputation, no company could afford to be silent while plaintiff lawyers leaked documents and information to television and print reporters. So more experts emerged in the public relations profession—many of them trained as lawyers—to develop communications strategies that would precede courtroom activity and then carry the company through a trial and/or to a settlement.

PUBLIC RELATIONS TODAY

The globalization of the media and the development of the Web have offered even more challenges and opportunities. Public relations functions are now the owners and operators of the company's Web site and, often, the company's Web communications strategy. Public relations professionals design and pro-actively manage large corporate Web sites containing massive amounts of information that once had to be printed in brochures and sent out in press kits. Reporters—once only reachable by phone, mail, or fax—now became available by e-mail, and conversely, reporters can now have quick access to in-depth and constantly updated information, statements, visuals, and video snippets any time of the day or night.

Today, the field of public relations involves activities, techniques, and subspecialties that parallel the social and technological complexities of the age. But the focus remains constant. Now it is called "reputation management," a reformulated statement of "image making." And while companies are more successful at managing political issues, the reputation of business in general and of most companies remains at an all-time low—as it was even before a series of corporate scandals (Enron, Tyco, WorldCom) raised new questions about corporate ethics and integrity.

Ironically, approaching its 100th year of existence, the public relations field also retains its own image problem. Phrases such as "flack" hang over the field, left over from movies and novels (e.g., *The Sweet Smell of Success* of 1957) in which the press agent is portrayed as amoral and scheming. There are more ominous phrases, such as "spin doctor," not unrelated to the profession's once lauded relationship to propaganda. Even the acronym *PR* continues to carry negative connotations, the reason why so many corporate departments now bear names such as Corporate Communications, Corporate Affairs, or External Relations. Countless professional confabulations have discussed the dilemma of the bad image of the public relations profession, but the experts in image making cannot seem to solve their own image problem.

BEYOND MESSAGE DELIVERY TO DIALOGUE

During the 1990s, the newly emerging ideology and methodology of corporate responsibility (sometimes corporate social responsibility) offered a new approach to the field of public relations. The underlying assumption of corporate responsibility—once articulated by Ivy Lee to John D. Rockefeller—is that a business cannot survive and be sustainable in the long term without the support of key constituencies. Those constituencies are not limited to those with economic ties (investors, employees, customers, suppliers) but include other critical social groups (the media, the government, communities, and what is now termed "civil society" and was once called interest groups).

The theory of corporate responsibility does not focus on the image of the company with these groups, however. It focuses on the concept of stakeholder engagement and the need to carefully listen to constituency groups as part of the decision-making process, attempting to address concerns as part of business development. It is a model where the company becomes a more transparent and open-minded entity, discussing issues and even business ideas with others so that social groups become involved actors in what is decided, while not, in any way, controlling the decision. The goal is not image or reputation but rather decision making that is compatible with the social and ethical concerns of communities that could be affected by it.

While the "managing reputation/image" model of public relations has always included the notion of "listening," this activity has been largely left to opinion research and to the intuition and accumulated experience of the public relations professional. More important, listening has been merely a step in the process of developing the message that then gets delivered by the most effective voices and techniques to get the particular perceptual outcome—for example, an issue belief, favorability for the company, and so on.

Now, according to the theory of corporate responsibility, listening has to be redefined as a serious kind of dialogue—a two-way conversation—where views are shared, common ground defined, and disagreements respected. The quality of the relationship is paramount, not the perception of the company.

This approach creates new challenges for the public relations field, which, as of 2005, only some companies and industries had embraced—and only in some narrow issue areas. It changes the job of the public relations function to not just carry messages to the outside but also bring the outside in. In this way, business management is more likely to make decisions that are compatible with societal expectations and values.

This redefinition of the function requires that public relations professionals become more adept at give-and-take exchanges and at finding common ground, not in a context of a negotiation but in a context of dialogue and respectful sharing. This is a different skill set from that which has generally guided the profession—namely, the ability to develop influential messages (in print and in visual and aural forms) and deliver them creatively to intended audiences.

BECOMING MORE BUSINESSLIKE

While public relations functions learn to operate within the new corporate responsibility paradigms, it is unlikely that they will stop doing what they have long existed to do. Companies will continue to need core public relations activities—media relations, internal communications, Web site management, corporate identity and positioning, financial communications, issue monitoring and management, government affairs, contributions, and community relations—all being performed at the leading edge of technology and of communications theory and practice.

These public relations activities are increasingly managed in ways that parallel other core business functions. Long-term and short-term plans are developed as part of the business-planning process. Desired outcomes are agreed on and often expressed in perceptual terms—that is, a particular audience will hold a particular belief—or in terms of an action that an audience will take as a result of a belief: for example, purchase shares in the company. As in any business plan, the situation analysis is laid out, and strategies are outlined along with tactics (messages, messengers, and media).

Measurement can occur at several levels. *Output* is a measurement of the activity of the function: issuing press releases, making contacts with government officials, writing speeches, or improving the Web site.

Impact is a measurement of target audience exposure to the messages. This measurement parallels the field of advertising where reach, frequency, and gross rating points can be used as readings of how often an intended audience target is exposed to the message. Impact in public relations can be measured in terms of both message accuracy (described through word counts and subjective analyses of whether media coverage accurately delivered the desired message) and the number of people exposed to the media that carried the information.

The most elusive measurement is *outcome*—that is, whether all the public relations activity (the output) reached the audience the right way (the impact) to actually create or sustain the desired belief. Opinion research can be used to measure outcome (e.g., Did the percentage of believers increase?), but often public relations professionals are not eager to have their work judged on their ability to move public opinion. This reluctance then raises the question of whether the public relations profession will allow itself to be measured on its core mission, which is to influence opinion.

The movement of public relations into more of the business mainstream, including the use of business tools such as planning, objective setting, strategy articulation, and measurement, has not yet closed the gap that most public relations professionals—all the way back to Ivy Lee—would like to have closed. That is the gap that keeps them somewhat to the side in critical decision making. Public relations professionals yearn to have a "seat at the table" earlier in the decision-making process. They know that the adage "Actions speak louder than words" is valid, and that no "spin doctor" or "message delivery strategy" can turn a bad corporate behavior into an acceptable one. In the end, good public relations can help a company, but it can never replace—or cover up—bad decisions.

—Jim Lindheim

Further Readings

Argenti, P. (1994). *Corporate communication.* Boston: Irwin.

Breakenridge, D., & Deloughry, T. J. (2003). *The new PR tool kit: Strategies for successful media relations.* Upper Saddle River, NJ: Financial Times Prentice Hall.

Caywood, C. L. (1997). *The handbook of strategic public relations & integrated communications.* New York: McGraw-Hill.

Marconi, J. (2004). *Public relations: The complete guide.* Mason, OH: South-Western Education.

Shafer, P. (1994). *Adding value to the public affairs function.* Washington, DC: Public Affairs Council.

White, J., & Mazur, L. (1994). *Strategic communications management.* Cambridge, UK: Addison-Wesley.

Public Relations

PUBLIC RELATIONS ETHICS

The ethical issues of public relations arise because public relations is not just a set of techniques to disseminate information. There is always a perceptual objective to be achieved, and ethical dilemmas abound in how that objective is achieved.

Codes of ethics exist within the public relations profession at various levels—in trade associations (The Public Relations Society of America, The Council of Public Relations Firms, the International Association of Business Communicators, etc.), in public relations agencies, and within the public relations departments of companies. Except in the specialized area of government relations, there are few laws that govern how public relations professionals go about their objective of persuasion. Enforcement of codes is sporadic, and sanctions are few. The codes that exist cover a variety of issues (protecting confidentiality, avoiding cultural offense, financial management), but three areas remain ethically ambiguous: (a) truthfulness of information, (b) relations with the media, and (c) motivation of third-party support.

TRUTHFULNESS OF INFORMATION

The public relations industry makes a variety of statements about a commitment to supply information that is accurate and honest and known not to be false. Some of these statements go further to require that public relations professionals make an effort to confirm the accuracy of the information they are communicating and to correct any misinformation that is transmitted.

The ethical gray areas include what might be termed "lying by omission" or "being factually correct while leading to a misimpression." In both cases, there may be a commitment to "telling the truth" but perhaps not the whole truth. Indeed, only a slice of the truth might be presented, and this might be done in a fashion that knowingly leads the audience to a conclusion that they might not have reached if they had the "full story."

Such activities are very common in public relations (as they are in marketing), since public relations can involve "spin"—that is, finding the best thing to say and avoiding discussing the negatives. In some cases of regulated communications, such as FDA regulation of pharmaceutical information, there are both guidelines and a watchdog over this parsing of the truth. But even with regulation, the line between acceptable and unacceptable can be muddy.

RELATIONS WITH THE MEDIA

The public relations profession has a symbiotic relationship with the media. Public relations people want their messages and stories in the press, and journalists need information and access.

In some parts of the world, direct payments to journalists for press coverage are a matter of course. In most countries, however, such "pay-for-play" practices are forbidden by the ethical codes of the media. However, there are some subtle distinctions in what *pay* may mean. Many—but not all—media outlets forbid reporters from accepting any travel reimbursement or entertainment from a company or an agency. But reporters can be invited to speak at conferences, sometimes for honoraria; and moonlighting reporters have been known to accept writing or video-editing jobs through companies that they own.

Most media also create an institutional barrier between their desire to sell advertising to a company and the company's desire for good media coverage. Nonetheless, many public relations professionals know when purchasing of ads will help with favorable coverage, and many media are now offering advertising in "special issue sections" (e.g., a report on environmental issues) where advertisers also will get coverage.

In early 2005, a major industry scandal erupted when a syndicated "columnist/commentator" received a government contract for his advertising firm to help explain a government program. The work also included speaking well of the program as a commentator. While the controversy led to apologies and the discussion of new rules for government public relations contracts, the practice is not rare. Various experts who widely comment through their own columns or TV appearances as specialized reporters (e.g., "our travel reporter") have contracts with companies to provide favorable comment. No disclosure of these relationships is required by public relations codes of practice.

The 2005 scandal also led to a focus on video news releases (VNRs) issued by government agencies. A VNR is designed to be a fully produced news segment that a TV news show can simply slip into its news program. It includes a "reporter," who may or may or may not appear on camera, and some government VNRs may include an "interview" with a senior government official that is actually a scripted appearance. In the 2005 controversy, reform proposals ranged from forbidding government-produced VNRs altogether (even for important public information programs) to requiring a visual disclosure on the entire tape. Government has no ability to require such disclosure on VNRs produced by the private sector.

THIRD-PARTY SPOKESPEOPLE

Many public relations efforts involve motivating third parties (e.g., respected experts, happy consumers, celebrities, or interest groups) to carry a message to the media or directly to the intended audience. This may involve simply finding such people and encouraging them to make their views known. At the other end of the ethical spectrum is the paying of spokespeople, preparing and training them, writing their words, and "pitching" them to the media, all without disclosure of who is providing this support.

Strategies can also include the support of "coalitions," which are essentially front groups that will buy advertising, serve as spokespeople, and sometimes lobby a particular issue. Such support can include the re-creation of such groups or providing special grants to existing nonprofit groups to support specified activities on behalf of the company. Sometimes these relationships are publicly disclosed, sometimes not.

Disclosure is usually the ethical remedy suggested for these third-party practices, since it seems to be acceptable to pay a spokesperson or provide a VNR or even have a financial relationship with a business owned by a journalist if these relationships are fully disclosed. To date, however, the public relations industry—and some in the media industry—have resisted such a "sunshine" approach since the effectiveness of numerous public relations tactics would be greatly reduced if the mechanisms behind them were revealed.

—Jim Lindheim

Further Readings

Caywood, C. L. (1997). *The handbook of strategic public relations and integrated communications.* New York: McGraw-Hill.
Public Relations Society of America. (2000). *PRSA member code of ethics.* New York: Author.
White, J., & Mazur, L. (1994). *Strategic communications management.* Cambridge, UK: Addison-Wesley.

REPUTATION MANAGEMENT

Reputation management is a term that has recently gained broad recognition, referring to methodical efforts by business managers to influence perceptions about their businesses. However, the notion that reputation can and should be managed has been around since ancient times. Reputation, which can apply to institutions or to individuals, is analogous to perceptions of character—and while it sometimes is assumed that having a reputation is a good thing in and of itself, an institution can have a good or bad reputation just as a person can have a good or bad character, and reputation measures are as multifaceted as are the purported elements of character. Socrates said that the way to earn a good reputation was "to endeavor to be what you desire to appear," optimistically suggesting a confluence of reality and perception. Although Socrates emphasizes the importance of good moral character to reputation, his remark on its face is not inconsistent with Machiavelli's concession that sometimes political and economic success require a reputation for being heavy-handed and conniving while nonetheless being well respected.

It is clear from these historical views that there is an element of reputation management that is concerned with public relations but that that is not all there is to reputation management. As managers grow more sophisticated about performance management and markets grow more transparent about performance measurement, reputation has become one of those so-called soft characteristics of a business that are believed to have a material impact on market value. Therefore, as analysts, the media, and other stakeholders express interest in corporate reputations, business managers seek ways in which to influence them.

REPUTATION INDICES

What companies have the "best" reputations? Not only is there never full consensus on an answer to this question among the many reputation indices that have been released by the media and other parties, but also, there is no full congruence on what it means to measure reputation. However, there are generally some companies, brands, and individuals that tend to perform well (or poorly) across indices, whether they purport to measure reputation, respect, admiration, brand, or some other variation on a theme. So while reputation indices differ substantially in approach and outcomes, they share the goal of measuring stakeholders' perceptions of business entities.

Most business reputation indices focus on company reputations, although clearly brand reputation influences company reputation and vice versa, while the reputations of individual executives can reflect or less often clash with the reputation of the enterprise. One aspect of reputation measurement methodologies that leads to important differences in results concerns the survey population. Perceptions of the general public tend to differ from perceptions of, for example, chief executives, stock analysts, the business media, or other specific expert populations, while perceptions also vary as a result of other factors, including respondent nationality, economic class, and other demographic indicators. These indices do not always measure a company's internal reputation (among its employees), which may be as important as its external reputation but may be the result of significantly different factors.

These differences among survey populations and methodologies lead to different attitudes about what matters to corporate reputation. Reputation generally is sometimes mistakenly equated with a reputation specifically for corporate responsibility, which in some studies is merely one factor among many that constitutes overall reputation. While the rise of socially responsible investing has increased the potential impact of corporate social performance on corporate financial performance, not all investors (or reputation indices) place equal weight on the importance of social responsibility to corporate reputation. In general, the factors that constitute various reputation indices vary significantly enough from study to study and there is no general agreement even on a typology of factors. Certain factors focus primarily on financial success and efficiency, others on strategy and governance, corporate social responsibility and trustworthiness, product innovation and quality, brand and name recognition, and even on how well the company does with regard to managing its reputation (e.g., through communications and public relations, marketing, or political maneuvering). While a good reputation may be seen as inherently valuable, often these studies seek to make a descriptive connection between a good reputation (however defined) and good financial performance.

As a general rule, the reputation studies that generate wide publicity generally concern companies that have well-established, often global, reputations (such as automobile manufacturers or life insurers). Companies that serve niche markets may have established reputations with their stakeholders but may remain relatively unknown to the broader investing public (such as auto parts manufacturers or reinsurers). Conversely, companies that sell consumer products to a cross section of society tend to be reputation sensitive because they rely on name recognition with consumers who are often also investors. Sometimes, entire industries can be swept up in a wave of excitement or criticism because of their association with external events that may not be entirely within their control: For example, the dot-com boom of the late 1990s led to irrational overvaluation of many Internet start-ups, while energy companies may suffer reputation loss when the price of crude oil leads to a rise in gas prices.

PERCEPTION VERSUS REALITY

The debate about the meaningfulness and importance of reputation—and by implication the meaningfulness and importance of managing reputation—links back to an ancient tradition that has often distinguished between perception and reality. From Plato's divided line that helped to explain his theory of forms and form-sense distinction, to Bishop Berkeley's antimaterialist claim that "to be is to be perceived," to Descartes' mind-body division, philosophical epistemology and related psychology have suggested that human beings (and other animals) engage with and respond to the world they perceive, not necessarily the world that is actually out there. Kant's synthesis in a critical philosophy that said that the version we see of reality is inescapably colored by our cognitive hardwiring, and more recently Wittgensteinian and postmodern thinking, to some extent say that the only world that matters is the one we think we are in—that is, the world of perception.

It may be argued that all investment and trading decisions made in the financial markets depend on perception, and the quality of these decisions is a function of the extent to which these perceptions match reality. Recent corporate governance reforms that focus on more comprehensive financial disclosure—in the aftermath of corporate conduct scandals that, not incidentally, adversely affected corporate reputation—are essentially an effort, accepting the traditional perception-versus-reality distinction, to bring perception closer to reality by giving investors more reliable real information on which to base their opinions and decisions.

Reputation Management

Even more than other financial market perceptions, however, perceptions of reputation are perceived to be particularly ripe for distortion. That is to say that to the extent that reputation is seen to be important, reputation management has been criticized for being intentionally manipulative of stakeholders' perceptions. Unlike financial statements, which can be reasonably assured through the financial audit process applying generally accepted accounting principles, reputation measures are often more difficult to quantify, sometimes relying on emotional associations with products, brands, and companies. When WorldCom was disgraced by an accounting scandal, one reputation-enhancing step that the company took was to change its name to MCI, the name of one of its legacy acquisitions that had less unfavorable associations for stakeholders (later, the MCI name went away in an acquisition). Johnson & Johnson, a company that has long performed well in many reputation indices, evades the general disrepute of the pharmaceutical industry sector, in part because its most recognizable brand-name products, baby powders and shampoos, have historically sentimental associations for many stakeholders.

These examples suggest simple reputation management techniques from which business managers can learn, but they reinforce the perception-versus-reality distinction and several associated concerns of reputation management, such as the potentially important difference between being a good company (having quality products and services, reliable financial performance, etc.) and being a known (prominent) company. Furthermore, to the extent that a good company is one with a favorable ethical reputation, there is alleged to be an important difference between good ethics (being socially responsible because it is morally right) and good business (which sometimes includes being socially responsible because it is perceived to be strategically advantageous).

MANAGING REPUTATION

Another complicating factor in reputation management is the question of what causes what. Does a good reputation enhance financial performance, or does good financial performance enhance reputation? Or is the relationship overstated? In the final analysis, reputation management comes down to giving deliberate attention to the perceptions of stakeholders in making business management decisions, something good managers should be doing anyway. Managing reputation well rarely involves giving equal weight to each stakeholder, but it does require prioritizing, understanding, and then acting to influence the ways in which key stakeholders' perceptions can affect such important business drivers as attracting and retaining human capital, increasing brand distinctiveness and market share, lowering the cost of capital, stimulating favorable analyst and media coverage, and so on.

The business case for reputation management has been said to be a market premium that attaches to a good reputation. Since the market value of a business is not simply a matter of what that business is today but also what investors expect from it in the future, a gap in reputation can distinguish otherwise similar companies' future prospects in the minds of investors. This perspective on reputation management may categorize reputation as an intangible or "shadow" asset, but an asset nonetheless. Reputation has been credited by risk managers as constituting a "reservoir of goodwill" when something goes wrong. However, the value of reputation as an asset is impermanent, and the reservoir is not bottomless. Market perceptions can be fickle, and a single event can transform a reputation, for better or worse. The downside of a prominent reputation is that while it may help in an up market, it can magnify liability in a down market, emphasizing the extent to which a company is vulnerable to events beyond its control—external events, competitor failures, or supply chain mismanagement. All these factors might challenge the perceived value of reputation management, whereas they led to Warren Buffett's famous remark in support of taking steps to manage reputation, "It takes twenty years to build a reputation and five minutes to ruin it."

Machiavelli's pragmatic approach to reputation notwithstanding, Buffett's folk wisdom emphasizes the importance of ethical reputation, because even if certain stakeholders (e.g., shareholders) want management to be aggressive in its bargaining position with other stakeholders (e.g., employees and customers), each influential stakeholder's perception of the business depends on assurances that it will be treated fairly. If management has a reputation for dealing dishonestly with regulators, the negative consequences will extend beyond direct fines and penalties, potentially draining the reservoir of trust the management may once have had with shareholders and the communities in which the company operates. Thus, reputation management experts tend to coalesce around the importance of business ethics and social responsibility to reputation, even if there is no broad consensus on the exact meaning of these concepts in practice. On a related point, they also commonly advise transparency in communications with stakeholders, reasoning that a sound business should have little to hide along with conventional wisdom that when there is something worth hiding, the cover-up usually causes more trouble than the problem itself.

Just as stakeholders' knowledge of the business is important to a fair evaluation of reputation, management's knowledge of who its stakeholders are and what matters to them is critical to effective management of reputation. The benefits of sound reputation management are not separate from sound business performance but rather integral to management's ability to deliver what many stakeholders want—increasing shareholder value, worthwhile products and services, good jobs, social and environmental benefits, and so on. Stakeholder dialogue and monitoring of stakeholders' interests contributes to management's knowledge and ability to balance and, where necessary, prioritize these interests to the extent they cannot equally be satisfied. When there are trade-offs between product quality and price, cost of production and environmental degradation, local community benefits and low-cost-country sourcing, and other conflicting stakeholder interests, it can be as important for management to have a credible story to tell as it is for management to make an informed decision.

Stakeholder engagement, a term that is often associated with maintaining a dialogue between a corporation and its moral critics, is in fact just a variation on investor relations that recognizes that Wall Street analysts are not the only stakeholders with the media power to express an opinion about corporate management. Stakeholder engagement is a form of reputation risk management that seeks to exert greater management control over the perceptions of others, and managers who view reputation as an opportunity and a risk employ other reputation management techniques that are modeled on risk management techniques, such as identification of key reputation drivers, scenario planning, reputation measurement and monitoring, and the installation of early warning systems.

Finally, in determining how to approach reputation management, it is important for management to ask what kind of reputation it makes sense for the business to have, and how prominent a reputation it needs to have. It is rarely possible to have a reputation for being the highest quality, lowest cost seller of a given product or service, so it makes sense to target reputation to the market the company is best positioned to serve. And given that reputation poses potentially as much risk as reward, it is reasonable to seek that reputation among those that matter to the business while seeking to stay out of the broader limelight lest that bring unwanted attention.

Together, these techniques are valuable reminders that reputation is manageable to the extent that it is based on substantive behaviors but never wholly within any one individual's or company's control. It may be practically useful to distinguish between perception and reality to call attention to the importance of attending to stakeholders' interests, but it is at least as important to recognize that a lasting corporate reputation also requires a grounded sense of corporate purpose that is not buffeted by sometimes ephemeral stakeholder demands and that helps sort out those demands. The notion of reputation management emphasizes the interdependence and potential inseparability of companies from the industries, communities, and markets in which they operate. While this interdependence has led some corporate critics to demand a stakeholder-driven conception of strategic management, it also demonstrates the extent to which capitalist societies rely on business for production and distribution of basic goods. It further suggests that as much as the financial markets are driven by perception, the real exchange of goods and services in the marketplace is evidence that business is integral to social well-being and not just an institution whose reputation is on exhibition for social scrutiny.

—Christopher Michaelson

Further Readings

Dowling, G. (2001). *Creating corporate reputations.* Oxford, UK: Oxford University Press.

Fombrun, C. J., & van Riel, C. B. M. (2003). *Fame & fortune: How successful companies build winning reputations.* Upper Saddle River, NJ: Prentice Hall.

Rindova, V. P., Williamson, I. O., Petkova, A. P., & Sever, J. M. (2005). Being good or being known: An empirical examination of the dimensions, antecedents, and consequences of corporate reputation. *Academy of Management Journal, 48*(6), 1033–1049.

Staw, B. M., & Epstein, L. D. (2000). What bandwagons bring: Effects of popular management techniques on corporate reputation, performance, and CEO pay. *Administrative Science Quarterly, 45,* 523–556.

Reputation Management

PART IV

Special Topics in Marketing Ethics

163

INTELLECTUAL PROPERTY

ntellectual property, as distinguished from real property, pertains to products of the mind (or intellect)—it refers to those rights or entitlements that attach to intangibles such as artistic expressions and technological inventions. Protection is afforded to intellectual property to encourage development of ideas, expressions, and processes for commercial gain.

TYPES OF INTELLECTUAL PROPERTY

There are various types of intellectual property. Distinctions are made according to the nature of the proprietary innovation.

Copyrights

Intellectual property such as computer software, video games, songs, and movies are granted legal protection in the form of a copyright. A copyright is a set of exclusive legal rights accorded to the expression of a particular literary, artistic, or scientific work. Any moral rights are separate and distinct from the legal rights. The purpose of copyright law is to protect and promote creative endeavors by deterring unauthorized use.

Copyrights are not granted automatically. For material to be protected, it must reflect some degree of originality. Furthermore, copyrights are not indefinite; in fact, they typically expire after a predetermined period of time (typically, 50 years).

A fair use exception excludes some uses of copyrighted material from legal protection. To determine whether the fair use exception applies, the purpose of the use is considered, along with the nature of the work. Copyrighted material is often given fair use treatment when used for educational purposes. Also considered are the proportion used, compared with the size of the whole, and the effect of the use on the potential market for the copyrighted material.

The granting of copyright protection is defended on public policy grounds. First and foremost, copyright law provides an incentive for creators to share their ideas with the public, and, at the same time, it militates against intellectual piracy. Through copyright law, copyright holders can enforce their rights through civil lawsuits.

Patents

Patents are issued with regard to systems, processes, and other inventions. New mechanical contrivances, for example, are appropriate subjects for patent protection. A patent offers the patentee exclusive rights for a defined period of time—often 20 years—in exchange for sharing information with the public about the protected systems, processes, or other inventions. The proprietary right allows the patentee to restrict others from making, using, or selling the patented invention until the term of the patent expires.

A condition for a patent to be granted is that the patentee provide a written description of the invention in sufficient detail so that another person could reproduce that invention. Once a patent is granted, the patentee's rights can be enforced through the vehicle of civil lawsuits.

Four reasons are generally offered to justify the protection of intellectual property rights: disclosure, innovation, product investment, and design development. Generally, patents are given to encourage inventors to share information about their inventions. Through disclosure to the public domain, inventors are able to build on the inventions of others. Without the protection of patents, inventors might be reluctant to share their creations with the public.

Patents are also widely considered economically beneficial. The promise of exclusive rights to an invention is believed to promote innovation of new systems, processes, and devices. This encourages companies to invest in research and development up front because of the anticipated financial returns often linked to the patenting of successful inventions.

Finally, patents arguably provoke new innovations in that, once a patented invention exists, competitors are inspired to develop new designs to work around the patented invention. In this way, the patent system promotes technological progress and economic growth.

Trademarks

A trademark is a distinctive symbol or sign to which commercial value is attached because of the connection between the symbolic representation and organizations, products, or services. Trademarks distinguish organizations, products, and services from those of their competitors. Traditionally trademarks have taken the form of names, phrases, symbols, designs, and images.

The primary purpose of a trademark is to identify organizations, products, and services in the marketplace. Rights are enforced to protect the ability of organizations to benefit financially from their investment in distinguishing their products and services through a brand image from those of competitors. For rights to be enforced, however, trademarks must be registered.

To be registered, a trademark must be distinctive. Fanciful designs and made-up words (i.e., *Kodak* as a camera company) are often de facto eligible for trademark protection. Similarly, arbitrary words (i.e., *Apple* as the name of a computer company) are also considered acceptable, although apparent trademark infringements, as with Apple Records, must sometimes be resolved through negotiation and, often, compensation. Suggestive words (i.e., *Salty* for sailing equipment) can serve as legitimate trademarks, whereas descriptive or generic marks (i.e., *Salty* as used with saltine crackers) are not protected.

Unlike copyrights and patents, trademark rights do not expire within a predetermined time period. For rights to be enforced, however, the trademark owner must continue to use the trademark.

Public policy considerations underlie the granting and enforcement of trademark rights. In fact, trademarks are generally considered to benefit consumers. While companies are able to reap the financial benefits of establishing strong brand reputations and linking those reputations to identifiable trademarks, the consumers benefit from making more informed decisions about the companies, products, and services in which they invest.

ETHICAL CONSIDERATIONS

The granting of intellectual property rights is often controversial. Assigning rights to intellectual contributions creates negative rights, in that rights attributed to intellectual property involve excluding others from using that property. This can arguably stifle competition and inhibit consumer choice and artistic appreciation.

Furthermore, intellectual property rights are distinguishable from the rights that attach to real property in that their abridgement does not result in harm, other than perhaps the financial loss of opportunity costs to the innovator. Even this is not certain, however. Many musicians, for example, argue that Internet-based file-sharing actually increases their name recognition and the popularity of their songs. When intellectual property is shared or copied, there is no tangible loss.

Not all information, expressions, or ideas are eligible for intellectual property protection. Some argue that the choice of what is protected is arbitrary, serves commercial interests, and is not linked to inherent moral entitlements.

CONCLUSION

It is generally assumed in the United States that free market societies must protect intellectual property to reward innovation and promote economic growth. Individuals and businesses assume and expect that their information, expressions, and ideas deserve the protection of copyrights, patents, or trademarks. The emergence of the Internet, however, has introduced increasing challenges to this framework. On the one hand, technology facilitates the infringement of digitized intellectual property. At the same time, the Internet increases the exposure of intellectual property to other cultures that have different values and regulations pertaining to intellectual property, its use, and its protection.

—Tara J. Radin

Further Readings

De George, R. T. (2005). Intellectual property and pharmaceutical drugs: An ethical analysis. *Business Ethics Quarterly, 15*(4), 549–575.

Di Norcia, V. (2005). Intellectual property and the commercialization of research and development. *Science & Engineering Ethics, 11*(2), 203–219.

Lea, D. (2006). From the Wright Brothers to Microsoft: Issues in the moral grounding of intellectual property rights. *Business Ethics Quarterly, 16*(4), 579–598.

Reed, E. D. (2006). Property rights, genes, and common good. *Journal of Religious Ethics, 34*(1), 41–67.

Resnik, D. B. (2003). A pluralistic account of intellectual property. *Journal of Business Ethics, 46*(4), 319–335.

Stark, C. D. (2005). Patently absurd: The ethical implications of software patents. *TechTrends: Linking Research & Practice to Improve Learning, 49*(6), 58–61.

Werhane, P. H., & Gorman, M. (2005). Intellectual property rights, moral imagination, and access to life-enhancing drugs. *Business Ethics Quarterly, 15*(4), 595–613.

Intellectual Property

ELECTRONIC COMMERCE

E lectronic commerce, also known as "e-commerce," refers to the marketing, distribution, sale, and exchange of products and services via the Internet and encompasses a multitude of Web-based (often called "virtual") commercial transactions. Through e-commerce, funds are transferred, supply chains are managed, and data are collected. E-commerce depends on and is the result of the application of new technologies to traditional forms of business. The commercial transactions that result are considered virtual or simulated—in contrast with traditional, or "real," brick-and-mortar transactions—because they take place invisibly. The *e*, for "electronic," reflects the technological systems that facilitate commerce, and e-commerce thus entails the complete network of systems and processes that enable commercial transactions to take place electronically via the Internet.

E-commerce is a vehicle through which businesses reach out to a virtual marketplace of customers united by need, desire, and/or mere curiosity. It enables firms to transcend barriers such as time and geography and thereby allows businesses to reach a broader audience than might otherwise be possible. It also provides businesses with the opportunity to collect massive amounts of information about their stakeholders—particularly their customers. Finally, use of the Internet by firms enables them to exercise significant control over operations and marketing.

At the same time, e-commerce can serve as a Pandora's box for firms, for there are just as many, if not more, obstacles as there are opportunities for businesses as they operate in the virtual world. Because the Web is largely unregulated, the Net creates an illusion of freedom for businesses and individuals and lulls them into the idea that conventional business practices and the law no longer apply. Businesses and individuals have sometimes discovered the hard way that customary business practices are important and that the law and the public can be unforgiving when people feel violated by online transactions.

HISTORICAL DEVELOPMENT

E-commerce has evolved considerably during the past 30 years. The term *electronic commerce* originated in the 1970s in connection with technology that enabled the electronic transfer of data in commercial transactions. Electronic Data Interchange (EDI) and Electronic Funds Transfer (EFT) are two examples of the technology developed during this time. EDI facilitates the computer-to-computer exchange of information over private or public networks and remains even today the primary data format for electronic transactions. EFT, in a similar fashion, is used for financial transactions. It, too, continues to exist, albeit expanded far beyond its initial use.

During the 1980s, businesses began to rely increasingly on such electronic means of exchanges to enhance the efficiency and minimize the costs associated with their transactions. Individuals became more familiar with electronic exchanges as automated teller machines (ATMs) proliferated and grew in importance and popularity and as the use of debit and credit cards became more widespread.

It was not until the 1990s, however, that the term *e-commerce* took center stage as the Internet became widely accessible and commercialized, particularly with the establishment of the .com registry, which establishes ownership and regulates the use of domain names. From that time onward, businesses began accessing new and untapped markets, and individuals were able to engage in commercial transactions without having first to establish a physical presence. This heralded what has become known as the "dot-com" era, because of the multitude of Internet-based start-up companies that emerged in a short period of time, along with the use of e-commerce by traditional brick-and-mortar companies.

The term *dot-com* commonly refers to the extension ".com" in a Web address or domain name and indicates a Web site that is commercial in nature. Although .com remains the most commonly recognized extension, other domain names are also available. The extension ".biz," for example, was introduced in 2001 and is restricted to business use. Specific countries have adopted their own extensions, such as ".au" for Australia, ".br" for Brazil, ".co.jp" for Japan, ".com.mx" for Mexico, and ".co.uk" for the United Kingdom.

The Dot-Com Bubble

The late 1990s witnessed a tremendous surge in the emergence of dot-com companies, and a new era began to take shape as businesses adopted Internet addresses, either as their main market presence or as a way to augment existing business. This move had a profound positive effect on Western stock markets, particularly in the United States. Between 1997 and 2001, markets grew suddenly and to unprecedented levels, and this created a speculative bubble that has become known as the "dot-com bubble." A bubble occurs when stock prices boom in a particular industry and speculators, recognizing the rapid increase in share price, invest further, not because they believe the stock is undervalued but in anticipation of continued growth. This bubble is called the dot-com bubble because it was linked to the emergence of a new group of Internet-based companies, commonly referred to as "dot-coms."

Stock values of Internet-based companies soared on the crest of a tremendous wave of opportunity and enthusiasm. Triggered by the shocking rise in value of Netscape's initial public offering (IPO) and allegedly manipulated by some of the world's leading investment banks and venture capitalists (CS First Boston, Goldman Sachs, Morgan Stanley, Merrill Lynch, and others), speculators hoping to get rich quick drove up the stock values of Internet-related businesses. Millionaires were born overnight as venture capitalists invested billions of dollars to fund incipient ideas, while traditional business models seemed to be largely set aside if not altogether abandoned. Low interest rates in 1998 and 1999 increased the availability of capital for entrepreneurial, Internet-based ventures. It was during this time that a number of today's Internet-based leaders emerged, including Amazon.com, eBay, Google, and Yahoo!

The Dot-Com Crash

The ethereal and fragile nature of the bubble quickly became apparent, however, as the bubble burst almost as quickly as it had grown. Between 1999 and 2000, the economy began to slow as the Federal Reserve increased interest rates six times. The failure of these businesses had a cascading effect such that, by 2001, the dot-com boom was over and many of the enterprises viewed so promisingly just a year before were now considered "dot-bombs."

The dot-com crash put hundreds of companies out of business almost overnight and cost thousands of people their jobs. Investors lost millions of dollars. In 1999 alone, there were 457 IPOs of stock of private companies—most of them linked to the Internet and technology. Of those IPOs, 25% doubled in price the first day their stock was traded. By 2001, there were only 76 IPOs, none of which doubled in price the first day of trading. Between March 11, 2000, and October 9, 2002, the NASDAQ fell 78%. The lesson of e-commerce was clear: It holds the potential for tremendous opportunity, but the path toward realizing that potential is fraught with challenges and not that far removed from traditional good business practices.

ETHICS AND E-COMMERCE

By 2006, the dot-com market gradually began to rebound. The popularity of enterprises such as Skype (an Internet-based telephone service) and YouTube (a vehicle for Internet-based video sharing) signaled a renewed growth in technology. Even so, ethical issues continued to nag the sector. The unbridled opportunism and manipulation of markets during the bubble had never been fully addressed, and the lure of windfall profits never completely left the psyche of some speculators, despite the legal, financial, and social costs of such behavior.

With the implosion of the dot-com bubble, questions have arisen regarding whether or not e-commerce calls for a new set of ethical guidelines. On the one hand, many maintain that e-commerce is unique and needs an ethic separate from mainstream business and marketing ethics. Others claim that e-commerce is just another form of business and should be subsumed within the broader fields of applied ethics. The chief assertion here is that the problems associated with electronic commerce are merely new manifestations of old business issues that can be addressed adequately through established ethical processes. E-commerce simply contextualizes, in new form, traditional considerations such as fair pricing, distribution, responsible advertising, and respect for privacy.

Not surprisingly, considerable debate has ensued regarding the Internet as a new or variant form of business. Questions persist regarding the Internet's encroachment on individual privacy, but concern for privacy has been a prominent theme in other contexts for decades. The mistake that many companies make lies in framing questions in e-commerce as new territory, for in doing so, they deprive themselves of the years of experience in dealing with those same sorts of issues in the brick-and-mortar marketplace.

Electronic Commerce

Distinguishing Features

While the fundamental difference or sameness of e-commerce is disputed, virtuality—a defining characteristic of e-commerce—certainly alters the dynamics of commercial transactions. While being online might not render it necessary to create a distinct code of ethics for e-commerce, it is important to recognize the presence of significant attributes that exacerbate concern about this way of doing business.

Availability of Information

Information is a valuable commodity, and corporate use of the Internet for marketing purposes presents managers with a pressing problem regarding how to handle the metaphorical mountain of information that the Internet makes available to them. Because firms cannot afford to market their products to everyone, managers must cull through information with a strategic purpose in mind. In other words, it is not enough to acquire information; that information must be handled in such a way as to create value for the firm. To aid in this process, support businesses have emerged whose primary purpose lies in collecting information to be sold for marketing purposes. In addition, businesses themselves are becoming increasingly adept at collecting information about customers and then selling that information to other firms.

Unrestrained information gathering is a concern to many people, especially those who care about individual privacy protection. In their view, while information gathering per se is not necessarily worrisome, how that information is used matters. The magnitude of the information available via the Internet coupled with the temptation to misuse it has exacerbated privacy concerns among a number of stakeholders in e-commerce. Because the Internet enables businesses to distribute widely the data they collect, the monitoring, control, and use of information have become focal points of concern.

Lack of Transparency

As odd as it might seem, an online presence often diminishes corporate transparency. While e-commerce allows firms to harvest large amounts of information about people, it also enables corporations to cloak themselves and their practices in deceptive anonymity.

Although many firms volunteer information about their goods and services, a significant number do not. Xfleas.com, for example, is a low-cost distributor of pet supplies. Although its Web site states that the company only sells products licensed in the United States, the only information available about the company is an e-mail address, a mailing address, and a fax number. There is very limited information about the specific products offered, and no information is provided about expected delivery times and other particulars associated with purchase and delivery.

Although customers might choose not to patronize such a company, many do so without being bothered by the lack of transparency in their transactions. Any qualms they might have are overridden by the lure of comparatively inexpensive products. In this case, the product offered is a 12-month supply of Interceptor, a popular heartworm preventative, which costs $25.54, including shipping. This compares favorably against Interceptor at $38.98 with $3.99 for shipping from 1-800-PetMeds, another popular Internet competitor—and so individuals willingly give their information to Xfleas.com.

Absence of Accountability

Accountability is noticeably absent in e-commerce as well. This can be a concern for customers who anticipate the possibility of mistaken delivery or defective products. Xfleas.com, for example, does not post any sort of return policy on its Web site. While it is uncommon for companies not to publish a return policy, they are not required to do so, and many opt out of this. Even in situations where the company does publish an explicit return policy, customers still encounter problems. Policies can be placed on Web sites such that they are not easy to find; the style in which policies are written can render them difficult to understand and/or apply; and the policies themselves can be replete with loopholes.

Product delivery is another area where accountability can be absent. Delivery is often delayed. Sometimes the product shipped is not the one that was ordered. It is frequently impossible to reach someone by phone or e-mail to handle or respond to complaints. While customers can choose which companies with which to do business, the reality is that the absence of accountability remains a significant concern regarding online transactions.

Perception of Vulnerability

The physical and metaphorical distance between firms and their customers, coupled with the ongoing flow of information (both accurate and deceptive), enhances Internet users' feelings of vulnerability. Customers complain about failed transactions and the lack of easy means of redress. Similarly, firms constantly strive to weed out customers who do not honor their debts. Other stakeholders express similar concerns about their vulnerability when engaging in online transactions.

In the end, stakeholders of all sorts recognize the value of information afforded by the Internet as well as the fact that the volume of information gleaned can be overwhelming and lead to inaccuracies, deception, increased financial risk, and feelings of vulnerability. The presence of these attributes serves to impose an obstacle to online trust. Ironically, it is trust that is arguably the linchpin for successful e-commerce. It is therefore essential for e-commerce ethics to incorporate consideration of such attributes in making ethical decisions regarding e-marketing.

Data and Discrimination

As destructive as improper use of data can be by brick-and-mortar enterprises, it is even more dangerous in the electronic domain because of the lack of formal restraints. Even so, a number of companies, failing to exercise proper judgment, have found that laws and ethical norms are unforgiving when it comes to the exploitation of personal data for commercial purposes.

DoubleClick and Data Miners

DoubleClick introduced people to "cookies," the term for information users leave behind as they surf the Internet. Cookies contain records of the keystrokes that Internet users enter and are stored on personal computers. They provide a record for return visits to Web sites, and the information they contain enables companies to construct profiles of customers.

Not long ago, DoubleClick, through the manipulation of cookies, created an extensive database of 100,000 online customers. When this was discovered, the company received harsh criticism by those who were unknowingly profiled. Early customers/surfers who had agreed to share information about themselves with DoubleClick had done so with the assurance from DoubleClick that their information would remain confidential. People felt betrayed and became outraged when DoubleClick attempted to merge with Abacus Direct, an offline marketing company with a database of information on 88 million households in the United States. Even before DoubleClick had the opportunity to use the data, the proposed merger alerted people to the dangers of intrusive target marketing that databases such as these could trigger.

Interestingly, although the DoubleClick merger issue was heavily publicized, it was not the first instance of such activity. Earlier, in 1998, Geocities was sued for selling personal information to third parties after guaranteeing its Web site users that their information would not be shared. Toysmart, too, was sued in 2000 for similar behavior in violating its privacy agreement during bankruptcy proceedings when it attempted to sell personal information to settle its debts with creditors.

While this type of activity occurs more frequently within e-commerce, where data can be more easily and opportunistically collected and disseminated, it echoes a similar situation relating to a database that Lexis-Nexis offered in the mid-1990s. At that time, Lexis-Nexis established what it called its P-TRAK Person Locator service. It provided address information along with aliases, maiden names, and social security numbers for millions of people in the United States. Although there is no public record of a lawsuit, the P-TRAK service was short-lived. Even though the data had been collected through legitimate means, their availability and accessibility posed a significant threat to the public. Both situations underscore the message that it is not the legitimacy or manner of obtaining the data that is necessarily determinative but their susceptibility to being used for manipulative or malign purposes that renders such databases questionable.

Amazon and Price Discrimination

Amazon has used data monitoring to develop customer profiles that it uses toward multiple ends—ostensibly to enhance customer service. For instance, Amazon uses historical purchase information to tailor Web offerings to repeat customers. Interestingly, there are serious questions about the accuracy and reliability of this sort of customer-driven information. When customers input the information themselves, it is often accepted without verification. Although this is troubling in itself, the underlying assumptions are even more problematic. With regard to purchases, not every single purchase can be interpreted as indicative of a customer's overall taste. Some purchases, for example, are made as gifts, others as one-time extravagances. In the end, Amazon was constructing profiles that appeared accurate but very likely were not.

In addition, Amazon allegedly used data profiling to set prices. In September 2000, Amazon customers discovered that they were charged different prices for the same CDs. Although the company claimed that the price differentiation was part of a randomized test, the result was price discrimination that appeared to be based on demographics. In other words, Amazon appeared to be redlining, or "e-lining" (redlining via the Internet)—a practice of price discrimination that differentiates financial opportunities on the basis of demographics such as race. Redlining is widely considered both unethical and illegal.

In the end, Amazon found that its use of information derived from online sources led to all sorts of complications. In this regard, Amazon is not alone.

Kozmo and Delivery Discrimination

Kozmo is another e-tailer identified as an e-liner. This company—a provider of 1-hour delivery services—excluded certain neighborhoods as a result of its racial redlining practices. In short, it refused to deliver merchandise to customers in undesirable neighborhoods, identified by their zip codes, which were predominantly black. Again, such behavior is considered legally and ethically inappropriate, for it deprives classes of people of opportunities available in the marketplace.

PayPal.com and the Global Marketplace

PayPal's less publicized e-lining behavior is particularly disturbing because of its influence on global e-commerce and its extensive relationships with people in different countries around the world.

E-commerce tends to be unique in that it renders geography virtually moot. PayPal, an e-commerce giant, emerged as a way of streamlining payments in arms-length purchases. As a disinterested third party, PayPal links parties for payment purposes in secure transactions. PayPal can link anyone, anywhere. The problem is that PayPal became selective with regard to the people with whom it chose to do business. In doing so, it effectively redlined groups of people on an international scale. In the United States, businesses can redline neighborhoods; in the global marketplace via the Internet, the ramifications are huge because e-businesses can e-line entire countries. This is what PayPal did by eliminating or not allowing transactions with parties in countries that are disfavored.

PayPal attributed its reluctance to do business with people in certain countries to the rampant corruption, lack of infrastructure, and risks associated with not receiving payment. While it is true that particular countries are notorious for "carding" (passing off illegally obtained credit card numbers), the problem was that the people of entire countries were denied access to a service and thereby forcibly limited in their access to e-commerce (since PayPal is a major e-payment tool). PayPal effectively engaged in discriminatory behavior, even though that behavior was for a legitimate business purpose (i.e., the minimization of financial risk). Unfortunately, although such behavior is considered illegal in the United States, there is no legislation to prevent it in e-commerce and in the global arena. PayPal thus engaged in practices via e-commerce that it could not have legally engaged in as a brick-and-mortar company in many countries, including the United States.

E-TRADE

An emerging area of concern is that of e-trade. E-trade refers to the online trading of securities and financial products. Buyers and sellers connect through the Internet in e-marketplaces. It used to be that stock markets were physical locations where buyers and sellers met to negotiate prices. The Internet renders this moot.

Although NASDAQ set up the first electronic stock market in 1971, it took more than 35 years for the New York Stock Exchange to automate its trading process. This step is significant in that it signals the potential end of traditional trading room floors. If this is true, it is imperative that those involved in this business enhance online security and privacy measures, both to preserve trust and to protect customers.

CONCLUSION

The e-marketplace remains an amorphous domain, rife with both promise and danger. Where neither legislation nor regulation provides clear direction and where moral norms are not clearly defined, businesspeople must determine for themselves how to navigate through ambiguous ethical situations. The examples of companies such as DoubleClick, Amazon, Kozmo, and PayPay underscore the problems associated with the emergence of new technologies and online transactions. The experiences of these companies also suggest good reasons for the need to establish and articulate guidelines for e-commerce, whether they are the same as or different from existing brick-and-mortar business principles.

—Tara J. Radin, Martin Calkins, and Carolyn Predmore

Electronic Commerce

Further Readings

Calkins, M. (2002). Rippers, portal users, and profilers: Three Web-based issues for business ethicists. *Business and Society Review, 107*(1), 61.

De George, R. T. (1999). Business ethics and the information age. *Business and Society Review, 104*(3), 261–278.

Donaldson, T. (2001). Ethics in cyberspace: Have we seen this movie before? *Business and Society Review, 106*(4), 273.

Hemphill, T. A. (2000). DoubleClick and consumer online privacy: An e-commerce lesson learned. *Business and Society Review, 105*(3), 361–372.

Koehn, D. (2003). The nature of and conditions for online trust. *Journal of Business Ethics, 43*(1/2), 3–19.

Kracher, B., & Corritore, C. L. (2004). Is there a special e-commerce ethics? *Business Ethics Quarterly, 14*(1), 71–94.

Laczniak, G. R., & Murphy, P. E. (2006). Marketing, consumers and technology: Perspectives for enhancing ethical transactions. *Business Ethics Quarterly, 16*(3), 313–321.

Peace, G., Weber, J., Hartzel, K. S., & Nightingale, J. (2002). Ethical issues in ebusiness: A proposal for creating the ebusiness principles. *Business and Society Review, 107*(1), 41–60.

Radin, T. J. (2001). The privacy paradox: E-commerce and personal information on the Internet. *Business and Professional Ethics Journal, 20,* 145.

MARKETING TO CHILDREN

The marketing of products to children is not a new phenomenon, and certainly, the historical record is rife with examples of popular product campaigns geared toward children. However, recent decades have seen an unprecedented expansion in marketing efforts aimed at children. Such efforts involve both direct and indirect forms of marketing to children. Direct marketing to children involves advertising and related activities geared toward soliciting children's awareness of and interest in specific products. Indirect forms of marketing to children involve similar efforts devoted to creating consciousness of products designed for younger persons among parents and others responsible for purchasing products for children. The average child now views tens of thousands of television and print advertisements every year, and magazines, television shows, and Web sites aimed exclusively at children provide a fertile medium for marketers to appeal to this audience directly. Indeed, the line between entertainment and advertisement is now routinely blurred in the television programs and movies viewed by children, which are often closely connected to marketing campaigns that sell toys, games, and other products centered on the characters and themes of these shows. Furthermore, marketing departments have become increasingly sophisticated in their attempts to appeal to children, often making use of extensive market research on the buying habits of children and the expertise of child psychologists in developing marketing strategies.

Essentially interconnected with the expansion of marketing to children is the increased disposable wealth of children, who now directly spend billions of dollars every year on toys, games, and other products. Children are also indirectly responsible for influencing billions of dollars in adult expenditures on food, clothing, vacations, and assorted goods and services. There is, thus, no doubt that children represent an important element in the modern consumer economy. In this sense, some have seen the expansion in direct marketing to children as simply responding to the increased purchasing power of this segment of the population. Nonetheless, this proliferation in the number of products marketed to children as well as in the techniques used to market these products has raised a number of concerns about the ethical status of many of these efforts. While some of the concerns raised about marketing efforts directed at children reflect more general questions about marketing ethics, others rest on more specific concerns with the practices of marketing to children. Ethical concerns of the latter type often stem from considerations of the differences between adult and children consumers. Because of these differences, most ethicists argue that higher ethical, and often regulatory, standards are appropriate for the marketing of products to children.

SUITABLE FOR CHILDREN?

A number of the concerns raised by marketing directed at children turn on the kinds of products that such marketing involves. Questions of an ethical nature have been raised in this direction about marketing campaigns that involve products that are dangerous, inappropriate, or useless. While it may be legitimate to assume that adult consumers have the capacity to rationally evaluate the relative merits and risks of products on their own, children, particularly those of a younger age, lack the understanding and experience necessary to independently judge the worthiness of many products. There is good reason for, thus, believing that even in a market economy children should be provided additional protection against the marketing of harmful products. Differences exist though in terms of the marketing of products of questionable suitability for children and, thus, as to which products, and to what extent, marketers should be restricted or regulated in appealing to children.

The clearest cases of ethically problematic marketing campaigns directed at children are those that involve products that are inherently dangerous. The most notorious cases involve products such as cigarettes and alcohol, which are not only harmful but which children are not legally permitted to purchase either. Despite such legal restrictions, there have, nevertheless, been several cases of marketing campaigns involving such products that were apparently directed toward children and teen-aged youth. A particularly notorious example of such a case was the advertising campaign used to market Camel brand cigarettes through the use of the "cool" cartoon figure Joe Camel. Critics argued the use of this Disney-like cartoon figure to market cigarettes was designed to purposely appeal to a younger audience. Eventually, under pressure from the Federal Trade Commission (FTC) and various interest groups such as the American Medical Association, R. J. Reynolds agreed to discontinue use of the

Joe Camel character. In a similar vein, critics have contended that marketers often appeal to children of unsuitable age in advertising movies, video games, and other media that contain sexual and violent content of an age-restricted nature. Certainly, any company that does purposefully market such products to children is engaging in an ethically dubious practice. At a minimum, if a product has been deemed to be inappropriate for persons under a certain age by law or regulation, marketers have a moral and legal responsibility not to target younger persons in their advertising campaigns.

Controversy also exists concerning the marketing of products to children that pose less direct harms. For instance, a number of groups have expressed concerns over the extensive marketing of soft drinks, snacks, sweets, and fast-food products to children. Given the poor nutritional value of most of these products, these critics argue that children are being encouraged to adopt unhealthy eating habits that can have long-term health consequences. Other marketing efforts directed at children have been targeted by critics for selling products that present unhealthy or unrealistic images to children. For example, some critics have argued that many of the dolls marketed to girls present them with a female body image that is unrealistic and that in doing so contribute to the self-image problems that are widespread among young females. Finally, some critics simply express concern over what they see as the widespread marketing of products to children that, while not harmful, have no positive educational, social, or personal value either. These critics argue that high-pressure advertising campaigns often exploit the naivety of children in marketing worthless products to them.

ADVERTISING TECHNIQUES

Questions of the last-mentioned sort raise further considerations about the means by which products are marketed to children and, in particular, to the methods of advertising. Here, two issues have been given particular prominence in discussions of marketing to children. One involves the pervasiveness of advertising to children and the other the means by which advertising appeals to children. As to the first point, a number of ethicists have expressed worries about the extent to which advertising has infiltrated nearly every childhood activity. They argue that, on a daily basis, children are bombarded with advertisements on television, the Internet, in public spaces, and even at schools and other community institutions. Defenders of the marketing industry have traditionally pointed to the role of parents in filtering what children see and argued that the primary responsibility for monitoring the consumer habits of children belongs with the family. However, critics suggest that the strength of this argument is weakened by a consideration of the ubiquitous nature of advertising to children in contemporary society that makes it nearly impossible for parents to adequately monitor and counter these commercial influences.

The second issue turns on the kinds of methods that advertisers use to appeal to children. Here, many critics worry about the extent to which emotional appeals and image advertising can influence younger consumers who can be expected to have less maturity and less developed judgment than adult consumers. The FTC, which is responsible for protecting consumers from deceptive advertising practices, has generally recognized this in applying more stringent standards to advertisements directed at children than to those aimed at adults. Despite this more strident regulation by the FTC of advertising to children, a number of critics argue that much of the advertising that is directed at children still makes use of emotionally manipulative techniques in appealing to younger consumers. For example, some critics have charged that advertising directed at children often plays on the fears, insecurities, and unrealistic expectations of children to influence their decisions about products. To the extent that children are more easily swayed by purely emotional appeals, such advertising can be seen as unduly manipulative.

Advances in technology have also raised concerns about the ethics of marketing to children. Of particular prominence here have been questions about the various methods by which marketers target children online, a number of which have come under scrutiny in recent years. Sophisticated marketers have the capability to track the online activities of children and to develop advertising personalized to individual users. Interactive advertising sites for children often also blend entertainment and advertising in a near seamless fashion, and various banner advertisements redirect children who click on them to company-sponsored sites. Such practices tend to intensify questions as to what extent children have the capacities to identify the advertising appeals intermixed with such online activities and to resist their influence. Online marketing techniques can involve the solicitation of various forms of information from and about children and their online habits as well. The collecting and selling of such information raises further ethical questions about protecting the privacy of children online, who are less appreciative of the importance of informational privacy.

REGULATORY AND INDUSTRY RESPONSES

A number of efforts have been made by the government, industry groups, and individual companies to initiate regulations and policies that address some of the specific ethical concerns raised above. At the federal level, the Children's Television Act of 1990 can be seen as a response to the increasing commercialization of children's television programming. The act requires that television stations carry a designated amount of programming for children that contains an educational and information component. In 2000, the Children's Online Privacy Protection Act was also passed. This act requires that commercial Web sites that are aimed at children less than 13 years of age obtain parental permission before collecting personal information from a child. At the industry level, the National Advertising Review Council, an organization formed through the auspices of a number of national advertising trade associations and the Better Business Bureau, established the Children's Advertising Review Unit (CARU) in 1974 to review and evaluate advertising directed toward children. The CARU has developed a set of self-regulatory guidelines to promote honesty and responsibility in advertising to children and also has included special provisions directed toward protecting children in the online environment. Some companies and marketing firms have also sought to adopt specific policies and codes of ethics with regard to marketing to children as well, including a few large corporations that have traditionally had a significant role in marketing their products to children. For instance, in 2005, Kraft Foods announced the adoption of a set of standards for marketing to children that included setting nutritional standards for foods advertised to children between 6 and 11 years of age.

BROADER SOCIAL ISSUES

Issues surrounding the proliferation of advertising to children and the uses of associative advertising also spill over into larger debates about the social impact of marketing to children. In this vein, some commentators worry that the tendency by marketers to target younger and younger children and to do so in increasingly numerous and sophisticated ways poses a more general threat to human flourishing and important social values. First, critics of this stripe contend that by inculcating desires for unnecessary and potentially harmful products in children from an early age, particularly through associative and image advertising, marketers threaten the ability of children to develop as fully rational and autonomous persons. Second, some have tied concerns over marketing to children to more general concerns with consumerism. By encouraging children to become fervent consumers at an early age, some contend that rampant marketing efforts directed at children stymies the development of personal virtue and the appreciation of noncommercial social goods.

Others have argued, however, that such social critics overestimate the influence that advertising has on individuals as well as the extent to which the values inherent in such practices are necessarily enemies of human flourishing. They believe that blanket assertions about the manipulative nature of such advertising are overstated and claim that advertising plays an important role in allowing children to become reflective decision makers by providing them with information about available products. In doing so, such defenders argue that advertising can actually aid children in formulating a sense of their own wants and preferences, as well as introduce them to the workings of a free market economy.

Debates over such broader social issues will no doubt continue into the foreseeable future. In attempting to sort them out, though, further research is called for in at least three directions. First, further empirical investigation into the effects of advertising on the psychological and social development of children is needed for a proper evaluation of claims concerning the scope and strength of its influence. Second, from the normative point of view, parties on all sides of the debate need to further explicate and defend the views of human values and social goods that underlie their positions. A complete treatment of the ethics of marketing to children will necessarily depend on a robust account of the nature of personal and social value. Finally, even with regard to unethical marketing practices, care must be taken to distinguish between those cases that pose a serious enough threat to children as to warrant government regulation from those practices that while perhaps ethically dubious are not sufficiently problematic as to call for regulatory restrictions.

—Daniel E. Palmer

Further Readings

Brenkert, G. (1999). Marketing ethics. In R. Frederick (Ed.), *A companion to business ethics* (pp. 178–193). Malden, MA: Blackwell.

Chonko, L. B. (1995). *Ethical decision making in marketing.* Thousand Oaks, CA: Sage.

Lippke, R. L. (1989). Advertising and the social conditions of autonomy. *Business and Professional Ethics Journal, 8*, 35–58.

Moore, E. S. (2004). Children and the changing world of advertising. *Journal of Business Ethics, 52*, 161–167.

Nebenzahl, I. D., & Jaffe, E. D. (1998). Ethical dimensions of advertising executions. *Journal of Business Ethics, 17*, 805–815.

Paine, L. S. (1983). Children as consumers. *Business and Professional Ethics Journal, 3*, 119–146.

Wong, K. L. (1996). Tobacco advertising and children: The limits of First Amendment protection. *Journal of Business Ethics, 15*, 1051–1064.

Marketing to Children

MINORITIES

M inorities can be defined depending on specific context, but generally minorities make up either a subgroup that does not form a majority of the total population, or a group that, while not necessarily a numerical minority, is disadvantaged or otherwise has less political or economic power than a dominant group. The most prevalent form of minority groups, that is, ethnic minorities, comprised less than 20% of the United States in 1980, and yet the projections are that by 2040, half of all Americans will be those now referred to as "minorities."

Minorities can also be classified by gender, disability, age, religion, sexual orientation, and other criteria. Although the ratio of men to women is balanced in most societies, given the lower economic status and lack of opportunities of the latter group has led some to equate them with minorities. Similarly, the elderly, while considered an influential group in many traditional societies, have been reduced to a minority role in terms of their economic and social contributions. Finally, the Disability rights movement has contributed to an understanding of people with disabilities as a minority group.

MARKETING TO ETHNIC MINORITIES

In an increasingly global world, businesses are recognizing the need to reach out to minority groups. Companies such as AT&T, Sears Roebuck, and Coca Cola were some of the pioneers of such practices. The three major ethnic minority groups in the United States—Hispanics, African Americans, and Asians—currently account for almost 30% of the population, and they cumulatively account for 20% of the total spending power in the country. In 2004, corporate America did not effectively market to this segment of the market, since only 2% of the more than $200 billion spent on advertising was allocated to the ethnic media. In a study sponsored by the Association of National Advertisers (ANA) in 2004, an overwhelming 89% of the advertisers said that they were practicing multicultural marketing while 85% were involved in specifically creating separate ads for separate ethnic markets. The greatest challenge faced by the agencies cited in the study was the measurement of results (38%), funding (34%), and a lack of market research (13%).

The 2005 Yankelovich *MONITOR* Multicultural study found that 70% of blacks and 53% of Hispanics are very concerned about marketers' methods and motives. Furthermore, 50% concur that most marketing has no relevance for them and that they wanted marketers to be more attentive, in a sensitive and culturally appropriate manner. The results also suggested that for Hispanic consumers, marketers should use both Spanish and English to facilitate the infusion of the brand message with cultural familiarity and relevance. In many countries, companies such as L'Oreal, Alberto-Culver, and Proctor and Gamble–owned Wella have introduced several ethnic minority–specific products in categories such as cosmetics and hair care.

DRAWING A FINE LINE BETWEEN PATRONIZING AND TARGETING

While targeting minorities is encouraged to enable them as consumers to have greater access to products available to mainstream customers and to offer greater efficiencies to marketers, doing so has a sinister connotation, when minorities are perceived as "vulnerable." This has even a worse connotation if the products that are being targeted are potentially harmful. For example, many consumer activists and federal officials took action in the last decade when internal documents from R. J. Reynolds and Brown & Williamson Tobacco Corporation showed how these companies had targeted minority youths, particularly with their menthol brands. Similarly, C. Heilman Brewing drew fire when it extended its Colt 45 malt liquor line with Power master, a high-test malt, toward African American consumers. In other cases, politically incorrect marketing strategies have come under scrutiny, for example, when a high alcohol content malt liquor, "Crazy Horse," named after a famous Sioux Indian warrior, was marketed to Native Americans in the early 1990s.

On the contrary, avoiding minority groups, also known as "redlining," by denying bank loans and insurance policies primarily to minority households has also come under a lot of criticism. Retail redlining, when major firms do not serve customers in minority neighborhoods, because of unprofitable operations, has also been severely criticized by federal agencies and activist groups. Related research, as well as television newsmagazines such as *Dateline* and *20/20,* has shown that African Americans wait longer for customer service in the retail industry than customers of other races. Balancing the demands of hiring and treating minorities fairly, marketing customized products without patronizing or exploiting vulnerabilities, and providing attentive customer service are some of the major challenges that firms face today with regard to their minority stakeholders.

—Abhijit Roy

Further Readings

Brenkert, G. G. (1998). Marketing to inner-city blacks: Powermaster and moral responsibility. *Business Ethics Quarterly, 8*(1), 1–18.

D'Rozario, D., & Williams, J. D. (2005). Retail redlining: Definition, theory, typology, and measurement. *Journal of Macromarketing, 25*(2), 175.

Grier, S., & Deshpande, R. (2001). Social dimension of consumer distinctiveness: The influence of social status on group identity and persuasion. *Journal of Marketing Research, 38*(May), 216–224.

Hymowitz, C. (2005, November 14). The new diversity. *Wall Street Journal,* pp. R1, R3.

Lee, K., & Joo, S. (2005). The portrayal of Asian Americans in mainstream magazine ads: An update. *Journalism and Mass Communication Quarterly, 82*(3), 654.

Macchiette, B., & Roy, A. (1994). Sensitive groups and social issues: Are you marketing correct? *Journal of Consumer Marketing, 11*(4), 55–64.

McKay, P. F., & Avery, D. R. (2005). Warning! Diversity recruitment could backfire. *Journal of Management Inquiry, 14*(4), 330.

Minority report. (2005). *Marketing Management, 14*(6), 7.

Quinn, M., & Devasagayam, R. (2005). Building brand community among ethnic diaspora in the USA: Strategic implications for marketers. *Journal of Brand Management, 13*(2), 101.

Tharp, M. C. (2001). *Marketing and consumer identity in multicultural America.* Thousand Oaks, CA: Sage.

Trends—Ethnic minority products: Beauty should be skin deep. (2005, May 19). *Marketing Week,* p. 36.

Wentz, L. (2004, November 1). Marketers hone focus on minorities. *Advertising Age, 75*(44), 55.

Yankelovich Monitor multicultural marketing study 2005. (2005). Retrieved from www.yankelovich.com/products/multicultural_2005.pdf

CROSS-CULTURAL
CONSUMER MARKETING

M arketing activities that originate in Western countries span the globe and reach many cultures. Questions of cross-cultural ethics arise when marketing practices that are acceptable in one country are inappropriate in another.

Consumer marketing, which is impersonal and directed at a mass audience, may be distinguished from relationship marketing, which is based on personal contacts. This is an important distinction because many of the cross-cultural problems surrounding consumer marketing arise precisely because much of the world has traditionally relied on relationship marketing.

World cultures tend to be either rule based or relationship based. Rule-based Western cultures rely on a legal or regulatory system to enforce what are seen as universal rules of fairness. Non-Western norms tend to place human relationships at the center of things. While relationship marketing developed in both kinds of cultures, consumer marketing is very much a product of the West and is an inherently foreign practice in relationship-oriented cultures. Even relationship marketing is done differently in the two kinds of cultures. These differences can present ethical challenges.

CONSUMER MARKETING IN RELATIONSHIP-ORIENTED SOCIETIES

Impersonal consumer marketing requires consumers to trust products and believe advertisements created by strangers, which is unnatural for people who traditionally place their trust in friends and family rather than on an economic or legal system. As a result, consumers may have neither the skills necessary to identify safe and effective products nor a functional legal system that regulates them. Global firms may find it legal and possible to sell dangerous pesticides, high-tar cigarettes, unwholesome baby food, or unsafe equipment that would be unmarketable in some Western countries.

Mass marketing can also inject culturally inappropriate products, prices, and promotion into local cultures. "Morning after" pills may become available in strongly Roman Catholic countries, or the market prices of life-saving drugs may be far beyond the means of most people in economically less developed countries. Advertisements may contain sexual material or portray disrespect for parental authority that is frowned on locally. Conversely, local custom can draw multinational enterprises into supporting practices contrary to their own values. Ultrasound machines may be used locally to identify unborn female babies for abortion and donated organs may be reserved for high-status individuals.

RELATIONSHIP MARKETING

Even relationship marketing differs in rule-oriented and relationship-oriented cultures. Non-Western business cultures typically value loyalty to one's associates, boss, or company. Suppose, for example, that a Western purchasing agent has been interacting with Asian suppliers but changes jobs. The Asian partners may view the agent as immoral for failing to follow through on personal commitments, even though his or her departure from the company may be perfectly normal from a Western point of view.

Western business culture, on the other hand, typically values playing by the rules more highly than personal loyalty. Asian businesspeople, for example, may respect intellectual property obtained from Westerner business partners with whom they have a long-term personal relationship, but they may feel free to use it for their own purposes when there is no such relationship. To the Western mind, relationships are irrelevant when it comes to law.

ADDRESSING CULTURAL DIFFERENCE

One approach to accommodating cultural difference is to try to design a single product or promotion that is compatible with a wide range of markets. A growing trend, however, is to do the opposite. Although global communication and distribution technologies are often viewed as a force for homogenization, they actually reinforce regional differences. Multiple cable and satellite channels enable regionally specific programming, and direct advertising through the Internet reaches highly refined market segments. Sophisticated manufacturing plants and supply chains fill highly customized orders on a global scale. It is rapidly becoming possible for marketers to respect local cultural norms wherever they do business.

—John Hooker

Further Readings

Schlegemilch, B. (1998). *Marketing ethics: An international perspective.* London: Thomson Learning.

Srnka, K. J. (2004). Culture's role in marketers' ethical decision making: An integrated theoretical framework. *Academy of Marketing Science Review.* Retrieved from http://www.amsreview.org

Cross-Cultural
Consumer Marketing

MULTINATIONAL MARKETING

Multinational marketing involves the domestic firm extending its products into multiple foreign markets. Multinational marketing examines the discrete differences between domestic and foreign markets. These foreign markets in many cases operate differently than the domestic markets. Firms have to account for another tier of marketing attributes to understand the foreign market. Several factors make the environment for multinational marketing more complex. The marketer has to initially recognize that each country is a sovereign entity. Basically, the country decides how it is to be run without any direct intervention from another country. The country is run in a manner that accommodates the government's political interest. The government has an overbearing influence over the environmental factors that affect a firm marketing in a foreign country. First and foremost, a firm must obtain permission from the government to either produce and/or sell a good in the country. So for a firm to be engaged in multinational marketing, it must know how to operate within another type of framework. The factors that shape this new framework can be broken down into categories that involve but are not limited to social, political, legal, economic, governmental, cultural, language, customs, and topological factors. These factors help institutionalize the characteristics of the country, and the firm must adapt to these principles by learning how these factors affect the delivery of marketing goods to consumers.

In many ways, marketing products globally is the same as marketing them at home. Regardless of which part of the world the firm sells in, the marketing program must be centered on a sound product or service that is properly priced, promoted, and distributed to a carefully selected target market. In other words, the marketing manager has the same controllable decision variables in both domestic and nondomestic markets. Although the development of a multinational marketing program may be the same in either domestic or nondomestic markets, special problems are encountered during the implementation of marketing programs in nondomestic markets. These problems often arise because of the environmental differences that exist among various countries that marketing managers may be unfamiliar with.

In examining the differences between countries, the marketer must focus on how the consumer buying behavior is affected by the environmental forces.

Many of these factors create distance between how the firm currently markets versus what can be done in the new environment. The environmental factors change the buying behavior and pressure the firm into revisiting its strategy for marketing in a new market. Sometimes the market changes so much that the firm has to rethink its entire strategic approach to entering the market. Although the traditional marketing mix factors of price, place, promotion, and product still reign as the most important factors in marketing, their emphasis changes when engaging in multinational marketing. The global factors actually affect how these marketing mix elements are used by the marketer. The global factors in most cases change the good that is delivered to the consumer. This directly limits the firm from being able to extend its goodwill previously established in the good's original form.

For these reasons, most firms tend to establish separate marketing plans for doing business in different countries. This is the essence of what multinational marketing is all about. Creating a separate marketing approach requires the firm to come up with unique strategies to enter heterogeneous foreign markets. The marketer must integrate the marketing mix factors with the global environmental factors to cultivate an effective approach to market in a country. The firm must conduct an extensive analysis of the global factors to determine the strategy for entering the country. In most cases, it is difficult for a firm to standardize the market attributes found in each country. This occurs because each factor is so unique to the country that it creates problems for the firm. The firm has to make a key decision early on in the process whether it is going to be an importer or an exporter. Importers make the good in another location and sell it around the world. Of course, they are subject to tariffs, quotas, duties, and sometimes, licensing restrictions that might alter the good even more. Conversely, they can choose to be an exporter, which means that they produce a good in a country and sell it in that country. A firm that directly invests in a country takes on the highest level of risk associated with multinational marketing. They are subject to potential loss of assets and stringent rules for doing business in the country. If there is a high degree of uncertainty surrounding the country, a firm might decide to be an importer to mitigate the risk.

LANGUAGE

Distance barriers are created by language or labeling requirements when products are produced using a certain language in advertising the good. Although these changes may be subtle in nature, they can have a huge effect on a good. Firms have to consider what language barriers exist and how they can modify a good's image and goodwill. Firms don't want to lose value that they have created in a product. Although language is a significant barrier, the firm has to find a way to work within new guidelines to maintain value and satisfy country requirements. Also, language barriers can affect the manner in which a firm advertises in foreign markets. Depending on the advertising method, language may limit the effectiveness of the medium of communication. Sometimes the meaning of words changes when put into another language. So the firm has to figure out how to preserve the integrity of the meaning, while using a different language to communicate the message.

CULTURE

Another factor that the firm has to contend with is culture. Globalization has made accessing foreign markets easier. Culture is a problematic issue for many marketers since it is inherently nebulous and often difficult to understand. One may violate the cultural norms of another country without being informed of this, and people from different cultures may feel uncomfortable in each other's presence without knowing exactly why. For example, McDonald's prided itself on selling standardized hamburgers to a mass market of consumers. When they wanted to expand into the market in India, they would have a problem because beef is not an acceptable food for this culture. The Indian culture views the cow as a sacred animal and, therefore, Indians don't consume beef as a staple daily food as people do in the United States.

In some other cultures, what you see is what you get, and the speaker is expected to make his or her points clear and limit ambiguity. This is the case in the United States—if you have something on your mind, you are expected to say it directly, subject to some reasonable standards of diplomacy. In Japan, in contrast, facial expressions and what is *not* said may be an important clue to understanding a speaker's meaning. Thus, it may be very difficult for Japanese speakers to understand another's written communication. The nature of languages may exacerbate this phenomenon—while the German language is very precise, Chinese lacks many grammatical features, and the meaning of words may be somewhat less precise. English ranks somewhere in the middle of this continuum.

However, the culture that awaits the firms has not drastically changed. The firm must understand the cultural dimensions that exist and determine how differences can affect buying behavior. Culture is the pattern of behavior and thinking that people living in social groups learn, create, and share. Culture distinguishes one human group from another. Foreign culture includes beliefs, rules of behavior, language, rituals, art, technology, styles of dress, ways of producing and cooking food, religion, and political and economic systems. The firm must analyze these traits and compare them with their host country standards. This helps the firm have a better understanding of consumers from that market. Some products are far more vulnerable to cultural differences than others.

For instance, products that are nondurable ("perishable") are extremely sensitive to cultural changes. Some examples of these products include fresh foods, vegetables, clothing, carbonated drinks, dairy products, wines, meats, and other forms of textiles. On the other hand, durable products are less sensitive to cultural changes but may be affected by environmental factors. In European countries, there is a different standard for electricity, which means that the voltage on most consumer electronic devices is different. There are two basic standards for voltage and frequency in the world. One is the North American standard of 110 to 120 volts at 60 Hz, which uses plugs A and B, and the other is the European standard of 220 to 240 volts at 50 Hz, which uses plugs C through M. This environmental change in electricity forces the firm to change the electrical connection to meet the requirements in different countries. Also, automobiles have a different standard because of the various environmental factors pertaining to emission standards.

POLITICAL

Understanding the political environment of a country is essential to obtaining permission to access a country to sell goods. Given the sovereign nature of most countries, they have a high degree of discretion in deciding how they choose to be governed. Thus, the political environment of countries is a critical concern for the international marketer, and they should examine the salient political features of global markets they plan to enter. A nation's sovereignty from an international law's point of view is independent and free from external control; enjoys full legal equality; governs its own territory; selects its own political, social, and economic systems; and has the power to enter into agreements with other nations. It is in the extension of national laws beyond a country's borders that much of the conflict in international business arises. Nations can and do abridge specific aspects of their sovereign rights in order to coexist with other countries. The European Union, North American Free Trade Agreement (NAFTA), and MERCOSUR are examples of nations voluntarily agreeing to give up some of their sovereign rights in order to participate with member nations for common, mutually beneficial goals. The ideal political climate for a multinational firm is a stable and friendly environment, but often that is not present. Since foreign businesses are judged by standards as variable as there are nations, the friendliness and stability of the government in each country must be assessed as an ongoing business practice. For example, the European Union limited Chiquita Banana from selling large quantities of bananas there and placed tariffs on the banana as well. By limiting supply and increasing the price the European Union made Chiquita's banana unattractive compared with other bananas in the marketplace.

The most important of the political conditions that concern an international business is the stability or instability of the prevailing government policies. Political parties may change or get reelected, but the main concern for firms is the continuity of the set rules or code of behavior regardless of the party in power. A change in the government does not always mean change in the level of political risks. In Italy, the political parties have changed 50 times since the end of World War II, but business continues to go on as usual in spite of the political turmoil.

The most severe political risk is confiscation, which is the seizing of a company's assets without payment. Less severe is expropriation, which requires reimbursement, for the government-seized investment. A third type of risk is domestication, which occurs when the host country takes steps to transfer foreign investments to national control and ownership through a series of government decrees. A change in the government's attitudes, policies, economic plans, and philosophies toward the role of foreign investment is the reason behind the decision to confiscate, expropriate, or domesticate existing foreign assets. Some products are more politically vulnerable than others, in that they receive more government attention. This special attention may result in positive or negative actions toward the company. Unfortunately, there are no absolute guidelines for marketers to follow whether the product will receive government attention or not.

There are some generalizations that help identify the tendency for products to be politically sensitive. Products that have an effect on the environment exchange rates, national and economic security, and the welfare of the people are more apt to be politically sensitive. For instance, the United States has banned the use of lead-based paint in homes. The Japanese government banned imports of beef from the United States after the discovery of the first case of mad cow disease in Washington State. For products judged nonessential, the risk would be greater, but for those thought to be making an important contribution, encouragement and special considerations could be available.

ECONOMIC

The marketer must develop an understanding of the economic factors that will influence the environment. The economic factors involve the size of the economy, the purchasing power parity that exists in the market, stability of the currency, foreign exchange rate, rate of inflation, rate of interest, disposable income in the economy, and the rate of unemployment. These factors determine whether the market is suitable for the firm to enter in order to sell a product. The marketer wants to enter markets that are stable and growing. The factors contribute to explaining the business cycle in a country. The marketer has to look at the current stage of economic development the country is in. It may not be an attractive market for the marketers if they have to allocate a large sum of resources and time to develop the market. The marketer should be able to measure the return from investing in a country.

Ultimately, the firm wants to remove its profits from the country. So looking at forward contracts to guarantee a stable return is essential for multinational firms that decide to invest in a country. This directly ties back to the stability of the country in terms of ensuring that its foreign exchange rate is not undervalued. The marketer should have a good idea of how many months they should take with a forward contract. The more unstable the environment, the longer the contract should be to mitigate risk.

For example, in 2002 when Dell Computer decided to sell computers in China, it found out that the per capita income was some $1,000 compared with $36,000 in the United States. Also, less than 1% of the population had a credit card. The Chinese government controlled the content that was permitted on the

Internet as well. So Dell had to revise its strategy for selling its computers over the Internet in the Chinese market.

LEGAL

One of the greatest areas of concern for the marketer is in the legal area. The marketer wants to protect its intellectual property rights and must look at how developed the rules are in protecting a foreign firm's intellectual property rights. If the country does not allow the firm to enforce its rights effectively in the country, the firm stands the chance of losing a great deal of goodwill in their products. The marketer must examine the rules for advertising as well in the country. Sometimes a country may have specific limits on speech and the manner in which the firm can communicate a message. The country may have rules that limit guest workers and the type of workers that can be used in a country. Understanding the country's laws will help the marketer develop a multinational marketing strategy that works. In most countries, the biggest problem that firms run into is illegal use of their intellectual property rights (i.e., copyright, trademark, trade secret, and patents). Some countries don't have sophisticated rules in place to protect foreign intellectual property rights and thus their infringement is likely. For example, Yaqing, a Shanghai-based soft drink maker, lost a lawsuit last January against Coca Cola and its local bottler over the naming of a new beverage. Yaqing claimed the characters for Coke's Qoo fruit drink—"Ku-er" in Chinese—were too close to those of Yaqing's Kuhai drink. Yet a Shanghai court ruled that the two names were different enough for consumers not to confuse them.

CUSTOMS

The firm must examine the role of technology in the foreign country. Technology has allowed marketers to overcome certain barriers that in the past prevented them from entering certain markets. Technology has afforded many firms the ability to operate more efficiently over the long term. So an examination of the role of technologies in the multinational marketing plan is essential in today's environment. The multinational marketing firm pursues different strategies in each of its foreign markets. They could have as many different product variations, brand names, and advertising campaigns as countries in which they operate. Each overseas subsidiary is autonomous. Local marketers are given the authority to make the necessary decisions and are held accountable for their results. In effect, the multinational marketer competes on a market-by-market basis.

TOPOLOGICAL

Last, in the process of marketing products in multiple countries, the firm must recognize the subtle differences in the topology of the country. In other words, the terrain and climate of the country will have a great impact on how the firm distributes its products. It might not be conducive to sell products in a similar manner as the United States based on the structure of the environment. In some countries, it is not common to see large shopping malls. It is more common to see smaller stores that sell a broad range of products. Also, the mechanism for reaching customers will be affected by the topology of the country. In some countries, because of the mountains and steep hills it is difficult to reach customers with traditional methods of advertising. For example, using the radio, television, and cable television may be limited in some foreign markets. So this is yet another challenge that the marketer has to consider in developing their marketing plan for each country.

CONCLUSION

Multinational marketing is a process that firms recognize they need to grasp in order to market in other countries. A continual evaluation of environmental factors is key to understanding these new markets. Firms must develop a careful and detailed approach for reaching consumers in various markets. They must work with the people in each country and find their unique differences to avoid alienating themselves from the market. Firms should not take an ethnocentric approach to examining each market but rather selectively choose a market and examine the environmental factors. After determining the core differences, the firm should establish a strategy for entering the market. These elements are mandatory for a firm to be successful in another country. Unfortunately, there are no shortcuts in learning about another country. But there is enough history available to learn about the country and develop a strategy for doing business in the environment.

—Sylvester E. Williams, IV

Further Readings

Czinkota, M. R., & Ronkainen, I. A. (2003). *International business* (7th ed.). Mason, OH: Thomson/South-Western.

Keegan, W. J. (1984). *Multinational marketing management* (3rd ed.). Englewood Cliffs, NJ: Prentice Hall.

Ricks, D. A. (1983). *Big business blunders: Mistakes in multinational marketing*. Homewood, IL: Dow Jones-Irwin.

Yaprak, A. (2000). *Globalization, the multinational firm, and emerging economies*. New York: JAI Imprint.

PART IV: Special Topics in
Marketing Ethics

GREEN MARKETING

G*reen marketing* refers to a broad range of activities designed to generate and facilitate any exchanges intended to satisfy human needs or wants, with minimal detrimental impact on the natural environment. It involves adopting resource conserving and environmental friendly strategies in all stages of the value chain. Other synonymous terms such as *sustainable marketing* and *environmental marketing* have also been used to denote this term. They are perceived as cost-efficient, effective, and just tools of handling problems related to the impact of economic activity on the environment and are often a means of sustainable competitive advantage.

Several companies have proactively implemented green marketing programs to improve their business offerings in several different ways. Some recent notable examples follow:

- British Petroleum has committed to spending $350 million on energy-efficient products over several years and is aggressively promoting its environmental awareness programs.
- General Electric is spending $1.5 billion on its *Ecoimagination* in researching for less polluting technologies and promoting them as well.
- Starbucks recently announced the donation of $10 million over the next 5 years for clean drinking water around the world through the sale of its Ethos bottled water. The company already offers coffees that offer fair pay for growers and environmentally sound cultivation.
- 3M encourages employees to participate in its Pollution Prevention Pays program. Since 1974, the program has eliminated over $2 billion pounds of air, water, and solid waste pollutants from the environment.
- The largest home and garden center chain, Home Depot, has discontinued the sale of wood products from endangered forests since 2002.

In addition to firms, major global bodies such as the United Nations have urged better "green" planning by asking cities to hold tree plantings and clean-ups throughout the world. Even buildings, such as the presidential library for

Bill Clinton, offer a "green" focus and feature environmentally friendly construction. Industry-based associations are actively encouraging green marketing programs—the U.S. Green Building Council is responsible for certifying and promoting environmentally responsible and high-performance buildings, while the Green Seal organization awards green seals to products that meet rigorous environmental standards, which in turn helps consumers identify products that are environmentally safe.

HISTORY OF GREEN MARKETING

Although a major focus on green marketing began in the last three to four decades after the publication of Rachel Carson's *Silent Spring*, the history of green marketing in the modern era can be traced back to the 18th century when Benjamin Franklin urged France and Germany to follow England's practice of switching from wood to coal, which had saved what remained of their forests. Franklin also attempted to regulate waste disposal and water pollution in Philadelphia. He also left money in a widely publicized codicil to his will to build fresh water pipeline to Philadelphia due to links between bad water and disease, which ultimately led to the city's water department to be the first (in 1801) in America to supply drinking water to all its inhabitants.

The American Marketing Association held its first conference on ecological marketing in 1975 that attempted to bring together academics, practitioners, and public policy makers to examine marketing's impact on the natural environment. Concern for green marketing has escalated since the 1980s and 1990s after the growth of environmental ills such as ozone layer depletion, oil spills, and overflowing landfills. Since then, the U.S. Federal Trade Commission and the National Association of Attorneys General have been very active in monitoring green marketing claims as well as developing extensive documents examining green marketing issues.

MOTIVATIONS FOR GREEN MARKETING

There are several motivations for companies going green. Michael Jay Polonsky identifies five major reasons for firms' increased use of green marketing. They are as follows:

Lower Costs or Higher Profitability

Disposing of harmful by-products has resulted in substantial cost savings in many firms. In trying to minimize waste, firms often stumble across more efficient production processes that eliminate the need for some raw materials, thereby reducing costs. In other cases, instead of minimizing waste, these materials serve as another firm's input to production processes. Finally, developing more efficient new industries, for example, using oxygen instead of air in making steel, can enhance cost or profitability.

Competitive Parity

To keep up with the benchmarks set by the competitors, firms may try to emulate their environmental marketing position; for example, a manufacturer may stop deforestation in a sensitive area in response to a major competitor's similar action or a tuna manufacturer may stop using driftnets by following others.

Commitment to Social Responsibility

Many firms are beginning to realize that they are members of a broader global community and, therefore, must meet environmental objectives in addition to their profit-based objectives. As such, they take a proactive approach to embracing a philosophy of environmental social responsibility in their overall firm's culture. Some, such as the Body Shop and Ben and Jerry's, heavily promote their involvement in green marketing initiatives, while others such as Coke and Walt Disney World practice this philosophy and yet choose not to publicize it as much.

Consumer Demand

Several surveys have shown that both individual and organizational customers in most countries are becoming more concerned about their natural environment and are demanding firms to be responsive to these concerns. Photocopier companies such as Xerox, for example, introduced a "high-quality" recycled photocopier paper in an attempt to fulfill demands for less environmentally harmful products.

Governmental Pressure

Finally, governmental pressures are also being designed to "protect" consumers by reducing production of harmful products or by-products, modifying consumer and industry's use and/or consumption of harmful goods, or ensuring that consumers have the required information in evaluating the environmental composition of goods. Governments regulate the control of hazardous wastes, while most by-products are controlled through the issue of appropriate licenses. They modify consumer behavior by "inducing" consumers to participate in voluntary curb side recycling programs, or in other cases taxing them for irresponsible behavior. In the United States, agencies such as the Federal Trade Commission protect consumers by regulating misleading claims, thereby enabling them to make better-informed decisions.

PROFILING GREEN CONSUMERS

There are many ways of segmenting green consumers. For example, J. Ottman Consulting identifies three types of green consumers: "planet passionates," "health fanatics," and "animal lovers." Planet passionates are committed to maintaining a healthy environment and avoid waste and products with poor environmental records. Health fanatics, on the other hand, try to maintain a healthy diet and lifestyle by taking precautions against toxic waste, pesticides, sun exposure, and other environmental problems that might affect their health. Finally, animal lovers protect the rights of animals through vegetarianism, buying products labeled as "cruelty free" and "not tested on animals," and boycotting products such as fur and tuna.

Marketing research firm Roper ASW on the other hand divides the total population into five segments, out of which two segments are likely to buy green. "True blue greens" (9% of the population) are wealthy and educated and include environmental activists and leaders; "greenback greeners" (6% of the population) also share the same characteristics, yet are not always likely to sacrifice the comfort and convenience for the sake of the environment. Roper ASW publishes the Green Gauge Report about consumers' willingness to pay for green products, thus helping companies target their marketing strategies.

Finally, Ginsberg and Bloom have suggested that companies should follow one of four green marketing strategies depending on market and competitive conditions, that is, from the relatively passive and silent "lean green" approach to the more aggressive and visible "extreme green" approach—with "defensive green" and "shaded green" in between to be better prepared in helping their companies choose the most appropriate environmentally friendly approach to marketing.

GREENING THE SUPPLY CHAIN

Greening the supply chain refers to firms integrating environmental issues within the new product development process, which include predevelopment activities, supplier's business practices, and product design and development. Environmental responsive companies take proactive posture in requiring a significant level of environmental responsibility in core business practices of their suppliers and vendors. Many companies have even begun taking a more proactive stance in ensuring compliance of their suppliers at the second- and third-tier levels. General Motors (GM) in a recent media release perhaps articulated it best, when they said that working with their suppliers, they can accomplish much more to improve the environment than GM could alone. Empirically, there is demonstrated evidence of a proactive supply chain management role in corporate greening and environmental strategies. Suppliers too benefit by seeing greater operational efficiencies, cost savings, enhanced value to customers, increased sales, positive media attention, and positive ratings from socially responsible investment groups.

A recent report on the suppliers' perspectives on effective supply chain management strategies prepared by Business for Social Responsibility Education Fund talked with representatives from 25 suppliers in four industry sectors, that is, automotive, business services, electronics, and forest products, and found that an increasing number of companies are seeking to influence their suppliers' environmental practices. The types of environmental issues that firms are seeking to address with their suppliers varied by sector. Firms in the automotive and electronics sector received the most environmental requests from suppliers, while those in the forestry sector had mainly received requests to explain their environmental practices. The service sector had received the fewest environmental requests—most such requests came from the larger firms. Greening the supply chain themes include environmental responsiveness of top management, environmental policy, early product development activities, design for environment and life cycle assessment, cross-functional environmental coordination, supplier involvement, environmental database, specialist environmental knowledge, and environmental benchmarking.

RESEARCH FINDINGS, CAVEATS, AND CONCLUSION

The impact of green marketing on both marketing performance and consumer behavior has been thoroughly investigated. For example, research has shown

Green Marketing

that the market value of a firm declines slightly when green marketing initiatives are broadcasted. Announcements related to green products, recycling efforts, and appointments of environmental policy managers had insignificant effect on stock price reactions, while promoting green marketing produces significantly negative stock price reactions.

Consumers who have a positive attitude toward ecologically conscious living and negative attitude toward pollution are likely to buy green products. Further findings substantiate what is known as the "4/40" gap: Roughly 40% of consumers say they are willing to buy green products, but only 4% actually do. Environmentally conscious behaviors are most likely to occur when consumers perceive that their actions are likely to make a difference.

One must also be wary of "greenwashing" practices, which involves disinformation disseminated by firms so as to present an environmentally responsible public image. Such practices are usually promoted through the use of image ads, misleading product labels such as "all natural," "biodegradable," "organic," and so on, as well as public relations tactics such as having hollow mission statements and codes of conduct, sustainability reports offering only partial disclosure, hiring scientists who vouch for industry-funded research, feigning public support for hidden anti-environmental agendas as some major examples. Industry ombudsmen such as the Green Business Network and Green Life attempt to monitor and expose such practices and keep the public informed about what is legitimate and what is not. Green marketing can be a very useful and successful strategy for firms as long as they comprehend the underlying motivations of customers in choosing environmentally friendly products.

—Abhijit Roy

Further Readings

Bennett, S. J., Freierman, R., & George, S. (1993). *Corporate realities and environmental truths: Strategies for leading your business in the environmental era*. New York: Wiley.

Cairncross, F. (1992). *Costing the earth: The challenge for governments, the opportunities for business*. Boston: Harvard Business School Press.

Coddington, W. (1993). *Environmental marketing: Positive strategies for reaching the green consumer*. New York: McGraw-Hill.

Crane, A. (2000). *Marketing, morality and the natural environment*. London: Routledge.

David, R. A. (1991). *The greening of business.* Aldershot, UK: Gower.

Fuller, D. A. (1999). *Sustainable marketing: Managerial-ecological issues.* Thousand Oaks, CA: Sage.

Ginsberg, J. A., & Bloom, P. (2004). Choosing the right green marketing strategy. *MIT Sloan Management Review, 1*(Fall), 79–84.

Koechlin, D., & Müller, K. (1992). *Green business opportunities: The profit potential.* London: Financial Times.

Kuhre, W. L. (1997). *ISO 14020s environmental labelling-marketing: Efficient and accurate environmental marketing procedures.* Upper Saddle River, NJ: Prentice Hall PTR.

Makower, J. (1994). *The E-factor: The bottom-line approach to environmentally responsible business.* New York: Plume.

Mathur, L. K., & Mathur, I. (2000). An analysis of the wealth effects of green marketing strategies. *Journal of Business Research, 50*(2), 193–202.

Ottman, J. A. (1993). *Green marketing.* Lincolnwood, IL: NTC Business Books.

Polonsky, M. J., & Mintu-Wimsatt, A. T. (1995). *Environmental marketing: Strategies, practice, theory, and research.* New York: Haworth Press.

Prakash, A. (2002). Green marketing, public policy and managerial strategies. *Business Strategy and the Environment, 11,* 285–297.

Saha, M., & Darnton, G. (2005). Green companies or green con-panies: Are companies really green, or are they pretending to be? *Business and Society Review, 110*(2), 117–157.

Samli, A. C. (1992). *Social responsibility in marketing: A proactive and profitable marketing management strategy.* Westport, CT: Quorum Books.

U.S. Environmental Protection Agency, Office of Pollution Prevention and Toxics. (1993). *Using and misusing environmental marketing terms: An evaluation by EPA.* Rockville, MD: Author.

Green Marketing

GREENWASHING

*G*reenwashing, a pejorative term derived from the term *whitewashing*, was coined by environmental activists to describe efforts by corporations to portray themselves as environmentally responsible in order to mask environmental wrongdoings. While the term has been used within activist circles since the late 1980s, it was not until 1999 that it was added to the *Concise Oxford English Dictionary* and officially recognized as part of the language. Consequently, some of the literature relating to greenwashing uses more neutral terms to describe this and related activities, including "environmental advertising," "environmental public relations," "green marketing," and "green communications."

THE HISTORY OF GREENWASHING

The first instances of what environmentalists now call greenwashing appeared in the late 1960s as part of a corporate response to the modern environmental movement that was catalyzed by Rachel Carson's book *Silent Spring*. During the 1980s, the environmental movement gained momentum as a result of the Bhopal, Chernobyl, and Exxon Valdez disasters. By the early 1990s, polls suggested that consumers were more likely to buy products from a company that had a sound environmental reputation; corporations responded by portraying themselves, and more of their products, as environmentally friendly. By the mid-1990s, firms were spending millions of dollars on public relations activities aimed at "greening" their images and managing environmental opposition.

   The term greenwashing was originally confined to describing misleading instances of environmental advertising, but as corporations' efforts to portray themselves as environmentally virtuous have diversified and proliferated, so have charges of greenwashing. The term is now used to refer to a wider range of corporate activities, including, but not limited to, certain instances of environmental reporting, event sponsorship, the distribution of educational materials, and the creation of "front groups." (Front groups, such as the International Climate Change Partnership and the National

Wetlands Coalition, are organizations that pose as independent advocacy groups, but which in fact are funded by and promote the interests of a particular corporation or group of corporations.)

It is important to note that not all environmental advertisements or public relations campaigns can fairly be labeled greenwashing, as there are genuinely environmentally conscious companies that use advertisements and other means to promote themselves as such. The clearest cases of greenwashing occur when these media are employed by firms to proclaim (or in some cases merely imply) a deep-seated devotion to sound environmental practice (usually by pointing out some specific accomplishments in that field) in an attempt to distract from its otherwise lackluster environmental performance. For example, a company that advertises its sole laudable environmental initiative to distract from its more environmentally deleterious activities, or a company that, despite being a recalcitrant polluter, boasts about a marginal reduction in emissions at one of its factories, would be clear targets for a charge of greenwashing. Similar suspicions arise when corporations within environmentally problematic industries sponsor grassroots environmental events such as Earth Day, or when corporations with poor environmental track records distribute environmental education videos to schools.

WHY IS GREENWASHING PROBLEMATIC?

The characteristics that render greenwashing subject to ethical criticism are related to, but differ somewhat from, those of other problematic types of promotional activities. Although a range of advertising and public relations techniques have been criticized for their potential to manipulate or coerce consumers, to manufacture desires, and generally to deceive the public, a certain degree of "puffery" or exaggeration has come to be expected, and in some cases considered acceptable, in the marketing of products or services. However, the use of similar tactics to publicize good corporate conduct—and in particular, corporate environmental achievements—has been deemed more problematic. One possible explanation for this is that companies guilty of greenwashing are not just *exaggerating* their environmental accomplishments or contributions: They are claiming to be environmental champions when they are in fact environmental villains. Thus, the charge of greenwashing seems especially apt in instances where corporate environmental communications are not just exaggerated, but tastelessly ironic.

Greenwashing

Ethical worries about greenwashing extend far beyond the general unseemliness of the practice. One of the key concerns expressed by environmental activists is that greenwashing could result in unwarranted consumer and regulator complacency. Corporations that make exaggerated claims regarding their commitment to the environment might give consumers and government regulators false hope that corporations themselves are making great strides toward protecting the environment, leading consumers and policy makers to believe that current levels of mass consumption are sustainable and that further government regulation is unnecessary. Moreover, there is the fear that if one corporation in a particular industry gets away with greenwashing, other corporations will follow suit, thereby creating an industrywide illusion of environmental sustainability, rather than sustainability itself. A final worry is that greenwashing may engender cynicism: If consumers come to expect self-congratulatory ads from even the most environmentally backward corporations, this could render consumers skeptical of even sincere portrayals of legitimate corporate environmental successes. This could result in a failure to justly recognize the achievements of genuinely progressive corporations, thus eliminating one significant incentive for improving corporate environmental performance.

CONCLUSION

The concept of greenwashing should be of interest to a range of parties. First and foremost, greenwashing should be of interest to consumers. While many instances of corporate environmental communication are well-intentioned and truthful, not all are, and consumers who wish to "vote with their dollars" need to be aware of various kinds of corporate deception and spin. Second, environmentalists and corporate watchdogs, such as the Green Life and CorpWatch, are of course interested to spot, and point out, cases of serious greenwashing. The charge of greenwashing constitutes a significant and poignant piece of critical rhetoric (in the nonpejorative sense of "rhetoric"). Finally, students and scholars of business ethics should be interested in the concept of greenwashing, too. There has thus far been a regrettable shortage of academic attention to the concept, despite the term's prevalence and its normative richness. The charge of greenwashing represents a savvy, typically nonacademic criticism of corporate environmental communications. Academics ought to be attending to the significance of such lay evaluations: The growing prevalence of greenwashing as a practice, and as an accusation, signals a new complexity in the evaluation of corporate environmental performance.

—Melissa Whellams and Chris MacDonald

Further Readings

Athanasiou, T. (1996). The age of greenwashing. *Capitalism, Nature, Socialism, 7*(1), 1–36.

Beder, S. (2002). *Global spin.* White River Junction, VT: Chelsea Green.

Green Life. (2005). *Greenwash 101.* Retrieved June 30, 2005, from www.thegreenlife .org/greenwash101.html

Laufer, W. S. (2003, March). Social accountability and corporate greenwashing. *Journal of Business Ethics, 43*(3), 253–261.

Lubbers, E. (2002). *Battling big business: Countering greenwash, infiltration and other forms of corporate bullying.* Monroe, ME: Common Courage Press.

Stoll, M. L. (2002, November/December). The ethics of marketing good corporate conduct. *Journal of Business Ethics, 41*(1/2), 121–129.

CAUSE-RELATED MARKETING

Cause-related marketing (CRM) refers to a marketing activity that involves a company forming a relationship with a particular cause or causes for mutual benefit. CRM can be characterized as a strategic marketing tool employed to achieve both social and corporate objectives; it simultaneously benefits the company and a charity or similar cause. The cause could be general, for example, a concern for the environment, or specific, for example, when a percentage of the sales of a particular product are donated to an identified charity. From the company's perspective, the benefits include the opportunity to enhance their reputation, differentiate themselves from the competition, boost employee morale, raise brand awareness, increase customer loyalty, build sales, and attract positive publicity. From the perspective of the "cause," the benefits include increased revenue and public awareness of their activities.

CRM originated in the United States, where corporate philanthropy is typically characterized as "enlightened self-interest" or as "doing well by doing good." American Express is credited with being the first company to launch a CRM campaign in the early 1980s. Increasingly, companies are moving away from "no strings attached" donations toward joint ventures in which commercial sponsorship of charities is included within overarching corporate objectives, and it is becoming common for contributions to social causes to be funded by the marketing budget rather than a central philanthropic fund.

There are several concerns raised by CRM. Neither the short-term nor long-term effects of CRM on charitable income are known. While CRM campaigns appear to result in increased funding for the social causes involved, there are fears that traditional sources of income may be harmed by CRM. There is concern that CRM will undermine traditional donations as companies come to expect a return for their contributions. Moreover, individuals may be less likely to spontaneously donate to particular charities if the products they buy support social causes. There is also a question relating to the sustainability of income for social causes from CRM. When a company feels it has exhausted CRM's benefits it will move to more profitable campaigns leaving the social causes they previously supported to find alternative ways of generating income. If CRM does undermine spontaneous donation, then after the campaign ends the charity may be badly affected. This possibility raises the question of what, if any, ongoing responsibility companies ought to have to the social causes they have entered into CRM relationships with after the campaigns end.

On a more theoretical level, the concern is that CRM marks a shift from an intrinsic motivation for companies supporting social causes (i.e., supporting them because it is the right thing to do) to an instrumental or prudential reason for doing so (i.e., supporting them to derive a benefit). At an individual level, CRM may undermine consumers' commitment to social causes because it is mediated through a market transaction that could lead to a sense of moral disengagement from social issues.

—Josie Fisher

Further Readings

Collins, M. (1993). Global corporate philanthropy: Marketing beyond the call of duty? *European Journal of Marketing, 27*(2), 46–58.

Hoeffler, S., & Keller, K. L. (2002). Building brand equity through corporate social marketing. *Journal of Public Policy and Marketing, 21*(1), 78–89.

Pringle, H., & Thompson, M. (1999). *Brand soul: How cause-related marketing builds brands.* New York: Wiley.

Smith, W., & Higgins, M. (2000). Cause-related marketing: Ethics and the ecstatic. *Business & Society, 39*(3), 304–322.

Cause-Related Marketing

APPENDIX

AMA Statement of Ethics

ETHICAL NORMS AND VALUES FOR MARKETERS

Preamble

The American Marketing Association commits itself to promoting the highest standard of professional ethical norms and values for its members (practitioners, academics and students). Norms are established standards of conduct that are expected and maintained by society and/or professional organizations. Values represent the collective conception of what communities find desirable, important and morally proper. Values also serve as the criteria for evaluating our own personal actions and the actions of others. As marketers, we recognize that we not only serve our organizations but also act as stewards of society in creating, facilitating and executing the transactions that are part of the greater economy. In this role, marketers are expected to embrace the highest professional ethical norms and the ethical values implied by our responsibility toward multiple stakeholders (e.g., customers, employees, investors, peers, channel members, regulators and the host community).

Ethical Norms

As Marketers, we must:

1. **Do no harm.** This means consciously avoiding harmful actions or omissions by embodying high ethical standards and adhering to all applicable laws and regulations in the choices we make.

2. **Foster trust in the marketing system.** This means striving for good faith and fair dealing so as to contribute toward the efficacy of the

exchange process as well as avoiding deception in product design, pricing, communication, and delivery of distribution.

3. **Embrace ethical values.** This means building relationships and enhancing consumer confidence in the integrity of marketing by affirming these core values: honesty, responsibility, fairness, respect, transparency and citizenship.

Ethical Values

Honesty—to be forthright in dealings with customers and stakeholders. To this end, we will:

- Strive to be truthful in all situations and at all times.
- Offer products of value that do what we claim in our communications.
- Stand behind our products if they fail to deliver their claimed benefits.
- Honor our explicit and implicit commitments and promises.

Responsibility—to accept the consequences of our marketing decisions and strategies. To this end, we will:

- Strive to serve the needs of customers.
- Avoid using coercion with all stakeholders.
- Acknowledge the social obligations to stakeholders that come with increased marketing and economic power.
- Recognize our special commitments to vulnerable market segments such as children, seniors, the economically impoverished, market illiterates and others who may be substantially disadvantaged.
- Consider environmental stewardship in our decision-making.

Fairness—to balance justly the needs of the buyer with the interests of the seller. To this end, we will:

- Represent products in a clear way in selling, advertising and other forms of communication; this includes the avoidance of false, misleading and deceptive promotion.
- Reject manipulations and sales tactics that harm customer trust. Refuse to engage in price fixing, predatory pricing, price gouging or "bait-and-switch" tactics.

- Avoid knowing participation in conflicts of interest. Seek to protect the private information of customers, employees and partners.

Respect—to acknowledge the basic human dignity of all stakeholders. To this end, we will:

- Value individual differences and avoid stereotyping customers or depicting demographic groups (e.g., gender, race, sexual orientation) in a negative or dehumanizing way.
- Listen to the needs of customers and make all reasonable efforts to monitor and improve their satisfaction on an ongoing basis.
- Make every effort to understand and respectfully treat buyers, suppliers, intermediaries and distributors from all cultures.
- Acknowledge the contributions of others, such as consultants, employees and coworkers, to marketing endeavors.
- Treat everyone, including our competitors, as we would wish to be treated.

Transparency—to create a spirit of openness in marketing operations. To this end, we will:

- Strive to communicate clearly with all constituencies.
- Accept constructive criticism from customers and other stakeholders.
- Explain and take appropriate action regarding significant product or service risks, component substitutions or other foreseeable eventualities that could affect customers or their perception of the purchase decision.
- Disclose list prices and terms of financing as well as available price deals and adjustments.

Citizenship—to fulfill the economic, legal, philanthropic and societal responsibilities that serve stakeholders. To this end, we will:

- Strive to protect the ecological environment in the execution of marketing campaigns.

- Give back to the community through volunteerism and charitable donations. Contribute to the overall betterment of marketing and its reputation.
- Urge supply chain members to ensure that trade is fair for all participants, including producers in developing countries.

Implementation

We expect AMA members to be courageous and proactive in leading and/or aiding their organizations in the fulfillment of the explicit and implicit promises made to those stakeholders. We recognize that every industry sector and marketing sub-discipline (e.g., marketing research, e-commerce, Internet selling, direct marketing, and advertising) has its own specific ethical issues that require policies and commentary. An array of such codes can be accessed through links on the AMA Web site. Consistent with the principle of subsidiarity (solving issues at the level where the expertise resides), we encourage all such groups to develop and/or refine their industry and discipline-specific codes of ethics to supplement these guiding ethical norms and values.